ALL ABOARD!

A History of Florida's Railroads

STEPHANIE MURPHY-LUPO

Globe Pequot

Guilford, Connecticut

For my sister, Paula Dianne

Globe
Pequot

An imprint of Rowman & Littlefield

Distributed by NATIONAL BOOK NETWORK

British Library Cataloguing in Publication Information available

Library of Congress Cataloging-in-Publication Data

Murphy-Lupo, Stephanie, author.
 All aboard! : a history of Florida's railroads / Stephanie Murphy-Lupo.
   pages cm
 Includes bibliographical references and index.
 ISBN 978-1-4930-1789-8 (pbk.) — ISBN 978-1-4930-1838-3 (e-book) 1. Railroads—Florida—History. I. Title.
 HE2771.F6M87 2016
 385.09759—dc23
                          2015030855

∞™ The paper used in this publication meets the minimum requirements of American National Standard for Information Sciences—Permanence of Paper for Printed Library Materials, ANSI/NISO Z39.48-1992.

CONTENTS

Acknowledgments iv
Introduction vii

Chapter 1: Before Rail
A Forbidding Territory, Too Far to Tackle 1
Chapter 2: Road Tested
Trails, Tramways, and Trains 19
Chapter 3: Yes to Yulee
The Force Behind the Florida Railroad 31
Chapter 4: An Act of Congress
Pen to Paper Transfers 500,000 Acres 43
Chapter 5: Tolls of Civil War
Death, Railroad Casualties, and Economic Ruin 50
Chapter 6: Reconstruction
Martial Law, Carpetbaggers, and Fraud 73
Chapter 7: Pioneer of Portent
William Chipley Warms to Pensacola 94
Chapter 8: Firmly Planted
"Henry and Friends" 107
Chapter 9: A Decisive Detour
St. Augustine Beguiles Henry M. Flagler 132
Chapter 10: Outsiders on Board
Reed, Walters, and Warfield 167
Chapter 11: Overseas Marvel
Flagler Tames the Florida Keys 195
Chapter 12: Plus and Minus
Loss, Gain, 1920s Boom, 1930s Fallout 228
Chapter 13: War and Peace
Hostile Takeover, Rational Mergers 260
Chapter 14: Private Places
Love-and-Less for All Aboard Florida 278

Bibliography 296
Index 300
About the Author 315

Acknowledgments

During a long career in journalism and a shorter span as an author, I found this book to be my greatest challenge. I am a native Floridian, so it was especially rewarding and enlightening to revisit the turf of past travels and those discovered through research.

It is truly amazing to realize that after living in Jacksonville, Fort Myers, Coral Gables, Pensacola Beach, Gainesville, Orlando, Fort Lauderdale, Boca Raton, and West Palm Beach, I had tons to learn and appreciate. Most of all, this exercise taught me that without bold, decisive railroad developers, what we love about Florida would exist, but no one would be here to appreciate it.

First, I'd like to acknowledge my husband, Gerard A. Lupo, a civil engineer and professional land surveyor who speaks the technical jargon I needed to understand certain concepts. More importantly, I am grateful for his patience and encouragement during the months devoted to this endeavor.

Rick Brautigan, a brilliant architect in Delray Beach and a total train nut, is a friend of long standing who made himself available to listen, clarify, and critique.

Gordon D. Gaster of Jupiter gave me a nugget of information a while ago which sparked my interest in parts of the state I needed to revisit.

Edgar M. Turner of Pensacola was generous with his anecdotes on business dealings with Ed Ball.

Garrison duPont Lickle of Palm Beach was willing and able to explain the nuances of some current railroad proposals.

Jay Van Vechten of Boca Raton enlightened me to no end on some personalities in the saga of Henry Flagler, one of Florida's greatest railroad figures.

Many thanks to retired financial advisor David L. Walby, a volunteer at Fort Pickens National Park on Santa Rosa Island. Also an author, he shared documents with me and encouraged me a lot.

Donald R. Hensley Jr., the editor of *Taplines*, was very responsive in answering my questions and shared some photos from his collection.

Sally Seay Smith of Pensacola, a close friend of many decades, was kind enough to translate some articles and photo captions written in Russian. Her husband, Dr. J. D. Smith, a career educator and former politician, was a helpful devil's advocate.

I appreciate the cooperation of Jim Kovalsky, president of the Florida East Coast Railway Society, for his expertise.

Thanks to Fenn Cawthon and Jean Clark Flowers, who shared anecdotes and photographs from a "railroad" road trip in the Panhandle.

Special appreciation is due author Gregg M. Turner for clarifying certain details.

Kudos to my editor, Amy Lyons, and other professionals at Globe Pequot for their dedicated attention to detail in shepherding this book to completion.

Finally, I want to thank Dick Buntrock of Lake Clarke Shores, for his praise of relevant books. He and I agree that Les Standiford's *Last Train to Paradise* should be appointment-reading for every Floridian.

WATSON'S
NEW
COUNTY, RAILROAD
AND
Distance Map,
OF
FLORIDA.
[1875]

EXPLANATIONS.
Rail Roads completed
" proposed
Canals
STATE CAPITALS
County Seats

INTRODUCTION

Who and what rode trains around Florida? It was quite a democratic mix:

The famous (Ulysses S. Grant, John Dos Passos, "the Queen of Chicago," Teddy Roosevelt and the Rough Riders, occasionally a president, often a US senator or congressman); the infamous Edgar Watson (and members of the Ashley gang of train robbers); and the garden-variety anonymous (visiting relatives or going to bury one).

Heroes and scoundrels, check; soldiers, pilots, and sailors; the super-rich, some big fish in little ponds, and those barely scraping by. Good and bad clergymen, sinners with clay feet; tipplers and teetotalers; truck farmers and plantation owners; desperados, shipwreck salvagers, cowboys, wranglers, and Indian chiefs.

On the train at any given time, one might find innocence, fraud, greed, feuds, larceny, and a plot to murder; sex, romance, tragedy, and thrills; ego, cargo, payrolls, and gold. Blind hope and vision without borders.

From day one, the Sunshine State held a special allure among the well-intentioned as well as a slew of scoundrels eager to exploit its assets and economic potential. The crazy quilt of stakeholders who made their mark is dizzying, indeed, even if one considers railroads alone.

What does it take to build a railroad?

Money and "land rights" in the old days versus the modern bugaboo of right-of-way. Railroad construction is not rocket science, but it does require precise engineering (rails do need to be exactly parallel). And it takes sweat to clear a forest or swamp, grade a roadbed, build bridges, culverts and trestles, switches, turnabouts, cross-ties and rails, spikes, plates, wells, tanks, crossings, and cattle guards *("I've been working on the railroad, all the livelong day . . . ")*.

Who built the railroads in Florida?

Slaves and immigrant laborers bore the brunt for construction and regular maintenance. Several chapters in this book deal with the leading developers and owners, some of the main players, some power brokers, and some women of influence, along with some reprobates in the mix.

Readers will learn about David Levy Yulee, Henry B. Plant, Henry M. Flagler, William D. Chipley, Sir Edward Reed, Julia D. Tuttle, and Bertha Honoré Palmer. But don't expect to master the "ampersand" dialect, that treble-like symbol that altered company names like a shell game. The ampersand is as ubiquitous in the rail realm as directions on a compass. Florida acknowledged hundreds that came and went in head-spinning fashion.

Expect some careening through acronyms. Maybe the first name and second name were reversed, or the name changed from "railway" to "railroad" to make a legal distinction.

Florida was shapeless without railroads, in that its chest was trapped between outsize shoulders, the hands couldn't reach the feet, the torso was in a blind spot, and Georgia was always turning the head around. Given this huge land mass, a minute population in the Colonial era, scant capital, and little more than primitive industry to prop up its economy, Florida was relatively slow to develop rail service.

But not that far behind such efforts recorded elsewhere. The first train left St. Joseph on the upper Gulf coast in 1836. Compare that debut with the first steam train in the United States, which was operational in 1829, and the Jamaica Railway Company's first complete railroad in 1843 (when Jamaica was still a British colony).

In fact, the first federal grant of land to assist a railroad was made to the territory of Florida. This occurred in 1835, when the number of Americans who had seen a locomotive was slim indeed, so Florida was making national history before it was a state.

How did people decide where to build a railroad?

Spanish trails, English outposts, and Indian camps gave early owners some hints about where to build: a trail from St. Augustine to DeLeon Springs and Titusville, for instance.

What was some of the lingo?

"Uncle Wes" was Western Union. "Second trick" was second shift—at least in this business. "Ghost train" was the payroll car, "whiskers" stood for seniority, and "rip-track" was where the engineer went for minor repairs-in-place.

Readers will find out more about Romeo and Juliette; how Robert Mugge persuaded Adolphus Busch to ship a trainload of beer to Tampa; and the why of railroad gauges (the distance between the parallel tracks is the gauge; early railroads used narrow gauge, 3 feet, while others used standard gauge, 4 feet 8½ inches).

Trains evolved from wooden platforms over a rutted roadbed to iron rails, then came the invention of the steam locomotive in 1797 in England. Early trams moved freight, but they were pulled by mules and oxen. In the earliest times, "train" passengers rode in a conveyance behind a team of horses.

Florida railroads began in a similar fashion—pulled by animals over rough roadbeds carved out of flat swamps and rocky ridges, and across rivers and lakes. Eventually one of those railroads would cross islands between Florida Bay and the Atlantic Ocean, accomplishing engineering feats that still fascinate more than a century later.

Many of Florida's railroads were developed by people from elsewhere who found an exotic tropical puzzle when they arrived and a melting pot of stakeholders. Hence, the inclusion of a chapter about the array of people here and in charge—or those with a say-so in how things unfolded.

This book was put together to show how hard it all was, so readers could marvel that railroads got built at all, and to show that railroads were the impetus for Florida's civilization and the capitalization of its economy.

Meanwhile, the pace of this story is meant to underscore the premium placed on Florida during centuries of European exploration, imperial saber-rattling, diplomatic claims, military confrontation, the territorial era after 1821, the Seminole Wars, and statehood in 1845 (confirming Thomas Jefferson's prediction that the United States could not keep its hands off Florida).

Upon statehood, Florida got 500,000 acres of federal land (plus another 20 million acres by 1900). Also bending and sometimes breaking development were the American Civil War and martial law during Reconstruction. The seesaw continued through the 1920s land boom, the busted threadbare '30s, and industrial modernization through much of the 20th century.

So at various times in this book, "Florida" refers to colonies owned by other countries, a US territory, a member of the Confederacy, and a state rejoined to the Union.

Florida railroaders showed the rest of the developed world the abundant crops easily cultivated here, often during seasons when the rest of the country shivered. Florida land was cheaper than Northern land, even farmland in the rest of the South, giving historians a reason to notice the swarms of homesteaders crowding the rail lines into Florida in the late 1880s.

Even President William McKinley visited Florida in 1897, when Henry Flagler invited him to see his domain—which was anywhere on the east coast south of Jacksonville.

As Sandra Wallus Sammons noted: "One [Henry Flagler] took the east coast and one [Henry Plant] took the west coast. Together the two Henrys helped make Florida what it is."

Florida was something of a crapshoot throughout the 19th century, especially before railroads made it possible to go from one coast to the other or north to south—and before engineers connected the dots of lagoons to form a passable inland marine route. Day-to-day was not unlike the Wild West. The only law to speak of was military here and there, and a local marshal. Decidedly more lawless in the interior than the coast, Florida outposts created situations often fact-checked pretty casually by whichever badge had to choose between justice or stayin' alive.

Early Florida was wild, man. Home to killer reptiles, wild boars, panthers and bears. If humans wandered around at night and did not get swallowed whole, they might see the glint of an eye in the darkness of a swamp, and hear the snap of jaws on a small creature's neck. Settlers built forts to keep out predators, and most forts were near a coast.

Obstacles to rail development included unpredictable, often inclement weather; lack of access to building materials; fitful financing; diseases (yellow fever, for one); pesky mosquitoes and poisonous snakes; and a labor force dealing with menacing wildlife and transient criminals.

The Spanish came here to prosper, not create a democracy. They had a caste system that dictated which classes of people paid taxes, including slaves, free blacks, and Indians. That is just one way in which disparate cultures shaped the landscape and decided what "Florida" would be by the time rail developers put an oar in the water.

Statehood brought along the Internal Improvement Fund in the mid-1850s, enabling developers to apply for land grants and offering a guarantee to pay the interest on their construction bonds. The first companies thus aided were therefore a platform for Florida's rail network in the future. At times, however, the state reneged on those bonds and Florida's reputation suffered.

Readers will not just see trains as museum relics, but also discover their influence in pop culture. As a movie poster set the tone in 1936: "All aboard for danger . . . excitement . . . romance . . . on the crack train of the Florida run!"

Not to be overlooked was the role of Florida trains in the realm of national sports. Baseball spring training was a whirlwind in Tampa alone—with the Chicago Cubs, 1913–16; the Boston Red Sox, 1919; the Washington Senators, 1920–29; the Detroit Tigers, 1930; the Cincinnati Reds, 1931–42, 1946–87; the Chicago White Sox, 1954–59; and the New York Yankees, since 1996.

Of course, waterways are one of the first hooks for people visiting Florida for the first time, and while the rivers and lakes gave developers countless headaches, it's easy to relate to the purple prose that Jefferson Browne penned in the 1890s about the daily variation of colors and hues in the waters of the Florida Keys, about fickle tints that "no brush can paint or pen describe." Browne cites olivine running into indigo blue . . . fading to milky whiteness after a storm . . . a patch of sea grass, into moss-agate, with light winds causing the surface to ripple like a stream of precious stones . . .

With that being reality, and no reason to embellish, it's easy to see why railroaders were hell-bent on bridging the transportation gap. Given the new passenger-rail wrinkle known as All Aboard Florida, it seems that they still are.

CHAPTER 1

Before Rail

A Forbidding Territory, Too Far to Tackle

ONE NEED NOT DIG DEEP TO GRASP WHY RAIL DEVELOPMENT IN FLOR
IDA was a flat-out, uphill train-wreck of a proposition. Littering the
downward slope were death, taxes, war, bond defaults, swindles, and land
grabs.

But oh, what a day, when a locomotive burst through bunting and banners
for the first time, signaling one more place no longer stranded in wilderness.

Before railroad bosses (er, visionaries) began to crack the code to open
this untamed territory to development, Florida was a peninsula with far-
flung, ancient coastal settlements and a vast, forbidding interior—dangerous turf for the faint of heart, where any stranger caught napping might
be chomped in half or swallowed whole.

Those in charge at first were Native American tribes. If one could
imagine a tapestry or stained-glass rendering of Florida then, it would be
vignettes depicting Indian cultures and livelihoods.

Next to rule, usually in league with, or sparring with, the Indians:
Spain, France, Spain again, Great Britain, and Spain yet again. Florida,
in fact, was settled by Europeans before they colonized the rest of the
mainland of what would become our republic.

In that respect, Florida was somewhat like the tail wagging the
Colonial-era dog. Throughout the state one encounters descendants of all

A tortoise meandering across a patch of sand reflects the nature of the soil in many places in Florida—one of many considerations involved in choosing a railroad route and grading the roadbed. STATE ARCHIVES OF FLORIDA, FLORIDA MEMORY.

the aforesaid societies, as well as African Americans who came to Florida willingly or otherwise.

Thus, every new venture, scheme, modest enterprise, or grand vision to come along faced a crazy-quilt of influences on how things got done. Knowing the lay of the land was tricky—given topography, demographics, weather, politics, and power-brokering—creating unique challenges for penetrating the interior.

SIZE MATTERS, SHAPE COUNTS

Square one for understanding rail development here is the size and shape of Florida—a peninsula both long, 447 miles north to south, and broad, 361 miles across the Panhandle. Total area, 65,795 square miles (way bigger than Cuba, larger than England and Wales combined). Land covers 53,927 square miles, and water flows or stands across 11,868 square miles.

Wetlands and marshes cover substantial portions of Florida—with freshwater systems inland and saltwater systems along the coast—and posed an engineering headache for railroad engineers. STATE ARCHIVES OF FLORIDA, FLORIDA MEMORY.

Most of Florida sags and sashays near sea level, which is why most buildings lack basements. The true "basement" is known in geologic circles as the Florida Platform—a watery shelf wiggling ever so slightly from the Atlantic Ocean to the Gulf of Mexico. Think prairie, marsh, hammock, and ridge rock, propped up in a shallow vase of lazy ooze.

In a modern atlas, the peninsula's iconic outline lounges over this rather wide, doughy "platform." Were it a valise, you could pack two land masses the size of Florida, with nary a wrinkle and room for sunglasses.

Water depth at the western edge drops from about 300 feet to more than 10,000 feet. This was vital information for mariners approaching Florida ports and harbors, before and after the ship's manifest was due to meet a rail connection.

UPLIFTING FEATURES

A few exceptions with respectable elevations are the Brooksville Ridge, 180 to 300 feet; the Northern Florida Highlands, 50 to 345 feet; and the Lake Wales Ridge, 185 to 312 feet. The latter ridge has a "wet desert" habitat, as its annual rainfall can surpass 50 inches.

We regard Ocala today for its rolling hills ideal for raising thoroughbreds. It's also home to the Ocala Uplift, a geologic runaway from Pasco County, straying almost to the Georgia line, then dipping a little south and shooting west to Wakulla. To the east is the Peninsular Arch, a plantain-shaped plate beneath the land mass, extending from Georgia almost to Lake Okeechobee (Lake O).

Whether schooled or unsophisticated, the earliest settlers, entrepreneurs, and industrialists faced the facts posed by these geologic features, as they determined what could be built and where. The nature of soil, water supply, and habitats for sea life, animals, and plants also were material considerations if one hoped to hunt, fish, farm, or raise livestock for a living (and send those goods to market).

FICKLE WEATHER, FOUL CONDITIONS

Regardless of the era, any enterprise in Florida depended on weather gods often in a foul mood. Scorching temperatures in summer. High humidity. A lengthy rainy season and almost six months with the possibility of hurricanes dictated the year-round routines for farmers, ranchers, builders, merchants, and shippers. Weather dictated whether a crop season was good, and weather set the pace for any construction.

Before rail, local commerce depended on water passage in unpredictable conditions. Cargo ranged from cotton, indigo, and other commodities to farm produce, oysters, fish, lumber, cattle, cigars, and naval stores.

Eventually the discovery of phosphate in central Florida's Bone Valley would figure prominently on any freight manifest (phosphate is an essential ingredient in fertilizer, and Florida has more of it than any other state).

Florida rail development began in the central Panhandle, where the woodlands provided oaks, bald cypress, yellow "longleaf" pine, black gum, southern magnolia, red maple, American holly, poplar, black willow, and river birch. Thus, it became a timber goldmine and the go-to source for early rail ties.

A SOGGY SITUATION

Tricked-out topography equals ribbons of rivers, lakes, and swamps lolling at the pace of Jell-O; sandy flats and treacherous sinkholes; ridges with steep grades; a blanket of dense forests, hardwood hammocks, and palmetto scrub; pockets of airy caverns; and underwater caves punctuating porous limestone bedrock.

There was no shortage of liquid thoroughfares to transport passengers and cargo, considering more than two-dozen major rivers, several thousand lakes, the Atlantic Ocean, and the Gulf of Mexico. Modes varied from seaworthy and river-sound vessels to horse-drawn stage coaches, oxen hauling wagons, and mule "trains" on strap rail (beasts of burden pulled a conveyance until they got weary; the team lay down, rested and resumed the journey when someone cracked a whip).

Certain rivers figured prominently as sites—and engineering headaches—for early rail lines: the St. Johns (Florida's longest river at 310 miles), the Apalachicola, the Suwannee, and the St. Marys among them. In Colonial and territorial times, these waterways were essential as a steamboat artery connecting the peninsula with cities in the South and across the Gulf to New Orleans.

The St. Marys River originates in the Okefenokee Swamp, thrusts into a southward loop, bends north again, and empties into the Atlantic Ocean at Fernandina. Forming a curious scar on a map, that irregular dip in the St. Marys watershed mimics the outline of Florida's phallic nub in miniature.

The river also defines part of the Florida-Georgia line, as if two wizened characters, a Spanish conquistador and an English planter, once stood on opposite banks looking out to sea. In fact, the St. Marys River

A foggy morning at Lake Seminole, where the Apalachicola River originates. The river formed from the confluence of the Chattahoochee and Flint Rivers flowing from Georgia. The river's path to the Gulf of Mexico played prominently in decisions about where to build a railroad bridge. STATE ARCHIVES OF FLORIDA, FLORIDA MEMORY.

was spelled out in the first Treaty of Paris of 1763 as the northeastern boundary of "East Florida." (England won the peninsula in that card game, for a while. Spain, temporarily, got Cuba.)

The Apalachicola River begins at Lake Seminole, where the Chattahoochee and Flint Rivers flow from Georgia. It winds south into Hathcock Bay, then reaches the Gulf of Mexico at the town of Apalachicola. The river played prominently in decisions about train travel—whether ox-wagon or rail.

The Brits carved "Spanish Florida" into two colonies and held them for two decades in the mid-18th century. The Apalachicola River was the boundary, with St. Augustine the capital of East Florida and Pensacola the capital of West Florida (for a time, that meant west to the Mississippi River).

A Saintly Sojourn

St. Augustine would, in time, change Florida rail history (as described in Chapter 9). But in the beginning, it was where Marquess Juan Ponce de León of Spain landed in 1513, poked around for a while, and moved on. That was par in those days, as most expeditions concentrated on coastal curiosities.

In 1565 Pedro Menéndez de Avilés, another Spaniard scouting for his king, set a serious benchmark, which is how St. Augustine remains the oldest continuously occupied European settlement in the New World. For the next two centuries, it was the seat of New Spain.

About 65 miles north, where the St. Marys River meets the Atlantic and splashes Georgia, a barrier island stretches for 13 miles. Amelia Island, the "Isle of Eight Flags," claims the only sky in the New World to frame silhouettes of eight flags. Fernandina, now Fernandina Beach, is the island's only municipality. (Chapter 3 describes Fernandina's fame as the eastern terminus of the first railway to connect the Atlantic coast with the Gulf of Mexico.)

Settled for more than four and a half centuries, Fernandina had sovereign "masters" and posturing saber-rattlers. Frenchman Jean Ribault landed in 1562 and hoisted a fleur-de-lis banner, which likely puzzled the Timucuan Indians in residence. He called the land Isle de Mai. A French accent was temporary, as the Spaniard Menéndez de Avilés overtook Isle de Mai three years later. Spain raised its flag of choice, the Burgundian Saltire.

In 1702 the British governor of Georgia sacked the mission and settlement, renaming the island "Amelia" after the daughter of King George II. Part of that time, the area was known as Egmont for an English earl's indigo plantation.

During the American Revolutionary War, Colonial forces invaded Amelia Island. After the British defeat, Spain got Florida back, for a while, ruling from 1783 to 1821 (the Second Spanish Period). Other flags over Fernandina were the "Patriots" flag, the Green Cross of Florida, and the flags of Mexican rebels, the United States, and the Confederacy.

In 1575, not long before his death, a Spaniard named Hernando de Escalante Fontaneda drafted a remarkable memoir chronicling his seventeen-year ordeal as a captive among Florida's Calusa Indians. He was enslaved in 1549 after he survived a shipwreck in the Florida Keys. Just thirteen years old at the time, Escalante remained among the Indians until 1566, when Menéndez de Avilés rescued him.

FOREPLAY FOR FLORIDA

For decades the United States had coveted Florida and extended some bold overtures to Spain. Years of courting led to the big handoff agreement known as the Florida Purchase Treaty, aka the Adams-Onis Treaty, or the Transcontinental Treaty of 1819.

Secretary of State John Quincy Adams and Lord Don Luis de Onis, Gonzales, Lopez y Vara, officiated, and the deal was finalized in February 1821. The United States assumed $5 million in citizen claims against Spain, while "His Catholic Majesty" ceded all his territories east of the Mississippi River.

Tallahassee became the capital of the territory. General Andrew "Old Hickory" Jackson, victor in the War of 1812 and hero of the Battle of New Orleans, was President James Monroe's choice for military governor. Florida functioned as a US territory from 1822 until statehood in 1845, under four governors: William Pope DuVal (later written as Duval), John Henry Eaton, General Richard Keith Call, and Robert Raymond Reid.

General Call—Jackson's former protégé—was at one time receiver for the General Land Office of Florida. Eventually, he owned the Tallahassee Railroad.

Land Grants, Land Grabs

In addition to money and engineering know-how, building a railroad requires ownership of land and/or right-of-way. In Florida, given sovereign footprints and tribal posturing, proof of title often was a crapshoot.

During Spain's rule of *La Florida*, the king bestowed generous land grants to reward loyal subjects. Even a Scot, George Fleming, who emigrated in 1785, received sizable parcels for assisting the Spanish military during its Second Period. In East Florida the Flemings farmed Hibernia, a St. Johns River plantation, while some Seton in-laws on the maternal side settled in Fernandina in the early 1800s.

The Arredondo land grant in north-central Florida illustrates well the plight of land surveyors and their clients who faced serious obstacles, especially when such grants were challenged. In this instance, the case of *United States vs. Arredondo* was argued before the US Supreme Court in 1832.

The beef was between the government and Don Fernando de la Maza Arredondo (and Son), subjects of Spain, living in Cuba at the time of the dispute. The prize in this contest was the right to sell or transfer, *in a timely manner,* an undivided parcel of 289,645 acres situated in what is now Alachua County, near Gainesville, roughly 52 miles west of St. Augustine and 36 miles west of the St. Johns River.

The Spanish government gave Arredondo the land in December 1817, according to a parchment signed in Havana.

The defendants' agents stated that a tribe of Seminole Indians had inhabited Alachua (an Indian word for "sinkhole") but abandoned it, and that Arredondo planned for 200 Spanish families to settle, raise cattle, cultivate the land, and have a beneficial relationship with Creek and Seminole Indians living on the outskirts.

One snag was about timing, as in deadlines imposed for the Spanish to either sell lands or otherwise dispose of those grants within three years of giving up claim to Florida. Further twists pertained to some deals with people who "bought" parcels from Spanish grantees or finagled tracts at silly prices when the Spanish ran out of time for extensions.

As described in Chapter 3, merchant Moses E. Levy, a Jewish émigré born in Morocco, was on the receiving end of a sweet deal with the Spanish circa 1820: 14,500 acres near Jacksonville and 38,400 acres in Alachua County. The latter parcel was part of the Arredondo grant, and Levy's agents signed for him in Havana.

In 1828 Arredondo filed a petition in the Superior Court of the Eastern District of Florida against the United States, citing a congressional act "providing for the settlement and confirmation of private land claims in Florida." He blamed skirmishes and wars with Indians, in part, for his failure to finalize the grants on time. The government countered with doubts about the grant itself, which "was made to the prejudice and injury of the Florida tribes of Indians."

Legal snarls, claims of fraud, and rural feuds turned up the volume of noise associated with Spanish grants. An obstacle to reliable land surveys, it formed a stifling overlay on state history. Once Florida was a territory, land agents in East and West Florida faced a vacuum of relevant evidence: missing records, damaged documents, and deeds the Spanish carried off to Cuba.

From the government's point of view, wily schemes were a parallel endeavor during the years it negotiated with Spain to cede Florida. General Call argued the point often in federal court, noting that justices were operating with the knowledge that "some of the grants, especially those after 1815, were done with intent to defraud the United States."

A Primordial Stew

Settlers arriving here usually brought a sizable posse. Florida archaeology illustrates the emergence of numerous complex Native American cultures—the truest "native Floridians."

The Timucua people likely migrated to northeast Florida and southern Georgia from the Amazon River rainforest. Unlike some tribes, they traded with the Spanish and adopted some of their ways. Their social structure of chiefs and a village council reflected a fairly progressive agricultural existence. Wild game rounded out their diet—with meat roasted on an open fire, *barbacoa*-style.

The Manatee River on the west coast is where Spanish explorer Hernando DeSoto arrived in 1539. When he marched an army through Timucuan territory, the hidalgos encountered numerous tribal villages. The Spanish survived largely on a diet of corn during their winter in the Panhandle—near what is now Tallahassee. One of the region's chief characteristics is rolling "red hills" along the border with Georgia.

The Timucua were Mound Builders, and their shell middens give modern archeologists a lot to study (a turtle-shell mound near New Smyrna covers 16 acres). San Juan del Puerto is the site of a 16th-century Franciscan mission for the Timucuan who lived on Fort George Island on the St. Johns River. The woodlands mask another large midden created over generations. The Lake Jackson Mounds north of Tallahassee famously mark the vicinity of the ancient Apalachee culture which thrived there.

The Choctaws, who had a decent rapport with the French, settled in the western Panhandle. They were among those forced to go to Oklahoma in the 1800s. Archeological finds reflect the "Choctaw Sea," which in antiquity covered the Choctawhatchee River and the river deltas of the Apalachicola and Ochlocknee Rivers.

Significant archaeological sites in the Panhandle confirm Paleo-Indians lived there about 12,000 BC (perhaps nomadic hunters in pursuit of mastodon for supper). Several distinct cultures began to range south from Georgia and the Carolinas in the 16th century.

RAWHIDE, RENEGADES, RARE BEEF

Livestock became a major portion of cargo business for rail operators, as ranching as a significant industry in Florida dates to the Colonial era (in fact, Florida engaged in cattle ranching earlier than other American locales). Among the first herds brought to these shores by Ponce de León and Don Diego de Maldonado, many escaped and adapted to a subtropical landscape and diet.

On the Spanish coastal plain of Andalusia, hired vaqueros on horseback marked cattle and moved livestock according to the seasons. Conquistadores then brought longhorns to the Caribbean and Florida.

Old Spanish Brands

Replicas of some Spanish cattle brands used in the colonial era. Florida was the seat of New Spain in the 16th and 17th centuries, and again after the Revolutionary War until it became a territory of the United States. Livestock descended from those early herds became an important part of the railroad business. STATE ARCHIVES OF FLORIDA, FLORIDA MEMORY.

The British brought herds as well. In England and Ireland, highlanders branded their livestock, herded them into pens, and roamed to find fresh pastures. Drovers and their dogs got the animals to market.

In the New World, the English and the Spanish revised cattle ranching to suit the tropics. The result created a significant industry for Florida's economy, and a pivotal piece of the railroad puzzle.

The nature of relationships between the Europeans and Native Americans helps explain how Indians got into herding cattle in Florida. Having brought diseases which wiped out numerous native settlements, the Spanish were hated among many surviving tribes. Indians often assisted the Brits in skirmishes against their common enemy, gaining their own herds as bounty.

As early as the founding of St. Augustine, cattle was a food staple for the colony. Spanish clergy posted to various missions taught Indians the skills to manage cattle. Thus, they too became cattlemen who traded hides, beef, and tallow with their neighbors. Those wrangler saddles fit settlers of every stripe, and they tackled some unforgiving turf to move herds and track strays in swamps and woodlands. As for equines used in cattle ranching, they were known as the Marsh Tacky, a smaller breed of horse, standing fourteen or fifteen hands and adapted for the subtropical landscape.

Although many tribes were content with live-and-let-live trade practices, numerous settlers perceived their families to be in danger in areas where Indians dominated the population. They routinely pressed local lawmen "to keep them safe." There were no official voices, however, to speak for the Indians who felt their lands, culture, and livelihood threatened by encroaching settlers.

Early cattlemen, whether American, European, or Indian, signed up for hazardous duty. They tangled with wild animals (panthers, bobcats, and bears), fought off rustlers, and feuded with each other. They endured cattle drives lasting months and traveled through unforgiving terrain, often in baking temperatures, frog-drowning rains, even hurricanes. Known variously as cowmen, cow hunters, or Florida "crackers" flinging an 18-foot bullwhip, they lived an existence best suited to loners.

The route to market began as a trek from the Panhandle or central Florida to Jacksonville, Savannah, and Charleston. By the 1830s they could herd livestock down to west coast ports such as Punta Rassa and Charlotte Harbor—destination, Havana. The "cattle call" along those wharves involved chutes to move the livestock aboard schooners. They were packed in like sardines on the hoof, sometimes 200 head per trip.

RESTLESS NATIVES

Although the best known among Florida's Native American societies, the Seminoles did not originate as one tribe. Allied with Creek, Miccosukee, and other natives of northern Florida and southern Georgia, they were somewhat united by the 1700s. Their common goal was to fight European invaders.

Once other tribes native to southern Florida were conquered by the Spanish and banished to Cuba, this Creek-Miccosukee alliance retreated south and into the Everglades. The federal government removed most Seminoles to Oklahoma, but hundreds remained in Florida's interior and form a sizable population all these generations later (the tribe also owns one of the state's largest cattle-ranching operations).

Ahaya, the first recorded leader of the Alachua band of Seminoles, grew up in north Florida near the Chattahoochee River. His war party helped the British in a raid against the Spanish at St. Augustine in 1740. A decade later he moved his people to an area where the fishing was good and game was abundant, and the tribe took control of sizable numbers of wild cattle. His village was located near what is now Payne's Prairie (named for one of Ahaya's sons).

Ahaya gained significant recognition apart from other tribes. His British allies nicknamed him Cowkeeper, for his sizable herd, and decided his community deserved its own identity. The British called them Seminoles, derived from a Spanish word, *cimarrónes* (meaning "runaways").

The British and Creek Indians raided the Panhandle, dispatching many Spanish cattle ranchers by the early 1700s. That left it to Indian settlers to sustain the cattle industry for the rest of the century.

"Black Seminoles" were runaway slaves who joined tribes of Indians. Seminole-style "bondage" differed from slavery in the antebellum South. Leaders of these black bands took direction from the Indians as if they were part of a militia. Under the more casual Seminole customs, slaves and free blacks lived in their own camps well apart from their "masters."

Blending their Gullah roots in a new environment, they spoke in an Afro-Seminole-Creole banter. They modeled their quarters on the Indian template of sleeping in chickees—elevated open-air platforms with a log frame and a thatched roof of palmetto fronds.

Born near St. Augustine around 1780, Micanopy became a Seminole chief in 1819 and proceeded to extend his tribe's reach, taking over vast tracts of land and cattle herds. He also hired as many as a hundred escaped slaves to work his properties.

HAVEN FOR AFRICAN AMERICANS

Florida's black heritage has been significant in many eras and many industries.

As early as the 17th century, slaves in Southern colonies were seeking their freedom from British plantation owners who relied on their labor. Spanish Florida became a safe haven for them, as the Spanish exploited the slaves' discontent by offering them refuge in exchange for avowing

Catholicism. Spain's larger goal was to disrupt their enemy's agrarian economy.

One permanent example of this ploy is near St. Augustine. Built in 1738 by a Spanish governor, Gracia Real de Santa Teresa de Mosé (now Fort Mose) was a free black community ("free" if you discount the exchange of secure sanctuary for service in the Spanish militia and religious fidelity).

In other instances, free blacks arrived in Florida with Spanish expeditions, working as scouts, gun-bearers, and soldiers. Earlier, they had assisted the Spanish, militia-style, in Central and South America.

SOUTHERN SANCTUARY

Even before someone properly documented them, "Floridians" indicated a checkered heritage, as the peninsula was a natural magnet for fugitives of many stripes: slaves who escaped from the North before the American Revolution; slaves on the run from the South; Maroons (Africans sold into slavery in Cuba who managed to escape and form independent settlements); white criminals on the lam, dodging warrants in other territories; islanders from throughout the Caribbean and émigrés from Central and South America (reflecting a mix of native Indians and Europeans); and deserters hiding out during a war.

Protestants and Catholics were wallpaper across the South, and our pre-Revolutionary makeup included many more Jews than some people realize—and not the Miami Beach variety of the 1940s and '50s, or the condo-commando crowd from the 1970s onward. These Jewish families appreciated an opportunity to live in the New World apart from persecution—no matter where they lived before—and their strategy was keeping to themselves. According to one author, Dr. Joseph Andrews, the first Jewish settlers in the New World arrived from Brazil in the mid-17th century. A Sephardic group, they'd been expelled from Spain around the time Christopher Columbus was sailing westward.

BY UNORTHODOX MEANS

New Smyrna on the Atlantic coast was settled by a Scot, Dr. Arthur Turnbull, in the 1760s. In an ambitious maneuver, Turnbull brought in his own labor force, almost 1,500 "settlers" from islands in the Mediterranean (Minorca, Majorca, Ibiza, and Sicily) and from Smyrna, Crete, and the Mani Peninsula of Greece. His workers—said to be the first followers of the Greek Orthodox faith in this hemisphere—cultivated hemp, sugarcane, and indigo and fashioned primitive rum.

Had Turnbull treated them better, they might not have left him to watch his crops rotting in the fields. Alas, they bailed on him and sought sanctuary from the British governor in St. Augustine to the north, an early example of slave mutiny.

A Capital Choice

William Pope DuVal, born in Virginia, studied law in Kentucky and moved to Florida, where he became judge for the East Florida District. This happened the same year that Spain signed the papers to cede Florida. About a year later, President James Monroe appointed DuVal the first nonmilitary governor of the new territory. President John Quincy Adams reappointed DuVal, as did President Andrew Jackson (as a general, he had been Florida's military governor and DuVal's predecessor).

During DuVal's long time in office, he chose "Tallahassa" as the new territorial capital, citing its favorable location. He also signed the first act of legislation, which created four Florida territories and assigned a local court system.

DuVal was territorial governor for a dozen years (1822–34), a time when his reputation included peaceful dealings with tribes of Native Americans. He is the namesake of Duval County and numerous other place names in Florida. One of the most widely known is Duval Street in downtown Key West.

A Drum "Roll" for Ybor

It is possible to view one particular immigrant as someone whose heritage and lifetime pursuits blur the lines between Old World, New World, modernity, and legacy. That man was Vicente Martinez Ybor—born in Spain in 1818, emigrated to Cuba in 1832. A clerk who learned the cigar business in Havana, he began his own enterprise to manufacture proprietary cigars. These artfully rolled gems were called

A sketch of Vicente Martinez Ybor, a native of Spain who emigrated to Cuba, learned the cigar business and began his own proprietary enterprise. Sympathetic to Cubans rebelling against Spain, he moved to Key West, then Tampa. He also invested in street cars, fuel, and street paving. STATE ARCHIVES OF FLORIDA, FLORIDA MEMORY.

El Principe de Gales (Prince of Wales); at one time, the factory made 20,000 a day.

Despite his Spanish ancestry dating to the Moorish occupation of his homeland, Ybor was sympathetic when Cuban rebels stood up to Spanish rule. After he was compromised as a rebel sympathizer, he fled Havana in 1869, arrived in Key West, and took up where he left off in the cigar business.

Less than two decades later, Ybor moved operations to Tampa, where he and some compadres founded a "company town" just outside the city limits. Tampa later annexed the neighborhood named for him. Unlike pre–Civil War industries which relied on slave labor, cigar-making was deemed an immigrant's game, and Ybor brought them from both Spain and Cuba. He created an empire that further elevated awareness of Tampa (for a time, it was the world's leader in cigar manufacturing).

Ybor also invested outside his lane, creating companies in many sectors and investing in the city's streetcar line. His fuel distribution and street paving entities led to the Port of Tampa expansion. Thus, a Spaniard, by way of Havana, made it impossible to clip the end of a cigar and strike a match without thinking of Tampa and its transportation infrastructure.

The next chapter will describe a decade of embryonic stages in rail concepts.

CHAPTER 2

Road Tested

Trails, Tramways, and Trains

FLORIDA, AT TIMES, SEEMED A LAND OF *BELLUM AD INFINITUM*. PEACE WAS a rarity, given the occupation by American troops during the War of 1812, the awkward skirmishes of the "Patriot War," and more American troops during the First Seminole War.

As the longtime Colonial seat of "East Florida," St. Augustine was the natural choice for capital of the territory, and it remained so for three years after the United States acquired Florida in 1821.

About that time, Kentucky-born lawyer Joseph M. White moved to Pensacola. A territorial representative to Congress from 1825 to 1837, White proposed a survey for a rail line between St. Marks (an old Spanish fortress near the Gulf of Mexico, née *San Marcos de Apalache*, founded in the 1600s) and Augusta, Georgia. Congress declined.

An inkling for enlightened transportation surfaced in 1828, when the Territorial Council chartered the Chipola Canal Company. It gave the option to build a canal or a railway from the Chipola River in the Panhandle to St. Andrews Bay on the Gulf.

Alas, no rails. Nada.

SHOESTRING STRATEGY

Tallahassee had became the territorial capital in 1824. In 1831 the legislature approved the first charter for a Florida railroad. Called the Leon

A saw grass prairie in the Everglades separates storm clouds from their reflection in the water. This sensitive environment was considered for railroad development and rejected as a monumentally bad idea. STATE ARCHIVES OF FLORIDA, FLORIDA MEMORY.

Rail-Way Company, the profoundly undercapitalized venture got new backers and a new charter; it emerged a year later as the Leon Railroad Company.

In March 1835 the territory received the first federal land grant ever given to assist a railroad—one of many "firsts" recorded in national memory. The grantee, the Tallahassee Railroad Company, received a roadbed and 30 feet on each side, and the rights to lumber it might need for construction within 300 feet on each side of the 22-mile line. The company also got 10 acres of land at the terminus in St. Marks. Thus, work began to link the capital with a port on the Gulf in the peninsula's "Big Bend."

Financing came from Panhandle cotton planters in Leon and Jefferson Counties who needed to ship their crops to domestic and foreign textile mills. Another prominent market source were Florida lumbermen who needed to send goods to ports on the East Coast, the Gulf, and the Caribbean. Merchants also shipped naval stores (a term for resin-based goop such as turpentine, pitch, and tar, used to build and repair wooden sailing ships).

One prominent planter was Benjamin Chaires, a native of North Carolina who settled near Tallahassee after creating the survey for Jacksonville. His first Florida investment was a one-third share in a plantation on Amelia Island, complete with equipment, slaves, and vessels. Considered Florida's "first millionaire," Chaires set up Tallahassee's first bank and helped to spearhead the Tallahassee Railroad.

Born in 1786, Chaires died of yellow fever in 1838, just six years after beginning construction of Verdura, a rather large and spectacular example of antebellum plantations. Built in the Greek Revival style, it was situated on a high hill; twenty-five broad steps to the front portico, framed in pillars, magnified its inherent sense of arrival. The dominant focal point was ten brick columns, five on the east end and five on the west, eight feet apart and three stories high. Broad verandas gave the second and third floors outdoor "living rooms" on each end.

More than sixty slaves worked Chaires's cotton and corn fields, and crafted the bricks for Verdura. With thirteen rooms, it had a dozen fireplaces, a double staircase, and space to dance in an 80-foot ballroom. Located several miles outside town, the property covered more than

9,400 acres. After the death of Chaires, other family members lived at Verdura for generations. It was destroyed by fire in 1885. Those three-story columns are all that remain.

The Tallahassee Railroad took several years to complete, but the line began a partial schedule in 1836 and reached St. Marks a year later. The mule-drawn train was wooden cars riding on wooden rails with iron straps. By 1838 the line extended another 3 miles south to the oceangoing ships at Port Leon. That feat was short-lived, as a major hurricane leveled Port Leon five years later. Thus, the Tallahassee Railroad moved its terminal back to St. Marks.

In 1856 the Tallahassee Railroad replaced its wooden rails with iron. Concurrently, steam locomotives gave the mules some overdue pasture time. (In the Victorian era in England and North America, "iron horse" was a literary term to describe new-age steam locomotives. That did not actually apply to the earliest trains in Florida, but it sounded great on paper.)

The Tallahassee Railroad continued to make its mark, but it wasn't the first to operate.

FIRST IN LINE

As mentioned previously, the handoff from Spain to the United States had created numerous land-title disputes. Apalachicola, for one, was rife with legal hassles. Some land speculators there abandoned the city and busied themselves with creating an ambitious settlement on St. Joseph Bay by 1835.

The main snag in their plan to bolster commerce was the absence of any route to the heavily traveled commercial artery, the Apalachicola River. The Territorial Council granted a charter in 1835 for the Lake Wimico and St. Joseph Canal Company, giving approval to dig a canal from a new town on St. Joseph Bay to a lagoon on the lake—thereby connecting the ambitious whippersnapper St. Joseph with the boss-daddy Apalachicola River.

Leaders of the company opted to build a railroad instead. The charter was amended to the Lake Wimico and St. Joseph Canal and Railroad Company in 1836, somewhat after workers began grading the route.

The company built a wharf 1,800 feet into St. Joseph Bay, where vessels awaited its trains. At the point where the tracks reached Columbus Bayou on Lake Wimico, the company installed a second wharf and cotton warehouses, ramping up its steamboat business.

Up and running by March 1836, the Lake Wimico firm was the first railroad to operate in Florida. Graduating from horse-drawn trains, the company acquired two steam engines which ran on broad-gauge tracks with iron strapping atop wooden rails, attached to wooden cross-ties.

Within six months one of those engines would pull a dozen cars and hundreds of passengers from St. Joseph to the bayou-on-the-lake-by-the-big-river and points north. Reflecting the prominence of St. Joseph as the Panhandle's largest town at that time, it was the site where fifty-seven delegates to the first Constitutional Convention met on December 3, 1838, to draft a charter for Florida to join the Union.

Thus, the Lake Wimico company owned the first steam railroad in Florida. And according to company lore, the engines were a winter splurge. In the summer the locomotives idled in sheds and horses took up the yoke.

The railroad operated a mere five years, until 1841. A yellow fever epidemic that year, and the railroad company's financial woes, sent St. Joseph into decline, demise, and "ghost town" status. Hurricanes in 1843 and 1851 flattened what was left.

Once the Apalachicola Northern Railroad arrived in 1909, some courageous souls founded another settlement near St. Joseph. The former Old St. Joseph became known as Port St. Joe, so-named for a paper mill and real estate conglomerate to be described in Chapter 13.

Runaway Ambition

The boldest plan of the territorial era was a notion to build a 210-mile rail line from Pensacola in the Panhandle to Columbus, Georgia, a hub of navigation on the Chattahoochee River on the border between Georgia and Alabama. The aim was to cash in on those states' abundant cotton crops by transporting the commodity to Pensacola's deepwater port.

In 1834 the legislature granted a charter for the Florida, Alabama & Georgia Railroad, with a capitalization of $2 million. About the same

General Richard Keith Call was a native of Virginia who became a protégé of Andrew Jackson. Call was one of four governors at the helm while Florida functioned as a territory before statehood. He owned the Tallahassee Railroad for a while, and his legions of slaves labored to build two splendid plantations in the area. STATE ARCHIVES OF FLORIDA, FLORIDA MEMORY.

time, the state of Alabama chartered the Alabama, Florida & Georgia Railroad. In 1835 Florida accepted Alabama's charter and corporate name.

Beginning in the late 1820s, Pensacola had become the center of the universe for one William Henry Chase of Massachusetts, a precocious West Point graduate and former captain with the US Army Corps of Engineers. He had married a Southerner, Anne Paul Matthews of Louisiana, someone he likely met while stationed with the corps on several Gulf coast fort-building and bridge projects. After retiring from the corps, he immersed himself in a new vision for his adopted city.

Chase founded the Bank of Pensacola around 1829 and developed real estate interests in the city, all of which positioned him to become president of the aforementioned Alabama, Florida & Georgia Railroad. This was no casual choice, even for an engineer. Chase simply believed his own flair for hyperbole: "Railroads are the rivers of tomorrow, and canals will be the intercoastal connection between rivers." (Chase's own words from an 1829 brochure extolling the charms of Pensacola.)

According to the charter for the Bank of Pensacola, the territory authorized $500,000 in bonds to be issued to capitalize Chase's railroad. A later amendment allowed the bank to increase its outstanding stock to $2.5 million, "to be held in shares of one hundred dollars each." (Meanwhile, officers and directors of the bank were, for the most part, officers and directors of the railroad company. The territory guaranteed the bank bonds, which were to finance construction of the railroad. The Bank of the United States issued the bonds, while the territory placed a first lien on the Bank of Pensacola's capital stock, real estate, and assets and on the bank's stock in the Alabama, Florida & Georgia Railroad.)

When stock subscriptions for Chase's railroad opened, sales soon reached $1.5 million. The Bank of Pensacola, with the Territorial Council's blessing (and the governor's signature), got permission to issue bonds to raise cash to buy $500,000 in railroad stock. In 1835 the bank issued $500,000 in bonds, and those debt instruments—$1,000 each, paying interest of 6 percent per year—held special appeal for foreign investors. The charter also allowed the bank to issue additional bonds if needed to pay installments on its subscribed stock in the railroad company.

In April 1839 the Bank of Pensacola tightened the terms of its loan policy: If you had borrowed funds and wanted to renew the loan, you'd have to pay 20 percent of the principal instead of 10. Between July 1837 and December 1839, the bank had advanced $259,175, including interest, to the Alabama, Florida & Georgia Railroad. Author David L. Walby's research on Chase indicates that amount was in addition to the $332,840 the bank had already invested in the railroad—or more than $500,000 by 1840.

Favored with a free survey of a route and right-of-way through federal lands (thank you, Congress), Chase's railroad hired crews and began grading the line. Along the way, Chase decided Montgomery, Alabama, would be the northern terminus, which shortened the route somewhat but posed the extra step of acquiring the Montgomery and West Point (Georgia) Railroad. Construction then began on grading the line toward Montgomery.

In 1836 the Bank of Pensacola reported capital of $606,115. Of that sum, bond obligations and capital stock came to $500,000. With so much of its money committed to railroad stock, the bank had scant resources to make loans and generate business.

Enter the Panic of 1837, America's first major financial crisis, one rooted in irrational land speculation in the West and Northeast and a headstrong difference of opinion about national and state monetary policies. The Bank of Pensacola's reaction was to suspend specie payments (gold and silver coins) on June 5, 1837, a status that lasted for eighteen months.

Meanwhile, Chase et al. were concerned about a charter provision allowing the governor to withhold endorsement on additional bonds until he had proof of one railroad mile constructed for each ten bonds presented. In addition, the territory imposed the lien on each subsequent mile of railroad built until the bonds were redeemed.

The railroad's response to financial pressures was to sell its iron rails, spikes, and locomotives in 1838 and '39, thereby preventing the completion of the promised route and stations. That failure completed the Bank of Pensacola's "undoing," landing it in the column of failed lenders. Troubled investors sought help from the Bank of the United States, which was obligated to pay interest on the bank's railroad bonds.

Even worse, Florida's traumatized governor, General Richard Keith Call, and the Territorial Council decided no one had been authorized to endorse those railroad bonds or pledge the territory's credit. The fallout from the scandal was that shareholders and bond-holders lost their shirts, and too few miles of partially built track lay in a heap.

Dr. Junius Elmore Dovell, a professor at the University of Florida, and J. E. Richardson, an assistant professor, summarized the debacle in *History of Banking in Florida: 1828–1954:* "This Pensacola firm thus became a 'railroad construction' bank. The avowed purpose of the whole scheme was to bring in outside capital for development purposes. Bonds were sold in this country, England and Holland."

High hopes for the venture collapsed when it was revealed the railroad had graded just 10 miles for track construction, despite such generous advances from the company's own bank. The railroad company folded without ever sounding a toot of two longs, a short, and a long. (Other chapters will describe how Pensacola eventually got a railroad, and how Chase played a unique role during the Civil War.)

Despite such clues to a flawed strategy, Chase's legacy partly rests on his ability to propel the progress of Pensacola at a time when industrialization was critical. As Walby notes in *William Henry Chase, Uniquely American:* "The national destiny and the destiny of William Henry Chase were the same. He was not in the audience, he was on the stage."

Another author and historian, Gene M. Burnett, referred to Chase as "Pensacola's One-Man Economy," someone whose grand schemes made it possible for future generations to have a far more dynamic future: "The city came by an economic coil-spring in the 1820s, when Colonel Chase began a passel of fort-building around the Gulf."

Burnett's assessment is that the symbiotic alignment between Chase's military connections and private business interests would, in today's world, likely land him in jail.

FEDERAL FISHING

The US Congress showed interest in rail development in Florida as early as 1842, when representatives commissioned a survey for a rail route between the St. Marys River and Cedar Key on the Gulf (the impetus for that decision comes to light in the next chapter).

However much these early on-off efforts flailed about, the profound impact of railroads on Florida history is ironclad. Whether modest or grand undertakings, these passenger and freight routes peeled back the interior, giving existing industry a leg up and prompting new ones. Who could have imagined, then, the level of tourism, real estate development, and industry that would follow in those tracks?

Despite so many natural, political, and financial obstacles to rail development, Florida would become a tangled landscape of ampersands as developers and entrepreneurs finagled new names for chartered lines, imaginary lines, and mergers of going concerns.

ATSENA OTIE, CEDAR KEYS

Seminole Indians hunted and fished around a series of Gulf coast barrier islands known as the Cedar Keys. Spanish explorers in the 16th century favored "the Cedar Isles" (a Spanish cartographer in 1542 designated them *Las Islas Sabines*) as a pit stop to take on fresh water and drop ballast on the way home from Mexico. Pirates, the likes of Jean Lafitte, Captain Kidd, and William Augustus Bowles, loved the locale as well, for the deep natural harbor lying among keys named Seahorse, Snake, Way, and Atsena (Ah-SEE-a) Otie.

During the Second Seminole War, US Army General Zachary Taylor established "Fort No. 4" on Depot Key. Thus, 1839 is generally accepted as the beginning of permanent historic occupation in the Cedar Keys.

In 1843 Augustus Steele—postmaster for Tampa Bay and US Customs House officer for Hillsborough County—received a permit for Depot Key. Steele renamed it Atsena Otie, an Indian word for "Cedar Island." Steele bought the existing buildings, built some guest cottages, and opened a post office.

Someone created a plat for a town on Way Key in 1859. By 1861, when the Florida Railroad completed its line from Fernandina to Cedar Key, the latter was an important outlet to export lumber and naval stores. Ships from Siberia began to bring in graphite for pencil lead, to complement the local cedar being exported to a northern pencil manufacturer.

Most of Way Key, now called Cedar Key, housed the depot and the railroad terminal—putting the once-sleepy port on the map of commerce.

HUMAN CAPITAL

At the time territorial mandates took hold, bands of Seminoles lived in settlements between the Suwannee and Apalachicola Rivers. They raised sizable herds of livestock, with a "town" often having 1,500 head of cattle and hundreds of horses.

Seminoles had routinely engaged in amicable trading with settlers and ranchers, whether Spanish or British. As the territory developed, with news of its enormous potential, people in other states and territories coveted slices of Florida.

Slaves able to escape other areas flocked to Florida, too. Concurrently, British, French, and American pioneers established rice and cotton plantations in northern Florida. Here, as was the custom in much of the South, slave labor became the engine of a plantation economy.

FRENCH ACCENT

The late Clifton Paisley, author of *The Red Hills of Florida, 1528–1865*, noted the time line for the selection of Tallahassee as the territorial seat of government in 1824. Its fertile acreage had been choice turf for generations of Apalachee tribes. Paisley's book refers to maps by English cartographers in 1767 and 1778, who penned the names of two Indian towns, Tallahassa Taloofa ("Tonaby's Town") and Mikasuki ("New Town").

Another name shows up in the city's early days as well. Achille Murat, nephew of Napoleon Bonaparte, came to the New World when things went south for his uncle. Murat had a plantation in Jefferson County and was prominent on the ledger books of certain entities.

In the mid-1830s, for instance, Murat's name was noted as a director of the notorious Union Bank of Florida in Tallahassee and owner of several hundred shares of its stock. The "real estate mortgage bank," a pawn of one John Grattan Gamble, was among three deemed "creatures of domestic ingenuity and foreign cupidity"—institutions that had access to public assistance and abused the privilege. The other two were the aforementioned "railroad bank" of Pensacola and the Southern Life Insurance Company in St. Augustine.

In the case of Gamble's scheme to finance favored cotton planters, the legislature yanked the bank's charter in 1843.

HART'S DESIRE

Writing about the history of Jacksonville, John Cowart noted that settlement leaders were eager to connect their area with the Gulf coast as early as the 1830s. The leading proponent was Isaiah Hart, namesake of the town of Hart's Road (later Hart's Station). They proposed the Florida Peninsular and Jacksonville Railroad, with the first leg westward to Alligator (Lake City).

In the wake of Seminole Indian attacks, Hart and the other investors abandoned their project. Cowart estimated their losses at more than $1 million.

The following chapters will describe rail development from Jacksonville, as well as the man whose accomplishments prompted the town of Hart's Station to be renamed Yulee.

A TOWN WITHOUT A TRAIN

What happened to a town without tracks? Newnansville is one example.

The Dell brothers, who had visited north-central Florida during the Patriot War, returned to settle there in 1814. They built Dell's Post Office "downtown" in 1826. A few years later, the community council named the place Newnansville (in honor of Colonel Daniel Newnan of Georgia, a Patriot War "hero").

As the county seat, it prospered and grew into a hub for trade and a burgeoning plantation society. Most harvests were corn and cotton, and later citrus. However, in 1854 the town of Gainesville became the seat of Alachua County—as it was in line as a stop for the advancing Florida Railroad. After the courthouse packed up for Gainesville as well, the declining stature of Newnansville as a prominent locale was writ.

In 1884 another railroad bypassed Newnansville by a mile and a half. After a winter freeze devastated the citrus crop two years later, people in town "made tracks" to leave. They settled in Gainesville and that other nearby town with a rail stop, Alachua.

CHAPTER 3

Yes to Yulee

The Force Behind the Florida Railroad

WHEN DAVID LEVY YULEE DIED IN OCTOBER 1886, A EULOGY IN THE *Washington Post* reflected the man's role in Florida history: "As Senator from Florida, he was better known than the state he represented."

Yulee was known, alright, for being articulate, ambitious, astute, passionate, charmingly persuasive, savvy, and comfortable with risk.

He also condoned slavery—in fact, he owned slaves. In 1861 he signed "a Chattel Mortgage" on eighty such persons to secure $35,000 for his railroad company's operations. Slaves labored on his plantations and did the heavy lifting on his railroads.

Some have chalked up Yulee's moniker as a "Fire-Eater" to his incendiary speeches promoting secession from the Union. Others say it was because he had a high profile among the Fire-Eaters—a band of Southern extremists who tried to resurrect the international slave trade in the 1850s (as it was illegal in the United States after 1808).

Some have called Yulee a great Floridian, even the "Father of Florida's Railroads." Others deem him a bad actor who betrayed the trust of investors. How he managed both is a telling saga.

This son of the tropics was born June 12, 1810, in Charlotte Amalie, St. Thomas, at a time when the islands of the West Indies were owned by Denmark. His father, Moses Elias Levy, was a wealthy merchant descended from Jewish courtiers in Morocco who had served

US Senator David Levy Yulee, who established the Florida Railroad Company and its 156-mile line from Fernandina to Cedar Key. Born in the Caribbean, he was a territorial representative and became the first member of the senate upon statehood in 1845. Yulee also was the first senator of Jewish heritage. He owned slaves—who built his plantations and railroads—and he was convicted of treason for his actions prior to the Civil War. STATE ARCHIVES OF FLORIDA, FLORIDA MEMORY.

a line of sultans. His mother, Hannah Abendanone, was born in the Caribbean.

Both parents had a Sephardic ancestry; in fact, Moses Levy was a very observant Jew with a Zionist vision. From lore and historical journals, drama in the family seems inevitable.

For pure "escapist" value, consider one fictional tale about Moses Levy's mother: Rachel Levy, the daughter of a Jewish physician in England, was kidnapped by pirates, taken to Morocco, then sold to a powerful Muslim, Jacoub ibn Youli, to enlarge his harem. Pregnant with Youli's child, Rachel managed to get away and return to England. Her son, Moses, was David's father.

In reality, Moses was born in Morocco in 1781. His father was Elias Levy, a Jew, and his mother was Ha-Levi ibn Yuli. Moses and Hannah Levy divorced, and their son David spent his early years with his mother in St. Thomas. Moses got around Europe and the Caribbean, and built a successful shipping enterprise in lumber and weapons throughout the Danish Antilles and Cuba.

Among his roster of business associates were Spanish colonials in Florida who favored Levy with sweet land deals on their peninsula. Moses emigrated to Florida with young David about 1821 and took possession of 14,500 acres near Jacksonville (at Hope Hill on the west side of the St. Johns River) and 38,400 acres in what is now Alachua County. As noted in Chapter 1, both parcels had been part of a grant by the king of Spain to Fernando de la Maza Arredondo. Levy's agents closed the deal in Havana.

David began attending a boys' academy in Norfolk, Virginia, and anticipated going to college there. When Moses insisted he go into business instead, David went back to St. Thomas for a few months to visit his mother. Returning to Florida, he worked at Moses's Pilgrimage Plantation near Micanopy (learning the sugarcane business there would come into play later).

For years Spain and the United States negotiated the future of "the Floridas," having signed a treaty in 1819. By the time Spain ceded its colony to the United States in 1821, Moses was already well positioned to pursue his interests. A rarity in the South—a Jewish plantation owner— he intended to foster a homeland for Jews fleeing oppression elsewhere. He designed his plantation as a sort of communal "New Jerusalem."

Moses also was an ardent abolitionist, even publishing a pamphlet in London setting forth a plan to end slavery. He lauded the need to educate slaves, enabling, according to Florida historian and professor Chris Monaco, a "gradual" path to emancipation.

Paradoxically, Moses also owned slaves. But it was his philosophy about reforming an evil system that put him directly at odds with his son, forming the vortex for a lifetime of estrangement.

THE YULEE YAW

David, an avid reader and self-taught student famished for more learning, took off for St. Augustine to study law. Still using the surname Levy, he had learned the value of political connections while living in Newnansville, where he chummed around with farmers, laborers, even Seminole chiefs. He also was well acquainted with decision-makers in St. Augustine, having met territorial officials, many Spanish families, and east Florida power brokers.

David's mentor was Robert Raymond Reid, a territorial governor. At age twenty-two, David was admitted to the Florida Bar. Four years later, he became a representative to the Legislative Council, forerunner for the state legislature. Elected to the Constitutional Convention in 1838, he held a territorial seat in the US House of Representatives, a convenient position for obtaining a railroad survey for Florida. That was handy, as he'd been dreaming since the mid-1830s about what Florida needed most: a way to connect its east and west coasts.

Florida, David once claimed, would go from isolation to its real destiny: Once a railroad could be constructed, the state "will become a central point in the thoroughfare of trade and travel; and a new stream of population and wealth will swell the tide of our then rapid course to maturity."

David wasn't thinking small, as his vision had few boundaries. What he really wanted was a transit system of rail and steamships which would make all of *his* Florida as accessible as Europe. He was not without detractors, whether the jabs were political or personal—given his relatively unconventional background.

In 1841 some of his peers denounced David's eligibility to be a territorial delegate, vowing he was not a US citizen. A panel investigated the process whereby Moses Levy became a naturalized citizen, and debated whether that formality transferred non-alien status to his minor-age son.

The conclusion of the Committee of Elections, signed by W. Halsted, was this: "Resolved, That David Levy, Esq. is not a citizen of the United States . . . and that therefore [he] is not entitled to a seat in the House of Representatives as a Delegate from the Territory of Florida."

A month before the inquiry began, Moses Levy visited New York and gave a deposition to clarify his status. F. A. Tallmadge signed the document stating, "That deponent was naturalized soon after he arrived at St. Augustine in the year 1821 . . . That deponent was told in 1821, when he applied to be naturalized, that by the treaty with Spain, deponent being in possession of property in Florida, he was entitled to be naturalized."

Congress spent about six months of yawning, tedious discourse on the matter. David Levy cited his own view in the Court of Appeals of the Territory of Florida, in session in Tallahassee in January 1841: "That the rights of American citizenship accrued to me under the sixth article of the treaty of amity, settlement, and limits between the United States of America and the King of Spain, of the 22d February, 1819."

Thus, on March 15, 1842, the US Congress reversed an earlier conclusion and dropped the challenge.

AN UNPOPULAR STATE OF MIND

David Levy had already set about lobbying Congress for statehood. That was a hard sell, as many were opposed. One critic called it "a land of swamps, of quagmires, of frogs and alligators, and mosquitoes . . . where no one would want to immigrate, even from Hell."

Florida won the debate, and sent two members to the US Senate: James D. Westcott Jr. and David Levy—the first member of Jewish ancestry elected to that body. Senator Levy was chairman of the committees on naval affairs, post offices, and post roads.

Moses Levy could afford to be puffed up at his son's achievement— but a year later, events would make him choke on that pride. In 1846 David Levy married Nannie C. Wickliffe, the Christian daughter of a former governor of Kentucky. Unwilling to consider the perceived social implications of being known as Mrs. Levy (her father's oft-spoken sentiment), she persuaded her new husband to solve the dilemma. David renounced Judaism and changed his last name to Yulee, a version of Yuli, his grandmother's surname.

A further insult to Moses was David's promise to Nannie to raise their children as Christians. The couple's offspring were Nannie Christian Noble, C. Wickliffe Yulee, NN Yulee Reid, Florida Yulee, and Mary Yulee.

Moses was outraged at such a betrayal of faith and remained so the rest of his life. Which makes one wonder whether he grasped the reality that, despite having renounced Judaism, his son dealt with anti-Semitic prejudice throughout his political life.

SHIP TO SHORE, TRACKS TO BOTH

David Yulee, a Democrat, had other stressors. With the slavery issue dominating much of the political debate during this time and the Whig Party coming into power, he was narrowly defeated in his bid for a second term in the Senate in 1850.

Failing reelection, Yulee trained his attention to a growing obsession with a railroad to link the state's coasts. More than a decade earlier, he'd conceived a plan dependent on state participation. By 1851 he opted to package the financing from state and federal land grants, and proceeds from selling corporate stock.

Having settled in Fernandina, he formulated a plan based on two overarching motives: to shorten the travel distance for ships carrying cargo from Atlantic ports to those along the Gulf of Mexico, and to reduce losses from ships which often foundered in the tricky shallows of the Florida Reef and the treacherous Florida Straits between Key West and Cuba.

Yulee believed a rail line able to shave 800 miles off that risky shipping route could be highly profitable (estimates published in *The American Railroad Journal* indicated a rail route could reduce the shipping time to less than five days from New York to New Orleans). Rejecting the snarls inherent in state control, he devoted his energy to developing a private railroad under an umbrella entity, the Florida Town Improvement Company.

In 1853 the legislature gave Yulee's project a green light, approving a charter for the Florida Railroad Company to build a line from the Atlantic Ocean to a point on the Gulf of Mexico south of the Suwannee River. The charter granted a 200-foot right-of-way through state lands and alternate sections of land 6 miles deep on both sides of the railroad.

Having cobbled together some parcels in Fernandina for the eastern terminus, Yulee got busy getting title to about 1,000 acres around the Cedar Keys for the western node. Ostensibly the line would run from Fernandina to Tampa, with a branch to Cedar Key.

Yulee chose to build the rail terminus at Cedar Key first, postponing the Tampa leg—arguing that Cedar Key's port was deeper than Tampa's, that it was closer to Fernandina, and that it was closer to the shipping hub at New Orleans. (Actually, Cedar Key's harbor wasn't deep enough. Yulee's solution was a wharf and a system of trestles so the Florida Railroad could reach vessels waiting with passengers and cargo.) Some have speculated this strategy was due to Yulee's views on slavery, given Cedar Key's history as a hub for smuggling. Some also suggested it was to thwart competitors planning to build tracks with a different gauge.

Ever the dynamic multitasker, Yulee juggled business with his devotion to agriculture. In addition to deal-making and politicking, he had established Margarita, a 5,100-acre sugar plantation on Tiger Tail Island in the Homosassa River. Another family home was the Cottonwood plantation near Archer.

Construction on the Florida Railroad began in 1855. At the Fernandina end, Yulee didn't let the swamp south of "downtown" stop him. He had a boardwalk built across it and platted a "New Fernandina" with a harbor and railhead.

In the March 21, 1857, edition of the *Florida Times,* publisher Joseph F. Rogero penned a piece about the Florida Railroad's master plan: "We have been shown a map lately issued . . . which enables the observer to take in at a glance the present and future importance of Railroads in our State . . . Of necessity, from the peculiar geographical position of Florida, our state must eventually become the highway of the trade and commerce of a vast area of country."

TOWNS BEFORE RENOWN

It took a year for the Florida Railroad's footprint to cover the first 10-mile leg to Lofton. The line reached Crawford, another 20 miles, by November 1856, then Baldwin by 1857. Seven months later, tracks had gone another 24 miles to Reynolds. In 1859 the pace accelerated considerably, covering another 44 miles and reaching Gainesville, via Archer, by June 1. The year after, another 30 miles. Cedar Key was the caboose of the project, with the final 7 miles completed to the western terminus on March 1, 1861.

That relatively vast stretch totaled 156 miles and gave Yulee bragging rights to the first Florida rail line to link the two coasts. The mostly black laborers also could boast the distinction of taking on an expanse considered godforsaken by many, and overcoming the most mosquitoes, carnivores, and angry squatters of any other crew to date.

An elevation of the route is almost symmetrical, with Fernandina and Cedar Key brushing sea level, and the middle 45 miles or so grabbing air, ranging from 100 to almost 150 feet above sea level. A traveler of that era boarding the Florida Railroad in Fernandina could expect a twelve-hour ride to the Cedar Keys—lumbering over a primitive roadbed, navigating largely uninhabited terrain, and crossing wetlands, a high ridge, and more wetlands to reach the Gulf of Mexico.

Were pine forests rumbling by you, or the other way around? Breaking up the monotony of forested wilderness and hammocks were occasional junctions where connecting railroads passed. Finally, the destination itself appeared as if anxious to see who, after all, wanted to visit these isles sitting on a flat marsh like cupcakes on a glass platter.

Resembling a landscape of pop-up towns, new depots appeared in Hart's Road (renamed Yulee), Calhoun, Crawford, Starke (formerly Reynolds), Hampton, Waldo, Venables, and Sumner. Towns in the railroad's right-of-way were named variously over time, but not randomly: Baldwin was named for Dr. Abel Seymour Baldwin of Jacksonville, a physician, municipal advocate, and state legislator who headed the campaign for the Internal Improvement Fund in 1855 (he also was a railroad executive involved in a line from Jacksonville to Lake City). Callahan's namesake was mill operator Daniel Callahan. Trail Ridge, renamed Highland, overlay an old trail used by Indians in ridge country. The namesake for Gainesville was a general in charge of troops during the Second Seminole War. James T. Archer, acquainted with Yulee, got the nod for that town. And Bronson was named for US judge Isaac Bronson (Yulee had argued cases before him as a young lawyer).

"ABNER MCGEHEE," AT YOUR SERVICE

The shrewd, affable, former senator Yulee had crafted all the pieces to the puzzle. A labor force of his own slaves and a few hundred leased ones— along with some white men—had performed back-wrenching feats to chop through dense forests, build berms and trestlework over water and swamp, lay the rails, and move on. Some, of course, paid the ultimate price, only moving on to an afterlife.

At the outset of construction, the Florida Railroad had acquired only one, secondhand, eight-wheel engine. Of course, each locomotive has a persona, and the namesake for this one was Abner McGehee, owner of a sawmill. It had been ordered for the Montgomery Railroad in Alabama and was built by Rogers Locomotive & Machine Works in Paterson, New Jersey, in 1839. "Abner" was the muscle for laying much of the track from Fernandina to Cedar Key.

Joseph Finegan of Finegan & Company in Clay County, a member of the board of directors and an investor in Yulee's company, got the contract to build the railroad. (Within a few years, damning correspondence between the two would be a harbinger for accusations of treason.)

In April 1860 the *Tallahassee Floridian* published some lavender prose among its columns devoted to news of the day: "Soon the dim and gloomy recesses of those primeval and almost impenetrable forests will re-echo the startling scream of the locomotive, and their affrighted denizens will tremble with terror as the unusual sound penetrates their hidden lairs."

The newspaper also published the Florida Railroad Company's schedule in January 1861: a westbound freight train ran Monday, Wednesday, and Friday, from Fernandina to Callahan, and St. Marys, Georgia, then down to Baldwin, Gainesville, and Bronson. The Tuesday-Thursday-Saturday schedule for eastbound freight trains had daily connections at Baldwin for Lake City and Tallahassee.

Washington Encore, Adieu

Yulee was elected to another term in the US Senate in 1855, a fortunate perch from which to pursue his rail project. A federal land-grant bill which he promptly promoted was a boon for him and two other rail developers—with the Florida Railroad receiving 500,000 acres from the federal government, plus a lesser windfall from the state.

With financial woes after the Panic of 1857, however, Yulee's railroad was at risk. To avoid bankruptcy, he gave up a majority interest to a Northern syndicate of investors. Lawyer Edward Dickerson led the group, and steamship mogul Marshall Roberts put up much of the money. The new owners retained Yulee and Joseph Finegan to manage their investment.

Yulee had advocated secession while serving in the Senate during his first term, and again in the nonconsecutive second round. When he believed the states'-rights crisis and war to be close at hand, he went further for the cause—inching out on a limb that would seal his fate.

In January 1861 Senator Yulee wrote to Finegan to convey that secession and war were a certainty. He spurred Finegan to gather information about military installations and personnel in Florida—essentially to steer a state takeover of federal forts and arsenals. Paying forward his ticket to jail, Yulee also proposed the immediate formation of a confederation of Southern states.

The same month he penned these urgings to Finegan, Yulee resigned his seat in the Senate—walking out of the chambers with senators Jefferson Davis of Mississippi and Stephen Mallory of Florida. Yulee then proceeded to Fernandina.

Upon Florida's withdrawal from the Union, the Dickerson syndicate found itself on the "enemy alien" side of the ledger, permitting Yulee and Finegan to regain control of their company for a while. Some posed the notion—and the *New York Times* speculated aloud—that such a corporate power ploy had been Yulee's motive for promoting secession.

With its construction completed to Cedar Key just a few months prior to the outbreak of hostilities, the Florida Railroad ran only briefly before its assets became a war game—a tool for Confederate strategies and an easy target for Union attacks. (Chapter 5 will describe the wartime fate of those tracks—the building of which had broken backs but not resolve.)

Reasons for Yulee's choices before and during the Civil War are complicated. It has been said that he saw the war as a way to default on the railroad bonds he had sold. Or maybe he saw the conflict as a way to preserve his contribution to the potential of Florida. A staunch advocate for states' rights, he also was a loyal Floridian—inasmuch as Florida was physically appended to, and dependent upon, a seceding South. There also is the possibility that an alternative more palatable than secession might have gotten his ear.

Yulee was president of the Florida Railroad Company from 1853 to 1866, and the operation survived in various restructurings. (After threads and tied-up loose ends, the Florida Railroad morphed into a piece of the Seaboard Air Line Railroad. In some places still in use, those embryo lines serve CSX Transportation and the First Coast Railroad. The highway corridor of State Road 24, US 301, and State Road A1A closely parallels the former Florida Railroad.) Yulee also was president of the Peninsular Railroad Company, the Tropical Florida Railway Company, and the Fernandina and Jacksonville Railroad Company.

Yulee gave up his railroad interests in 1880 and moved to Washington, DC, where his wife had relatives. A few months after completion of the couple's mansion there, Nannie died. Six years later, Yulee died in New York City at the age of seventy-six.

Fernandina became a mature destination, quite popular by 1880, but the plans of later visionaries would leave it stranded in that era as an island unto itself. Likewise, Cedar Key would putter along as a laid-back anglers' haven, because the horizon's "radar" already registered the musings of future railroad barons.

Later chapters include more on why Yulee was charged with treason, and what happened to his railroad assets during and after the war. As for his legacy, he is the namesake for the town of Yulee in Nassau County and for Levy County in the west-central part of the state. The Amelia Island Museum of History considers Yulee to be the "Father of Fernandina Beach."

The town of Archer's historical society installed a monument to his achievements on the site of the original train depot. In the 1990s the same group launched Yulee Railroad Days as a local historic festival. The event grew across north-central Florida as a celebration of the Florida Railroad and the towns it spawned.

The regularity of rail traffic from post–Civil War through the 1920s—and the fact that entire communities owed their growth to the Florida Railroad—bolster Yulee's legacy. In purely physical terms, the evidence of rail tracks and roadbeds—in fact, some surviving coquina concrete culverts in Nassau County—may be seen as a timeless testament to the pioneers who rode those trains to a new depot in a town not yet on the map.

This is part of what keeps Yulee intact in our "social memory," according to one scholar, Maury Wiseman, author of the article "David Levy Yulee: Conflict and Continuity in Social Memory": "While different facets of Yulee's life have been promoted, repressed, or ignored, Floridians' memory of him as an important man in their state's history has never faded."

The next chapter will address the way statehood created a new realm of opportunity and boons for railroad developers and schemers.

WRITING ON THE WALL

Thomas Evans Haile and his wife, the former Esther Serena Chestnut, relocated from Camden, South Carolina, in 1854, settling with their children at a new home west of Gainesville. They had brought sixty-four slaves to establish a cotton plantation, to be named Kanapaha, choosing the property for its proximity to the planned route of the Florida Railroad.

They eagerly monitored the progress of tracks as Yulee's rail line worked its way in their direction. And Serena Haile's diary alludes to 1857, when the community built the Kanapaha Presbyterian Church, choosing a site that would be near the rail depot in South Arredondo.

The Historic Haile Homestead on Archer Road directs visitors to Serena Haile's diary, which reveals her rather unconventional custom of writing on the white plaster walls of the house.

Mrs. Haile and her children were carefree and expressive, creating "talking walls" in every room—spelling out the names of visitors, grocery lists, and home remedies. Several succeeding generations perpetuated the practice, adding poems, rhymes, and sketches.

CHAPTER 4

An Act of Congress

Pen to Paper Transfers 500,000 Acres

BECOMING PART OF THE UNITED STATES IN 1845 GAVE FLORIDA AN altered "state" of formal status. More importantly, the Act of Congress conveyed ownership of half a million acres of federal land. And within five years, the United States gave Florida another 10 million acres of swamp and wetlands.

Such enormous tracts had developers twitching with anticipation and scouting for backers. This, despite the gloomy national snapshot about the railroad industry. One historian said that in the year before Florida joined the union, other states had defaulted on $60 million in bonds, credit was unobtainable, and internal improvement projects in many states were stalled.

As mentioned previously, David Levy Yulee was one of the state's newly elected members of the US Senate. The other was James Diament Westcott Jr., a native of Virginia who was educated in New Jersey and became a lawyer. Andrew Jackson had appointed Westcott secretary of the Florida Territory, and Westcott was the US attorney for the middle district of Florida from 1834 to 1836. He served in the territorial house of representatives in 1832 and was a delegate to two state constitutional conventions.

Upon statehood, politicians and community leaders such as Yulee and Westcott ramped up the debate for more rail development. Gradually entrepreneurs began piecemeal projects in their regions.

In 1851 the state formed the Internal Improvement Board, a committee to identify worthy projects. Members included Governor Thomas Brown, some other state officers, and "delegates" from each judicial circuit. In its largesse, Congress had specified that the land grants were to be used for land reclamation. In turn, the Internal Improvement Board set about locating the designated lands.

A second committee got busy studying which tracts were best suited to specific improvements. Its members included Yulee, attorney James T. Archer of Tallahassee, and Dr. Abel Seymour Baldwin of Jacksonville, a member of the state legislature. They shared their findings with newly elected Governor James E. Broome (a native of South Carolina who owned large plantations and was married five times).

According to author Gregg Turner, the committee researched the ways that other states had stimulated rail projects and settled on a few key strategies: state gifts of land or money or both, using the proceeds of state land sales to buy railroad stocks and bonds, and granting "qualified firms state credit."

Yulee and Archer, who was state comptroller in 1855, worked with Broome to draft a bill which the governor signed on January 6, 1855. The law provided for "a Liberal System of Internal Improvements in this State." The favored financial strategy was grants of land, with the state guaranteeing the interest on bonds the railroad companies issued. Railroad hopefuls could sell the "free land" and use the proceeds to grade land and lay tracks.

Ultimately the state pledge to pay interest on those railroad bonds actually became a guarantee of ruin. That's because the state secured their payments of principal and interest by a mortgage pledging current and future state lands.

STATE OF AFFAIRS

Initially, however, the realm of railroads was awash in a sea change. The Internal Improvement Fund (IIF) board recommended a land-grant system to allow "qualified companies" to apply for development projects. Trustees of the IIF were the governor, the comptroller, the state treasurer, the attorney general, and the land registrar. The lands in question were, of course, those which Washington had given Florida upon statehood and thereafter. And the IIF had sole discretion to set prices for those lands and give grantees a waiver on taxes.

Dr. Baldwin, who had sat on the site-selection committee and campaigned for the IIF, promoted development of the Florida, Atlantic & Gulf Central Railroad (the "Central"). The company got a charter in January 1851 to build a line from the St. Marys River to the Gulf of Mexico, at some point west of the Apalachicola River. However, a yellow fever outbreak in Jacksonville deferred construction for a few years.

In 1855, when the good doctor became president of the railroad company, he petitioned the IIF, asking it to endorse a 60-mile section of his project from Jacksonville to Alligator (now Lake City). As author Turner points out, neighboring Columbia County issued $100,000 in bonds and invested the proceeds in railroad stock. The city of Jacksonville issued $50,000 in bonds and invested the proceeds likewise. Eventually Baldwin's company sold stocks and some of the 200,000 acres granted by the IIF. The Florida, Atlantic & Gulf Central also issued bonds, with interest payments guaranteed by the IIF.

Baldwin built a wharf on the St. Johns River, and Jacksonville gave it a free right-of-way. The city also kicked in some land for Baldwin's terminal buildings. Best of all, the company had a thirty-five-year reprieve on corporate taxes.

In 1857 John Pease Sanderson replaced Baldwin as rail company president. By 1860 the line between Jacksonville and Lake City carried passengers, mail and express parcels, merchandise, lumber, cotton bales, livestock, animal hides, farm produce, and naval stores. (One of the Central's locomotives—supplied by the New Jersey Locomotive and Machine Co. in Paterson—was named the Governor Perry, after Broome's successor. Another, the Jacksonville, was the workhorse for laying track.)

As Edward A. Mueller wrote in *Southeast Limited* in 2012, Baldwin was quite the renaissance man. Born in New York and educated as a botanist, he became a medical doctor and moved to Florida to improve his health. He played several musical instruments, dabbled in art, and was the official meteorologist for the Smithsonian Institution.

SINGULAR STATUS

It's obvious the IIF trustees played favorites—and that the potential for the railroad industry gave it the power to control a lot of legislation and the acts of many governors. Landowners and planters with the most money often got the contracts for railroad construction.

Yet the first companies blessed with such favors paved the way for an industry chugging into the future. Four companies took advantage of land grants in exchange for first mortgage bonds. They were the Florida, Atlantic & Gulf Central; the Florida Railroad Company; the Alabama & Florida Railroad; and the Pensacola & Georgia Railroad. The lands transferred to them totaled more than 1,750,000 acres.

The Pensacola & Georgia Railroad got its state charter in 1853 and subsequent permission to connect Pensacola with Lake City. The president of the P & G was US Representative Edward Carrington Cabell, a native of Virginia and a lawyer who settled near Tallahassee in 1837, establishing the Attatulga cotton plantation. (Perhaps he was more suited to business than serving the public; during eight years in Congress, he missed more than 34 percent of roll-call votes.)

The P & G project would unfold in sections. Cabell's board of directors settled on a preliminary plan to start construction at Tallahassee and work eastward to Bailey's Mill, then Madison, cross the Suwannee River, and terminate at "Lake City." Thus the work involved bridges and trestles in addition to track, rails, cross-ties, and crossing grades. Having the line across the river was strategic to connecting it with a line from Savannah, Georgia.

Work in Tallahassee began in 1856 and reached Capitola the following year. Just a few months before the Civil War began, the P & G was complete from Tallahassee to Lake City. As one of the IIF's grantees, Cabell's railroad had received 7,280 acres of gratis land for each mile of completed rail.

Meanwhile, Cabell had bought the Tallahassee Railroad from General Richard Keith Call in 1856. Before the P & G reached Lake City, however, Cabell moved to St. Louis. His successor was Panhandle planter Edward C. Houstoun, a native of Savannah. In 1858 the P & G also built the Tallahassee depot, which still stands.

A flurry of exuberance among rail firms imposing on Florida's generosity caused Governor Madison Starke Perry to issue a word of caution in 1859: "Railroads are useful, but State credit is a pearl above all price. It is easily tarnished and, to be kept without blemish, should be carefully guarded."

Taking Stock

As described in the previous chapter, David Yulee was president of the Florida Railroad Company from 1853 to 1866. He founded and built the line from Fernandina to Cedar Key, the first railroad to connect a Florida port on the Atlantic Ocean with another on the Gulf of Mexico. After six years of construction, the line provided service across 156 miles of the state's interior.

The Florida Railroad was a decided upgrade on rail equipment, with two sixty-seat passenger cars of au courant design, two baggage cars, fourteen boxcars, and twenty-one flatcars. In short, it was ready for commerce.

The victory came with a price, as Yulee's frail finances were more wobbly after the Panic of 1857. The company's board met on November 7 of that year, and the secretary's minutes indicate that directors believed it was time to reel in some cash: "Whereas, the work on the Florida Railroad having advanced to a condition which brings it into useful connection with the business of the interior . . . a point has been reached where [the Company] may hope to be met by the confidence and cooperation of the planters and merchants of the interior." Thus, the board directed the secretary to "invite subscriptions" to the company's stock and make the process convenient to prospective buyers.

Company secretary George W. Call notified the public that potential subscribers could visit Fernandina or send a letter. For each $100 share, the assessment was $10. At the time, the company reported ownership of sites in Fernandina and Cedar Key, and 750,000 acres of land appraised at more than $2 million.

Whatever the stock subscription raised, it wasn't enough for the Florida Railroad to stand on its own. To circumvent bankruptcy, Yulee allowed a syndicate of Northern investors to take a majority interest. As noted earlier, two of the principals were lawyer Edward Dickerson and steamship mogul Marshall Roberts.

More than 150 years after Yulee began his venture, a Florida newspaper revisited a key element that made the difference in his efforts and those of most other rail developers: "The link between African-Americans and the railroad in North Central Florida begins in the 1850s, when Sen. David Levy Yulee of St. Augustine envisioned a route linking the Atlantic and Gulf coasts. Needing inexpensive labor, Yulee leased an estimated 300 to 400 slaves from North Carolina and Virginia to construct a railroad . . . from Fernandina to Cedar Key," so said John Westerman in the *Gainesville Sun* in 2005.

FAMILY TIES

US Senator James Westcott had a rather accomplished brother who was a physician, surveyor, inventor, geologist, chemist, and freelance mailman.

Dr. John D. Westcott, a native of New Jersey, became surveyor-general of Florida in 1855. He financed the St. Johns Railway when it received its charter in December 1858. A demi-line of but 15 miles, it ran from Tocoi Landing on the east side of the St. Johns River to New Augustine, a village across the San Sebastian River from St. Augustine. The track of wooden rails and iron strap provided an alternative to riding a stagecoach from Picolata.

Tocoi resident Richard Floyd donated property for a depot to Westcott's company in 1859. Inland dwellers Francis Ferrira and John Hanson conveyed rights-of-way of 800 feet, enabling the railway alignment through their lands. That same year, about 13 miles of land was graded eastward from Tocoi and track put down for more than 5 miles. Westcott ordered new freight cars, a passenger salon, and a steam engine.

In 1860 the schooner *J. B. Bleeker* reached Tocoi to deliver more rail tracks, spikes, and rolling stock. The St. Johns Railway was on good footing. Westcott, meanwhile, also was physician to the Florida militia and had served in the Second Seminole War. After the declaration of the War Between the States, he was captain of the Florida Partisan Rangers Infantry and then a major in the Confederate army.

Westcott's adventures as an inventor are noteworthy. He did early experiments with the "saddle-bag railroad"—which he would display at the Centennial Exposition in 1876. It had a single track with "a shoe-like device" propelled in front of an engine driven by wheel traction. The "shoe" lay inside the track rather than straddling it and is considered the forerunner of the monorail.

Westcott also participated in surveys for the routes for the Florida East Coast Canal and Transportation Company, which built the Intracoastal Waterway in eastern Florida.

CHAPTER 5

Tolls of Civil War

Death, Railroad Casualties, and Economic Ruin

MADISON STARKE PERRY, A NATIVE OF SOUTH CAROLINA, MOVED TO THE territory of Florida, founded the town of Rochelle, became a prosperous planter, and got involved in politics. After terms in the state house and the state senate, he became governor in October 1857.

His administration is credited with promoting railroad development in his adopted state and smoothing over an ancient boundary dispute with Georgia. By 1860 he led a state containing the fastest-growing region in the South—the "Middle Florida" plantation country between the Apalachicola and Suwannee Rivers.

Governor Perry also had the ear of Florida decision-makers in Washington, DC, and others who were predicting which states might secede from the Union. A year after taking the oath as governor, he advocated for reestablishing Florida's militia.

He also called a convention into session in Tallahassee in early 1861. Of the sixty-nine delegates, most were conservative wealthy planters. Seven of them wanted to wait. The rest voted for secession on January 10, 1861.

NOT ON BOARD

Two prominent figures opposed secession on ideological grounds—believing there was no justification for any state to abandon the Union. One was General Richard Keith Call, who had been Andrew Jackson's protégé and served two terms as territorial governor (1836–39 and 1841–44).

The other was New York–born lawyer William Marvin. President Jackson had appointed him US Attorney for the Southern District of Florida Territory at Key West, where he served from 1835 to 1839. He also was on the Florida Territorial Council.

Marvin was then a territorial judge on the US District Court for the Southern District of Florida (1839–47). Upon statehood, President James Polk nominated Marvin to the US District Court for the Southern District of Florida. He sat on the bench from 1847 to 1863, then resigned (a further reference shows his role in trying to resolve the Yulee treason case).

CIRCLING THE WAGONS

Governor Perry promptly ordered federal troops to evacuate Florida. Earlier that week, Union forces at forts around the Panhandle had heard solid rumors that Perry had ordered Florida state troops to seize the federal arsenal at Chattahoochee and all coastal forts and installations.

Although Florida was far less populated than other seceded states, with a smaller militia, its rail and water transportation formed the spine of a strategic supply route for the Confederate army. Florida supplied farm produce and beef to troops in and out of state, as well as salt—which, in the pre-refrigeration era, was essential to preserving meat. Many boat captains were exempt from military service because their vessels smuggled Florida cattle to Cuba, where they bought supplies and collected payment for the bill of lading in gold coins.

Union forces set up an embargo around the entire peninsula to thwart blockade runners—all according to Washington's "Anaconda Plan." Early in the war, Union troops occupied the important ports of Cedar Key, Jacksonville, Key West, and Pensacola. Confederate troops, already in position in St. Augustine and Fernandina, were making moves on the Pensacola Navy Yard and forts in the vicinity.

After war activities damaged or destroyed rail lines, Florida farmers once again had no way to get their livelihood to pay for itself.

ARGUABLE ASSETS

The Civil War was openly unkind to Yulee's assets, and magnified a financial nightmare for the former senator.

The Cedar Keys, and portions of the Florida Railroad, fell into federal hands during a raid by the USS *Hatteras* on January 16, 1862. Union forces destroyed the rail depot and rolling stock, a wharf, the telegraph office, and a turpentine warehouse on Cedar Key (Way Key). In the harbor where ships had cotton and turpentine in their holds, Federal troops scuttled and burned four schooners, three sloops, and a ferry boat. Also lost were a battery on Seahorse Key and field works on Depot Key.

During the early part of the war, Cedar Key had been a critical source of salt production, with the locals using vats to boil seawater to supply the Confederacy. In October 1862 the USS *Somerset* raided a facility on Salt Key and destroyed sixty kettles capable of turning out 150 bushels of salt per day.

The US Army and Navy controlled the Cedar Keys for the rest of the war, after they destroyed 30 miles of Florida Railroad tracks leading from the islands. Remnants of original coquina and concrete culverts surfaced later as a reminder of a promising undertaking sidelined on an indeterminable detour.

Other skirmishes occurred between Union and Confederate forces in the Gulf islands. Federal forces also made frequent raids inland along the railroad and up the St. Marks and Suwannee Rivers to confiscate cotton and cattle.

DAMNING CORRESPONDENCE

As mentioned in Chapter 3, US Senator Yulee of Florida owned plantations which depended on slave labor; slaves laid the tracks for his Florida Railroad line from Fernandina to Cedar Key; and he was a fierce advocate for states' rights.

What isn't crystal clear is whether the latter position was based on an outsize belief that Florida's economic standing depended on the will of like-minded souls to fight for a respectable benchmark in the South. Moreover, is it possible Yulee believed it was his own destiny to be that standard-bearer?

On January 5, 1861, while still in Washington, the railroad honcho wrote to his associate, Joseph Finegan in Jacksonville, urging him to make sure the state government took control of federal forts, arsenals, and installations in Florida. He specified two forts in Pensacola and its navy yard, as well as the lone fort on Santa Rosa Island, as the highest priority.

In an excerpt, Yulee wrote: "What is advisable is the earliest possible organization of a Southern confederacy and a Southern Army. The North is rapidly consolidating against us . . . a strong government [of seceded states] . . . and a strong army with [Jefferson] Davis as General in Chief, will bring them to a reasonable sense of the gravity of the crisis."

(Finegan, a native of Ireland who served in the US military before moving to Florida, already appreciated the gravity of the crisis. About a month before he got that letter, he had led a group of Southern partisans to form the Fernandina Volunteers—pledging loyalty to the state as they awaited the outcome of the national debate. For a time, they garrisoned at Fort Clinch.)

Jefferson Davis also was still a sitting US senator from Mississippi. Later in January, he, along with Yulee and Senator Stephen Mallory of Pensacola, would resign from the US Senate and support the Southern cause in various capacities—Davis as president of the Confederate States of America; Mallory, a native of Trinidad, as Davis's secretary of the navy; and Yulee as a power broker and facilitator of intrigue.

At the 1861 annual meeting of his Florida Railroad, Yulee made a speech about his hopes for the future, given that war had interrupted his grand hurrah so soon after the line's completion: "[The railroad's] career will come, and then not the least in its destined achievements will be the creation of a new emporium of commerce in the South . . . Fernandina will be added to Savannah, and Charleston, and Norfolk, and Baltimore, as an Atlantic Seaport for business with fair claim to a good rank among them . . . It is of all the Atlantic ports the nearest and most convenient to New Orleans, a fact of no slight significance, for New Orleans ought to become, under the new political arrangements, the great entrepot of American produce, and the leading Centre of trade."

Despite Yulee's alignment with Southern values, he declined elective office in the Confederate States of America and chose to live at his

Fernandina estate and run his railroad. He also butted heads with Confederate commanders who wanted him to sacrifice some of the Florida Railroad's assets—tracks and equipment—in favor of lines that others considered more vital to the cause (in 1860, those assets included five engines).

As for Perry, his term as governor ended in March 1861, and he joined the 7th Florida Infantry Regiment.

TUG O' WAR

Until Florida left the Union, Doc Baldwin and John Sanderson remained active in the newly completed Florida Atlantic & Gulf Central Railroad. With Jacksonville a critical gateway, the company's rails often went "for the cause" and got iffy replacements. Despite dwindling finances and interrupted commerce, Sanderson managed to order two new engines during the war. One was named the R. E. Lee.

Sanderson was an "ultra secessionist" who had helped draft the papers making Florida's separation official. In 1862 he was elected to the Confederate Congress in Richmond.

Baldwin opposed secession but acquiesced to the passions of others. As a surgeon, he spent much of the war near "Camp Finegan," the colonel's headquarters in the vicinity of Lake City. By May 1865, Baldwin was a prisoner of war.

DUNES OF DESTINY

Santa Rosa Island is a skinny barrier stretch between Pensacola Bay and the Gulf of Mexico. Its west end insinuates itself into the bay's deep harbor, and its pristine snowy sands, scantily clad in thistled dunes, loll eastward in no particular hurry for 40 languid miles—hardly the setting for Civil War skirmishes, or even the Battle for Santa Rosa Island (October 8, 1861).

Beachfront real estate wasn't the prized target, however; it was Fort Pickens, which had been built at the west end of the island to dominate the harbor and guard the Pensacola Navy Yard.

The fort's namesake was Major General Andrew Pickens of the South Carolina militia, a veteran of several Revolutionary War battles. But it was two Northerners who were responsible for the fort's unique profile during the Civil War.

More than a generation apart in age, both were distinguished graduates of the United States Military Academy. The younger officer, US Army Lieutenant Adam Jacoby Slemmer, a native of Pennsylvania, had been on the faculty of the academy in 1856. That was the same year Major William Henry Chase, a native of Maine, declined the offer to be superintendent of West Point.

Just before the momentous showdown at Fort Pickens, Slemmer was part of Company G, 1st United States Army Artillery at the Barrancas Barracks on the mainland side of the bay, just west of the Pensacola Navy Yard. Major Chase was the commander of Confederate troops in western Florida. At the time, Pensacola had a population of about 2,900—and much of that growth stemmed from decades of Chase promoting the city's economy and financing development.

It is unclear whether Slemmer and Chase had met each other before 1861. Afterward, every officer on both sides of the conflict knew they displayed exceptional fortitude during a steely-eyed standoff.

When South Carolina seceded in December 1860, Lieutenant Slemmer was in charge of Fort Barrancas, as his superiors—Major John H. Winder and Senior Lieutenant Asher Eddy—were on leave. Chase, who had adopted Pensacola as his home, was president of the Alabama & Florida Railroad Company. Before resigning from the Army Corps of Engineers, he had been a master engineer who built Fort Zachary Taylor in Key West, several fortresses near New Orleans, Fort Barrancas and Fort McRee in Pensacola, and Fort Pickens on Santa Rosa Island. In short, he knew every inch of Pickens, inside and out.

At the time Florida withdrew from the Union, Fort Pickens had been unmanned for years but its location protecting the harbor made it a highly strategic target. Slemmer intuited that the island fort was both valuable and vulnerable to a rebel incursion, and that he could not guard two forts on opposite sides of Pensacola Bay without reinforcements.

As a precaution, Slemmer removed powder from the exposed magazines at Fort Barrancas and concealed it inside the fort. He also raised the Barrancas drawbridge and ordered tighter security. Near midnight on January 8, 1861, a squad of about twenty rebels approached Fort Barrancas, then fled when Union soldiers fired their muskets. According to an article in *Florida Historical Quarterly*, those may have been the first Federal shots fired in the war.

As David L. Walby writes in *The Battle for Santa Rosa Island*, Slemmer transferred his small Union garrison of seventy-six men to the island fort two days later, the same day Florida seceded. Two days after that, Major Chase led a rebel force that seized the Pensacola Navy Yard and demanded the surrender of Fort Barrancas a mile away. The undermanned Union commander surrendered the navy yard. Soon, Barrancas was in rebel control as well.

Within days Chase landed some troops on the dunes near Fort Pickens to parlay with Slemmer—hoping to intimidate the younger officer and persuade him to (a) give up the fort or (b) allow Chase to enter the fortress he himself had designed, so they could confer in a more amenable setting. Despite his vast experience as a persuasive negotiator and commander of highly skilled engineers and officers, Chase failed, possibly because he had mixed convictions. It is said that while reading his written demands, Chase became teary and his voice shook. Slemmer stood firm, however, refusing to surrender the fort or allow entry.

Chase withdrew—unaware that Slemmer's regiment was puny in number and light on matériel. Chase returned a few days later to entreat the lieutenant once again. No dice.

Meanwhile, Stephen Mallory had been dealing behind the scenes, right up until the moment in January 1861 when he and two colleagues walked out of the US Senate to join the Confederate cause. Mallory persuaded President James Buchanan and Secretary of State William Seward not to send Union reinforcements to Fort Pickens. In exchange, he promised that rebels would not attack the fort. Chase also acquiesced on a few points, allowing Slemmer's men to retrieve their company's mail on the mainland and receive provisions at the fort.

Walby says this skewed accord, the so-called Pickens Truce, lasted until April, when Colonel Harvey Brown and 1,700 Union troops arrived on the island to relieve Slemmer and his men. Until then, there were other tests of Slemmer's resolve, but to no avail.

General Braxton Bragg succeeded Chase as Confederate commander and got considerable rebel reinforcements in November 1861, upon completion of the Mobile & Pensacola Railroad. Chase had no further involvement in the war and went back to running his railroad—though likely looking over his shoulder. That's because Chase knew that his name and the word "treason" likely would end up in the same sentence.

President Abraham Lincoln's official papers include a letter dated June 20, 1861, to Lieutenant General Winfield Scott. Delivered by US Secretary of State William Seward, it notified Scott that the president was suspending the writ of habeas corpus for Major Chase, "lately of the Engineer Corps . . . now alleged to be guilty of treasonable practices against this government." Nonetheless, there is no indication Chase was put under arrest or required to answer for his actions against the Union.

Colonel Brown continued to defend the Union fortress against rebel incursions. With the US Navy's assistance, he steadily shelled Forts Barrancas and McRee and the navy yard on the mainland. In one extended bombardment, the navy yard burned, along with much of the neighboring village of Warrington.

Because of Slemmer's courage and able finesse, and Brown's follow-through, Fort Pickens remained under Union control throughout the Civil War. So did Fort Taylor in Key West and Fort Jefferson in the Dry Tortugas, 70 miles west of Key West.

Borrowing a Battery

Continuing his machinations on behalf of the Confederacy, David Yulee wrote to South Carolina Governor F. W. Pickens on July 20, 1861. Colonel Finegan delivered the letter asking a favor.

Yulee wrote that Finegan was assembling a legion to serve during the war, so that Florida would be well represented in the field. Alas, the state was "very much without armament and without much means in the treasury." He implored Pickens to "let Florida have, as a great favor, a battery of field artillery for a company of [Finegan's] legion. It could be loaned either to the State or Confederacy."

"90-Day Gunboats"

At the outset of the war, the St. Johns Railway route was under way. During the interrupted construction, the US Army and Navy confiscated its equipment.

In March 1862 three Unadilla-class US Navy gunboats—the *Ottawa*, *Seneca*, and *Pembina*—sailed up the St. Johns River and demolished the railroad dock at Tocoi Landing. The crews burned the company's rolling stock, demolished the steam engine, and confiscated the rails. What wasn't destroyed was shipped to Hilton Head, South Carolina.

At 158 feet, about the length of many of today's super-yachts, these hastily built "90-day gunboats" were two-masted schooners with single-screw engines. They were oceangoing, yet with a draught shallow enough to maneuver in inland waters in pursuit of blockade runners. The three at Tocoi Landing were among twenty-three which the Union commissioned.

Decline and Destruction

Any railroad operating at the outset of the war was in for a beating. Train routes gained extra business from military uses—moving troops and supplies—but lost ground in other ways. Operators had to abandon basic maintenance and witness the outright destruction of tracks and rolling stock.

Yulee's Florida Railroad become a Confederate resource and a political football.

In 1862 a Confederate colonel received an instruction to direct a force to destroy as much of the Florida Railroad and Jacksonville "road" (the Florida, Atlantic & Gulf Central) as he and his military authorities deemed sufficient to prevent Union advances into the peninsula's interior. Union attacks at Fernandina and Cedar Key had already banged up portions of the Florida Railroad. Although Union forces controlled those eastern and western terminal points, the Confederacy held most of the 156-mile line. Florida troops were intent on dismantling usable rails and shuttling them off to sites considered more valuable to Confederate troops and supplies.

In 1864, with rail iron scarce, the Confederate States of America confiscated some of Yulee's rails to create a line from Live Oak to

Lawton (renamed Du Pont), Georgia, where it would connect with the Atlantic & Gulf Railroad—a line running westerly from Savannah and just about parallel to the state lines. Yulee and Finegan fought this decision by filing an injunction against the state, an action that saved parts of the railroad but clouded their Confederate loyalties. Yet there were other instances when Yulee cooperated with the Confederate government to temporarily remove certain strategic tracks in the path of advancing "enemy" troops.

With company offices in Gainesville, Yulee commuted from his Fernandina home to work. This went on until March 1862, when Union troops forced the evacuation of Fernandina. Yulee and his family, along with Finegan, were on the last train off of Amelia Island. Many passengers were killed when the USS *Ottawa* shelled the train as it crossed the bridge to the mainland, but Finegan, Yulee, and his family were among the survivors.

Fifteen years earlier, Yulee had built a sugar plantation and home, Margarita, on Tiger Tail Island in the Homosassa River. After their flight from Fernandina, Yulee moved the family to Margarita, where he remained for the next two years—still commuting to the railroad office in Gainesville. His plantation's produce of citrus, cotton, and sugarcane were smuggled past blockaders until 1864—when Yulee learned Union troops had destroyed Margarita.

His family, who were visiting friends in Ocala, went to live at their Cottonwood plantation near Archer. In the final days of the Civil War, the dregs of the Confederate treasury arrived by train at Cottonwood. Federal troops found the train empty, triggering rumors of buried loot.

Also late in the war, Yulee assisted in briefly concealing the whereabouts of Jefferson Davis's baggage train—Davis having been captured on another train near Irwinville, Georgia.

Union Lieutenant Edward W. Denny certified the contents of Davis's personal effects, once they were seized June 15, 1865, at Waldo and forwarded to Hilton Head, South Carolina: one leather trunk with three woolen coats, one linen duster, three pairs pants, three woolen vests, one woolen "tippet," one small dressing case, two towels, one pistol—nine shooter, one case of ammunition, one pair woolen socks, one silk undershirt, two pairs woolen drawers, one silk scarf (necktie), one leather holster, two dressing robes, and eight "dirty" linen shirts.

A second box held a lot more socks, undershirts and drawers, one double-barreled revolver with molds, ammunition, tobacco and snuff, "case ornaments of brass," a brush, comb, razor-strap, boots, gaiters, slippers, toothbrushes, a pistol case, holsters with pistols enclosed, and cartridges. Denny repackaged certain other items: eyeglasses, a ring, private correspondence, miscellaneous papers, envelopes and notepaper, $20,000 in "rebel money," boxes of cigars, one portfolio, and portraits of Davis, his wife, Varina, and General Robert E. Lee.

Historians have used various rearview mirrors to reflect Yulee's views on slavery and secessionism. In one assessment, which is documented in the George A. Smathers Libraries at the University of Florida, Yulee favored a greater number of slave states and territories to balance the Union, "believing that without expansion, Southern states would become static and lose political clout."

In other words, it was about business. In the library's collection of Yulee's papers is the guide commentary by John R. Nemmers: "He firmly believed that further economic development in the South would lead to white immigration, thus nullifying southern fears of that time of 'Africanization' (a black majority of the population)."

In a 2005 article in the *Gainesville Sun,* John G. Westerman quoted author Chris Monaco on the onetime senator's motives: "Yulee was a fire-eater. He was very adamant about Southern rights, but he did change toward the end, and he did become much more tolerant."

RAID, "AFFAIR," OR SKIRMISH

In the Ambush at St. Marys River, at Barber's Plantation, Union Brigadier General Truman Seymour, commander for the District of Florida, led an army which lost the fight to the Confederates. The date was February 20, 1864, and marked Seymour's march westward toward Lake City—the largest town between the Atlantic Ocean and the Suwannee River, and the crossroads for rail routes to the north. The time line was critical, as President Lincoln was facing reelection and there were people at work in secret to coordinate a new Florida government loyal to the Union.

Portrait of Jacob "Jake" Summerlin (1820–1893). Summerlin was a youngster when he started working cattle and moved to central Florida at age 16, eventually earning a fortune as a cattle rancher in the area of the Kissimmee and Peace Rivers. A very wealthy man before the age of 40, he sold cattle to Cuba and to the US Naval Base in Key West. He owned large land parcels, including the well-placed wharf at Punta Rassa. During the Civil War, Summerlin smuggled beef to the Confederates by shipping it out of present day Charlotte Harbor. He also sold cattle to Union soldiers camped at Fort Myers. STATE ARCHIVES OF FLORIDA, FLORIDA MEMORY.

With his small army scattered among brigades at Jacksonville and elsewhere, Seymour directed the Federals to advance in three columns along a road running just about parallel to the Florida Atlantic & Gulf Central Railroad.

A few miles west of Sanderson, skirmishing began and continued for miles, with the Union army under the impression that the Confederates were on the run toward the railroad station at Olustee—about 12 miles east of Lake City. However, the closer to Olustee the Federals came, the more forceful resistance they met.

Colonel Finegan, positioned at the Olustee depot, had orchestrated that ploy, aiming to draw Federal troops into a trap. At the end of an exceedingly bloody siege, the Union lost the Battle of Olustee, and Seymour retreated to Jacksonville. The railroad was intact, for the moment, and Confederates resumed their supply line to ship Florida beef to their troops. (That defeat put a halt to Union efforts to bring Florida into the fold in time for the 1864 presidential election.)

The Battle of Olustee was noteworthy for the ratio of dead and wounded to those who participated in the battle. However, it was considered the only "major" battle of the Civil War in Florida. Other encounters between enemy forces included a few battles, fifteen "skirmishes," five "affairs," one or two "raids," and a couple "artillery duels."

Colonel Finegan had long appreciated the role of Florida beef to the Confederate cause, so he directed cattle baron Jacob "Jake" Summerlin to select thirty members of his Florida brigade to round up herds for shipment north. For a time, Summerlin's crew was able to drive 600 head a week to the rail yards at Baldwin. Between 1861 and 1863, Summerlin sold the Confederacy 25,000 steers at $8 per head.

Summerlin, always happier on the range than indoors, had hit his stride by the time war skirmishes had destroyed many Florida railroads. He teamed up with boat captains James McKay and A. F. Hendry to smuggle cattle to Cuba. Undeterred by the blockade and persistent Union gunboat activity, the smugglers eluded the enemy using shallow-draught boats to navigate the maze of the Ten Thousand Islands in southwest Florida.

Outfoxed by "War Eagle"

Having been thwarted by Colonel Finegan's troops, Union forces began raids into the heart of cattle country to disrupt herds and farming activities. One regiment entered from the Gulf and proceeded toward Marianna. Another column invaded the Alachua prairie. Concurrently, Confederate cavalry colonel John J. Dickison, known variously as "War Eagle" and "Swamp Fox," learned that Union forces had burned the rail tracks at Starke.

Dickison had made a name for himself already as a wily leader who understood Florida terrain. He may not have been able to defend the state's long-tall coastlines, but he was exceedingly agile in relocating cavalry needed anywhere in the narrow interior. He and his men confronted Federal forces in the Battle of Gainesville and routed the men of the 4th Massachusetts Cavalry. Union troops retreated to Jacksonville and Fernandina. They returned to Gainesville, but Dickison et alia repelled them again.

Also during the Civil War, the colonel accomplished a combat first in American history. In the conflict known as the Battle of Horse Landing in May 1864, on the St. Johns River south of St. Augustine, Dickison led his men in a surprise artillery strike on the USS *Columbine*, a Union gunboat. After taking the ship, they disabled and burned it. It was a rarity during the war for a Union vessel to be captured by land-based rebels. It's also said to be the only documented incident in US history of a cavalry unit sinking an enemy gunboat.

By December 1 of that year, the US Army suspended the blockade of certain ports, including Fernandina and Pensacola.

Torpedo a Dud-o

The *Richmond Daily Dispatch* of December 19, 1864, followed a recent headline from the *Quincy Dispatch:* "Yankees attempting to blow up railroad trains."

The story went on to say Union troops were using torpedoes for the job. About 15 miles from Baldwin, rebels found a torpedo with 68 pounds of powder on the track of the Florida Railroad. "It was buried in the centre of the track, and was to be fired by means of a lock and cap attached to a musket barrel . . . connecting with the torpedo by a gutta-percha tube."

Two trains had passed without incident, because "a piece of iron happened to be left between the hammer of the lock and the cap, which prevented the explosion when the cars passed over."

BATTLE OF CEDAR KEY

In February 1865, having cut their losses on the railroad route to the north, Union troops opted to attack from the Gulf terminus at Cedar Key. They marched inland and northward along the line of Yulee's Florida Railroad, making raids on various Confederate positions.

They decided to return to Cedar Key to ship the cattle, horses, wagons, and other loot confiscated from the interior. A small force of rebels suddenly attacked the Union troops, but the action amounted to little more than saber-rattling.

The Union commander dismissed the incident and resumed his march toward the port. A majority of the Federal unit crossed the bridge at Number Four Channel, heading for Cedar Key. However, Captain Dickison and his Confederate cavalry were hot on the heels of their advance squad. Leaving a small group to guard their horses, 120 rebels pushed forward in a line, with scant ammunition and one 12-pound cannon.

Pickets spotted the rebels and opened fire. Dickison returned in full. The Union lieutenant left to guard the channel had about thirty men, who used the Florida Railroad embankment as a breastwork. The rest of the Union force retreated from the Battle of Cedar Key.

A BRIDGE TOO FAR

Confederates routinely used the Tallahassee Railroad to move troops, supplies, and artillery to defend the city. And the railroad's red-letter day came on March 6, 1865.

The previous winter, Union troops focused on planning an invasion of Tallahassee and the region's cotton treasure. The capital was vulnerable, as Florida units were occupied elsewhere.

Union army Major General John Newton had led an expedition with the US Navy to engage and destroy Confederate troops after attacks at Cedar Key and Fort Myers. Intelligence indicated Newton's band was camped near St. Marks, causing alarm in the capital just 20 miles away.

However, some teenage cadets from a local military academy "manned up." They, along with a band of wounded-veteran volunteers, joined the defensive force. With the advantage of rail travel, Confederate generals Samuel Jones and William Miller were able to hasten their transport south to take on the advancing Union troops.

While the navy's ships were stalled on the St. Marks River, Newton's force reached a point where a bridge had been destroyed. Resuming the march, they tried to cross the river at another point. Events there became known as the Battle of Natural Bridge.

Union troops initially pushed back the rebels, but the partly amateur Confederate force used breastworks to shield themselves as they guarded the approaches and the bridge itself. Action lasted much of that day, but the Union army could not secure the bridge. Newton reversed his stance and sought the protection of the Union fleet at St. Marks.

As a result of the railroad's role in an unlikely standoff, Tallahassee became the only Confederate capital east of the Mississippi River to avoid Union attack. And it was the second-to-last to witness the American flag replacing the rebel flag at the end of the war.

This was the last official battle in Florida—and it punctuated the ultimate Union conquest. Some attribute the Northern advantage partly to the fact that armies in the South were largely cut off from Florida resources.

Brigadier General Miller addressed that fact in a letter dated January 2, 1865, to General Samuel Cooper, adjutant in Richmond: "The possession by the enemy separates our line of railroads in Florida from the ones of the Confederacy. Besides the necessity of getting [supplies] out of the State, it may be desired hereafter to remove the iron now on these railroads for use in the central parts of the Confederacy."

Miller cited more than 25,000 tons of iron in Florida, plus 18,000 tons on the link from Live Oak to Lawton, Georgia, and the Savannah & Gulf line. He suggested building a 22-mile railroad "over good ground, with easy grade," by way of Quincy to the Chattahoochee River. Miller pointed out that the route had already been surveyed as a continuance of the Pensacola & Georgia Railroad.

Existing iron at his disposal included 9 miles of iron from the Florida, Atlantic & Gulf Central, already removed and waiting at Lake

City, and 8 miles of iron from the Florida Railroad's line east of Baldwin. He suggested the remainder could be taken from the Tallahassee Railroad or the Florida Railroad's terminus at Cedar Key—although his letter referred to the legal dispute with Yulee over confiscation of his assets.

Requesting orders to proceed, Miller emphasized, "We need to get supplies of sugar, molasses, pork and beef out of state," where they are most needed.

ORDERS FROM HEADQUARTERS

General Finegan sent several orders from his east Florida headquarters at Lake City in 1864, all indicating Baldwin as a pivotal point: The commander of Bay Port was to make haste marching to Gainesville, catch a Florida Railroad train, and proceed to Baldwin. Captain J. Q. Stewart was to initiate a forced march of his entire company to Otter Creek and catch a Florida Railroad train to Baldwin. Captain M. J. Clarke, at Crystal River, was to move by forced march with a detachment of his company to Gainesville, and *take a train to Baldwin.*

Writing that same year from, yes, Baldwin, Finegan said his command had occupied the site the day before, as Union troops had retreated to Jacksonville after burning a warehouse with matériel. Before leaving, the Federals threw 120 boxes of ammunition into a pond. The powder was too soggy to salvage, but Finegan's ordnance officer recovered the musket balls.

Finegan predicted the Union troops would either reorganize on a grander scale or go elsewhere. They had brought a Florida Railroad locomotive from Fernandina to Jacksonville, using the Florida, Atlantic & Gulf Central. Therefore, Finegan said he'd have the use of two engines to supply his command.

Another officer received orders to take swift measures to "concentrate enough railroad transportation in telegraphic reach to move a brigade of infantry from Baldwin to any point on the Florida Railroad where their services may be needed." The orders cautioned that troop movement was a priority, providing the least possible interference in transporting supplies.

FAMILY TIES

David Levy Yulee was not the only person of influence who was jailed for treason related to Civil War activities, but he was among the last to be pardoned. And he spent more time locked up than anyone other than Confederate president Jefferson Davis.

As the war fizzled out, the former senator and some like-minded persons planned to petition Washington for readmission to the Union. Before they could express their intent, Yulee was arrested in Gainesville and spent about ten months in prison at Fort Pulaski, Georgia.

President Andrew Johnson had appointed retired federal judge William Marvin as Florida's provisional governor after the Civil War. Marvin wrote the president, petitioning for Yulee's release. His argument rested on Yulee's value to the state's economy, citing his essential position as head of a railroad company.

In a bit of irony, Yulee's fate rested largely in the hands of Joseph Holt of Kentucky, who had been President James Buchanan's secretary of war. Appointed the nation's first judge advocate general of the US Army, he had presided over trials following the assassination of President Lincoln. He also was Yulee's former brother-in-law. His second wife, Margaret Wickliffe Holt, who died in 1860, was the sister of Yulee's wife, Nannie.

Holt's response to Governor Marvin's appeal to grant Yulee leniency? "Icy disdain."

Financial woes had caused Yulee and his associates to forfeit a controlling interest in the railroad company—and his letter to Finegan was proof of intrigue supporting secession while still a sitting US senator. Some wanted him hanged for treason in 1866, but he was saved after a personal appeal by General Ulysses S. Grant, who pulled some strings to expedite Yulee's release in March of 1866.

Yulee, with his get-out-of-jail-free card, returned to Fernandina, headquarters of the Florida Railroad.

EMANCIPATION, PARTICIPATION

President Lincoln's Emancipation Proclamation took effect January 1, 1863, spelling out freedom for more than three million African Americans.

Most people on both sides of the conflict expected slaves to rebel immediately and leave the scene of their captivity. However, some historians say many if not most slaves remained on plantations, often taking on management roles in the fields and handling livestock. Some traveled to Jacksonville to join the Union army; others got state jobs to rebuild roads, rails, and bridges.

Dollie Nattiel was born around 1855 at Margarita, Yulee's plantation on the Homosassa River. Her mother was one of Yulee's dozens of slaves. When Dollie was a young girl, they moved to Cottonwood plantation. Her diary describes a two-story, weather-boarded house painted white with green shutters and a gable roof, on a hill a mile outside town. It faced east, its chimney at the north end, with fireplaces on both floors. The main house had eight rooms and a front porch. An open space separated the kitchen and dining room. Northwest of the house were two rows of shanties to house Yulee's slaves.

About half a mile away was a sawmill, where Dollie and other children frolicked in piles of sawdust on Sunday afternoons. Yulee's four children lived at Cottonwood in those days: Charlie, Margaret, Florida, and Mamie. Until the family's flight from Margarita, Yulee was often absent from Cottonwood for months at a time: "A lot of times Mr. Yulee would arrive by train to Archer and walk home." Dollie said Yulee was a firm but humane master with precise expectations: "[Slaves] had to keep themselves clean and looking good. Their quarters had to be kept looking nice."

Dollie's mother cooked for the Yulee family and sometimes served their meals. Her main assignment, however, was material to plantation profits: scaring off blackbirds who scavenged in the fields. She had ten or fifteen helpers, whatever it took to get that job done.

Dollie said Yulee gave most of his former slaves 40 acres of land near Archer.

HARDLY A RAILROAD, NOT UNDERGROUND

The Underground Railroad got its name because railroad jargon was the vernacular for how it operated. It was not "underground," just clandestine, and it was not a railroad, just people helping people run away from slavery.

They usually traveled at night, often in disguise, on trusted routes known as "lines." They stopped to rest and eat at safe houses known as "stations." Their guides, or "conductors," referred to the refugees as "passengers" or "cargo."

LEGACY OF LOSS

Defeat was the legacy for many generations of Floridians. About 5,000 of the state's 15,000 soldiers did not return home to resume industry, farming, or raising families. General Grant and other Union leaders promised them honorable treatment, but politicos in Washington were the arbiters of their fate.

Most Confederate veterans had never owned slaves. They had farmed small tracts and struggled to revive ruined fields or scorched lands. There is also evidence of a high death toll of veterans within a few years of war's end, from disease and poorly tended injuries. However, those Floridians were not given benefits for the disabled, as Union veterans were.

WAR ON WHARVES, NERVES

The Stone Wharf at New Smyrna Beach, which dated to the time of 18th-century pioneer planter Arthur Turnbull, was an early casualty of the war.

As Edward King wrote in 1875 in *The Great South: A Record of Journeys:* "When the war closed there was not a wharf left on the river. Federal and Confederate had warred and wasted, and today for memento there lies in the stream, some distance above Jacksonville, a sunken gun-boat, its engine gear just showing above the waves."

To the north, on Amelia Island, is Fort Clinch, named for General Duncan Lamont Clinch, a prominent officer during the Second Seminole War. Construction of the masonry fort began in 1847, at the mouth of the St. Marys River, with the aim of protecting the deepwater port of Fernandina. (No battles were fought at Fort Clinch during the Civil War, but it housed a garrison of Fernandina Volunteers at the outset.)

STARTING OVER

William Dudley Chipley (1840–1897) was the son of a Georgia preacher who attended the Kentucky Military Institute. After graduation from

Transylvania University, Chipley enlisted in the Confederate army in the Kentucky Infantry.

Promoted to lieutenant colonel and active in combat, he was wounded in two battles, at Shiloh and Chickamauga. At the Battle of Peachtree Creek in 1864, Chipley was taken prisoner and remained in Union custody for the remainder of the Civil War.

Chipley returned to Georgia, married, and set his sights on the railroad industry. In 1876 he moved to Pensacola and began to make his mark on the Panhandle. (Chapter 7 describes the scale of Chipley's contributions to his favorite city and the region.)

NEW PORT, NEW HOPE

The St. Marks River town of Newport is a good example of a once-thriving settlement which barely survived the devastation of the war. One of Florida's largest communities in the 1850s, it was settled in 1843 by survivors of a major hurricane slamming Port Leon, a cotton-exporting town where a tidal wave literally washed away the docks.

These stalwarts took the remnants of their lives 5 miles upriver, to the opposite bank, and established the aptly named Newport. State archives report the town had, within a few years, a bustling business hub with cotton warehouses, an iron foundry, and even a newspaper.

Railroads dipped into the port's business, and the advent of the Civil War put a bull's eye on Newport, as Union soldiers used the river to approach Tallahassee. As mentioned above, they were foiled at the Battle of Natural Bridge, 7 miles north of Newport. But that was after "they burned down all the warehouses and left the community in ashes . . ." notes Florida Memory archives. "Newport rebuilt after the Civil War, but never recovered its former prominence."

Another wrinkle that many generations witnessed involves San Marcos de Apalache, the second-oldest surviving Spanish fortification in Florida. In 1679 the Spanish governor began building wooden barricades where the St. Marks and Wakulla Rivers meet. Much later, it was a rendezvous for Indian tribal meetings. General Andrew Jackson seized and occupied Fort San Marcos in 1818. After a long period of nonuse, the rehabilitated fort was a sentinel for the arrival of a railroad to the port of St. Marks.

The Confederate army occupied Fort San Marcos during the Civil War. In 1865 rebel forces repelled an attack by the US Navy.

North, Then South

Locomotives and rolling stock often started out in one camp and ended up in another. One particular engine was built for the US Army during the Civil War. Later, the government sold it to the Nashville & Chattanooga line, where it became No. 52. It carried the same number as part of the Nashville, Chattanooga & St. Louis Railroad.

Master mechanic James Cullen rebuilt the engine in 1885. The Georgia Car & Locomotive Company bought it in June 1919 and sold it two months later to the Chical Lumber Company based in Pensacola. By then, renamed No. 12 was on duty for construction of a sawmill in Blountstown.

Swann Song

North Carolina native Samuel Ashe Swann moved to Fernandina in 1855, when Finegan & Company hired him as an accountant for its various projects, including the Florida Railroad. He married Martha R. Travere in St. Augustine in 1859, and the couple lived in Fernandina until Union troops captured the city. Swann moved the railroad company's headquarters to Gainesville, where he spent the rest of the war years. He also represented a lumber firm until returning to Fernandina to pursue other business interests in 1867.

As a "private" land agent, Swann negotiated land deals for the Florida Land and Immigration Company and Yulee's Florida Town Improvement Company. In July 1875 Swann sent out a circular describing his solution to a major dilemma—no takers for "the wild lands of Florida" that were a significant tax burden for the land company and the former bond-holders of the Florida Railroad Company.

Such widely scattered and "unsalable pine lands"—conveyed in 1867 and 1871 by James T. Soutter and John McRae—had for years burdened other owners of land along the railway. Swann's solution was to hire the Southern Land and Immigration Agency of New York to sell 359,000 acres of land by "floats," or land warrants, at 60 cents per acre net. He called his plan "a most excellent arrangement."

In other activities, as a special agent for the state's Internal Improvement Fund, Swann negotiated the 1877 sale of 3 million acres of state lands—an action caused by the state's bankrupt railroads, "especially the Florida Railroad Company."

Swann and Yulee frequently corresponded about the financial ordeals scarring their investments and endeavors. Swann also assisted the Confederacy by attempting to frustrate the Union blockade against Southern shipping. His letters indicate travel to Cuba to arrange for shipments of provisions to Florida and clandestine exports of cotton.

Communiqués to Swann reflect the growing list of tax sales as Northern investors vacated their properties and Southerners were forced to abandon homes and farms.

EPITAPH IN BLOOD
Professor J. E. Dovell provided a fitting summary of Civil War–era sentiments: "Each day brought news of another disaster; a century of sorrow was crowded into a year. The end of the war found the mass of people relieved that the bloody conflict was finished . . . The veteran who said 'Thank God it is over, one way or another' expressed the common feeling."

CHAPTER 6

Reconstruction

Martial Law, Carpetbaggers, and Fraud

IN THE EARLY YEARS OF RECONSTRUCTION, RAIL PROJECTS BEGUN BEFORE the war were idled in neutral gear. The industry, like its assets, was bent and broke—no capital, rusted-out or worn-out locomotives, crippled rolling stock, and scarce materials to make repairs. Even if a company had money to resume building, there was poor inducement—given the political, social, and economic disarray in Southern life under martial law.

In 1866 the federal government approved a five-year extension on those land grants made a decade earlier, expecting it would motivate railroad companies to complete their lines.

The Florida Atlantic & Gulf Central Railroad (the previously mentioned pet project of Dr. Abel Baldwin and John Sanderson) had made semi-adequate repairs after the war and was able to offer service between Jacksonville and Lake City every week. But the company was so short on capital, it couldn't meet bond payments or "sinking fund" payments to the Internal Improvement Fund.

By 1868 the company was desperate enough to sell "bad order" cars to the Pensacola & Georgia Railroad, by then headed by Panhandle planter Edward C. Houstoun. According to *Southeast Limited,* the lot included nine boxcars with bad trucks, six boxcars without trucks, one mail and passenger car, one coach, and a fifteen-car log train. The buyer would have needed to install new trucks, roofs, or doors and a paint job, plus new upholstering in the passenger car. Despite disruptions during the Civil War, the P & G Railroad had been able to add an extension westward from Tallahassee to Quincy. It also had participated in the extension from Live Oak to Lawton, Georgia (with connections to Savannah), giving it extra business during the war. Meanwhile, an out-of-state investor (described in the next section) had been buying "Central" stocks and bonds, aiming to become a major railroad speculator. By then plans were in place to auction the FA & GC Railroad. Using legal means to block the pending auction, the mystery player secured a delay. However, within a month of that fire sale of dinged and dented rolling stock to the P & G, William E. Jackson and Associates bought what was left of the Florida Atlantic & Gulf Central for $111,000 (about 20 cents on the dollar).

CAPABLE CARPETBAGGERS

During Reconstruction the Republican Party in the South included "carpetbaggers" (Republicans from the North) and "scalawags" (Southern partisans).

Before turning their attention to Florida rail investments, two particular scoundrels left another Southern state in a financial abyss after issuing $4 million in fraudulent bonds for a railroad project. They were carpetbagger and former Union general Milton S. Littlefield of New York and his scalawag mentor, George W. Swepson of North Carolina. The latter was president of the Western Division of the Western North Carolina Railroad.

In one of his many books, Gregg M. Turner quoted Hillary A. Herbert's description of Swepson from 1890: "the most adroit agent of corruption who was ever known in North Carolina." The Caswell County Historical Association penned its own assessment more than 120 years later: "George W. Swepson became one of the chief Scalawags of the Reconstruction period. His machinations in railroad bonds contributed in large measure to the financial ruin of [North Carolina]. He and his carpetbagger friend, Milton S. Littlefield . . . displayed open contempt for constitutional restrictions. As president of a railroad, Swepson openly bought votes in elections, and he gave away railroad stock that had been secured by state bond issues."

According to an article by Robert J. Wyllie in 1994, Littlefield and Swepson accomplished their agenda through "forged proxies, stock manipulation, bribes, crooked bookkeeping, and numerous other intrigues."

When North Carolina got too hot to be hospitable, Littlefield moved to Florida, while his cohort evaded inquiries from the home front. It was Swepson who had been buying those stocks and bonds of the FA & GC Railroad. In league with Houstoun of the P & G, he was able to gain control of his prize in July 1868. He promptly renamed it the Florida Central Railroad and granted the P & G a long-term lease. In 1870 the "Central" was folded into Swepson's Jacksonville, Pensacola & Mobile Railroad (which ran from Lake City west to Quincy).

Swepson must have thrived on controversy, based on Paul A. Fenlon's 1929 backstory, *The Notorious Swepson-Littlefield Fraud: Railroad Financing in Florida, 1868–1871:* Trustees of the IIF had ordered the FA & GC to be sold because its officers failed to make payments to the sinking fund. By then Colonel Sanderson was a director and Franklin Dibble was president. Weighing options, they chose a premise to "consolidate" operations with the Pensacola & Georgia Railroad. In theory, it was a practical solution because compatible connections meant lower operating costs. Houstoun of the P & G agreed to collaborate, while Dibble openly opposed the state's plan to sell his line.

Enter Edward M. L'Engle, Swepson's lawyer, armed with a measure to enjoin the sale before state trustees could coordinate one. Hence, Dibble's outward hand-wringing to block the sale had given Swepson the time to file an injunction.

Swepson got another leg up when Governor Harrison Reed called for a special session of the Florida Legislature in June 1869. There, Littlefield introduced a bill spelling out state benefits of $20,000 per mile to build a railroad from Quincy west to Mobile. The ever-charming Littlefield sweetened his spin on the merits during frequent soirées around the capital—wining, dining, and entertaining legislators, bestowing cigars, bubbly, and whiskey. Cash for some, promises of money for others.

So, the J P & M Railroad got authorization to build toward Mobile. The company had the OK to issue bonds based on $14,000 per built mile, and the state would exchange Florida bonds for corporate bonds—to be sold on the open market.

Initially two snags marred Littlefield's view of the path to victory: One measure gave the state a first lien on the existing line from Jacksonville to Quincy; another required the railroad to prove clear title to the assets it was pledging to secure the state bonds. Mere flies in the ointment, and only briefly, once Littlefield bribed a state employee to omit those two items from the recorded version of the bill—actions which the *Floridian* deemed "a cunning fraud, boldly and adroitly perpetrated." A month after the special session and their big win, the J P & M Railroad was incorporated in New York City.

Governor Reed, meanwhile, had referred to "the spirit of the age" as an environment that behooved men of courage to embrace industry and opportunities to advance Florida's economy. A less flowery account of that mood appeared in 1929, when author Frederick C. Hicks wrote *High Finances in the Sixties:* "'a fantastic era' . . . of speculative financing . . . legislative and judicial corruption . . . organized lawlessness . . . a mania for railroad building in a time of unstable currency."

Thus, the sale of FA & GC Railroad to William Jackson & Associates went forward, with a ninety-nine-year lease to the P & G. Swepson, meanwhile, challenged the sale as illegal because the railroad company was "bankrupt." That company, with assets of $1,207,000 and liabilities of $1,020,000, sold for $111,000.

Houstoun became a double agent—representing both Jackson and the state trustees. He added a third leg to the stool to represent Swepson in his July 1869 purchase of a controlling interest in a newly named entity, the Florida Central Railroad. Houstoun also got an agreement for free rent for the first year of P & G's lease.

Same song, shorter verse, on the proposed sale of the P & G and the Tallahassee Railroad. Houstoun, who was president of both, wrote John Sanderson informing him that Swepson had retained him as his agent in buying the P & G. Houstoun had already acted as Swepson's agent when he bought about $1 million in first mortgage bonds of the P & G and the Tallahassee railroads (using a deposit of $50,000 for the former, $10,000 for the latter).

Now, Dibble and his associates bought the P & G for $1,220,000 and the Tallahassee line for $195,000. Swepson offered Dibble "the use of" some bonds in return for $960,000 in securities. Dibble pledged $150,000 to Swepson, which was to come from the sale of new bonds. In addition, Swepson would get one-third of the capital stock of the Florida Central Railroad (formed from the two just-sold companies). Trustees of the IIF decided the bonds Swepson agreed to transfer to Dibble were acceptable toward the purchase of those two railroads.

Once again, the Fourth Estate expressed alarm. The Tallahassee *Floridian* said, "The trustees, in changing the terms of the sale . . . perpetrated a wrong against the Stockholders and general creditors . . . They violated law . . . and outraged justice."

In April 1869 Swepson *somehow* got appointed "confidential agent" of the IIF trustees, with authority to hold the outstanding first mortgage bonds of the P & G and the Tallahassee Railroad companies. Further, the state comptroller and attorney general were to hand over to Swepson all the money "that may be received" for the railroads, on behalf of the trustees. The same day, the trustees gave Dibble the deeds to both railroads.

Robert H. Gamble, comptroller, and Attorney General A. R. Meek reported they had received $806,000 of P & G first mortgage bonds and $153,700 of Tallahassee Railroad first mortgage bonds (at about 94 cents on the dollar), and that the difference represented by the bonds and the amount bid for the two railroads was turned over to Swepson "to take up the outstanding bonds." Swepson "paid" $472,000, which was directed to the IIF board.

The net result of this shell game among Swepson, Dibble, and the trustees was that the two railroads sold for $1,415,000 in "cash"; Dibble got the deeds by transferring less than half a million dollars in worthless bonds and a check that could not be cashed; and the state was defrauded of more than $750,000. Dibble transferred ownership of the railroads to Swepson, but he would get back ownership once Swepson got the promised $150,000 and that $472,000 earmarked for buying the two railroads.

A pivotal point on the dial of the whole scheme was the exchange of $4 million in railroad bonds for an equal amount of Florida bonds. This would seem to have given Swepson and Littlefield the power to sell

Florida bonds to anyone who wanted a stake in state-assisted railroads. The unlucky taker of almost $3 million of the bonds in 1870 was a Dutch syndicate which peddled them to naive investors. As Fenlon wrote, "This completed the implementation of the fiasco."

Also remarkable is that Swepson gained control of more than 200 miles of rail lines, all the locomotives and rolling stock, depots and warehouses, and about 1 million acres of land—without using his own money, as he had dipped into the treasury of a company he controlled, the Western Division of the Western North Carolina Railroad.

A collection of Swepson's correspondence contains a copy of a letter he wrote to A. J. Jones on February 12, 1870. Swepson's statements include a reference to the rumors surrounding his indictment: "I will not stand still and see Littlefield and myself assailed and have all the odium of these matters put on us and allow others to go free. I know what members of the General Assembly have been paid . . . enough to cause dismay. I know all the Rail Road Presidents who have paid to get their bills through . . . I cannot afford to be slaughtered by myself, or have only Littlefield's company."

Numerous historians have evaluated the roles of Swepson and Littlefield in the Carolina rail scandal. One account holds that Swepson had received $6.3 million of special tax bonds. The money was to pay for the state's subscription for two-thirds of the capital stock in the Western Division of the Western North Carolina Railroad Company and to start construction of the line. The net proceeds from bond sales was about $1.9 million, of which a small portion went to posturing a charade of actual construction on the track. According to C. K. Brown, who wrote about Swepson's investments in 1928, Swepson misappropriated the rest to invest $843,000 in Florida railroad securities.

An 1879 article in the *New York Times* stated that the governor of North Carolina had, a year earlier, entreated the governor of Florida to surrender Littlefield for prosecution. Governor George F. Drew complied, "and the warrant for his surrender issued." However, there were enough loyal policy-makers still in power in North Carolina to thwart the state's quest for justice. Neither Littlefield nor Swepson was convicted in either state.

RAIL OR BAIL

Meanwhile, there was mounting political pressure from Panhandle constituents in the form of an ultimatum. As reported in regional newspapers, if Florida failed to build the locals a railroad, the state of Alabama was ready to annex the counties of Escambia, Santa Rosa, Washington, Walton, Holmes, Jackson, Calhoun, and Franklin.

The threat accomplished the desired response. The legislature passed bills granting exclusive rights to the Jacksonville, Pensacola & Mobile Railroad Company. Critics said those "rights" created a monopoly and gave the company inadvisable advantages, such as cash between $14,000 and $20,000 per mile for the estimated length of the line, to be paid before construction began, and a land grant for the right-of-way up front, rather than according to a ratio of completed miles.

One such opponent was John Screven, president of the Atlantic & Gulf Railroad Company. *The Weekly Floridian* deemed the state's actions as encouraging a monopoly. The proposal also impinged on various landowners whose only benefit was having sites near the railroad.

In 1873 Florida Governor Ossian B. Hart gave an address which repeated the malaise of railroad companies failing to pay taxes and/or interest on their bonds. During the watch of Hart's successor, Governor Marcellus L. Stearns, lawmakers approved measures to protect the people from railroad speculators. Stearns pushed for laws to standardize the rules for incorporating railroads, for regulating the sale of rail tickets, and, notably, denying the Jacksonville, Pensacola & Mobile Railroad Company the ability to issue bonds.

THE ASTOR FACTOR

The St. Johns Railway was able to cobble together the means to resume operations by the late 1860s. Within a few years, it caught the eye of New York millionaire William Backhouse Astor Jr. (grandson of German immigrant-turned-millionaire fur trader John Jacob Astor). William enjoyed pursuits such as horse-breeding in Kentucky and yachting aboard his luxury vessel the *Ambassadress*.

What he apparently did *not* enjoy was time in Manhattan devoted to his wife's social calendar. Thus, Astor began wintering aboard the yacht in

Jacksonville, and soon took a liking and a business interest in building up the region and promoting tourism.

In 1874 he bought an 80,000-acre tract along the St. Johns River in Lake County north of Orlando. The seller of part of the land was the estate of Moses Levy (described in Chapter 3 as the father of David Levy Yulee). With some partners, Astor set aside 12,000-plus acres to create the new settlement of Manhattan, Florida (later renamed Astor). He built wharves to accommodate vessels in the Debary, Baya, and Clyde steamship lines and the Astor Hotel, which housed the town post office and the Clyde maritime agency.

Astor bought the St. Johns Railroad and rebuilt the war-torn line between St. Augustine and Tocoi Landing on the east side of the river. Short on metal supplies, he initially started construction with wooden rails covered with iron straps. Horses or mules pulled the railcars over the 15-mile route—a four-hour journey which cost passengers $2. The chance to observe wild animals sleeping on the path was a bonus.

By 1876 Astor retooled the railway, replacing the pine rails with iron. He bought steam locomotives and retired his mule teams. He also expanded his interests into citrus, especially grapefruit, which then was considered exotic in much of the United States. His son, Colonel John Jacob Astor IV, added the citrus to the menu of the Astoria Hotel in New York (a longtime hyphenate with his cousin's property, the Waldorf).

William Astor's railroad broadened its reach as the St. Johns & Lake Eustis Railway Company, a "land bridge" line southwestward from Astor to Lake Eustis, Lake Harris, and others in the "Great Lakes of Florida" region. The first 12-mile leg from Astor reached Summit in 1879, with another 15 miles to Eustis the following year. The next leg to Lane Park, another 7½ miles, was ready by 1883, with the final leg from Fort Mason to Leesburg completed in 1884.

Thus, Astor's convictions led to a passenger being able to board a steamboat in Jacksonville and catch one of Astor's trains inland, as far west as Leesburg. His investment paid off for a while, as the company earned an 8 percent dividend.

Meanwhile, West Tocoi on the west bank of the St. Johns River became a terminal of the Tampa & Jacksonville Railroad. Passengers

This photograph is of a sketch of alligators drawn in the mid-1770s by William Bartram. In 1765, he and his father, British royal botanist John Bartram, visited the vicinity of what would become the town of Astor on the St. Johns River. John's poetic prose appeared in "Travels," and William's drawings were considered very important in the field of natural history. STATE ARCHIVES OF FLORIDA, FLORIDA MEMORY.

going to St. Augustine caught a ferry for Tocoi Landing, to catch the railcar for the city. Between 1870 and 1892 the two Tocoi points also were the primary route from Jacksonville to St. Augustine.

Of course, Astor wasn't the first or last to appreciate his environs. In 1765 British royal botanist John Bartram and his son visited the vicinity of what would become the town of Astor on the St. Johns River. Writing in *Travels* about his tour, Bartram said: "This blessed land where the gods have amassed into one heap all the flowering plants, birds, fish and other wildlife of two continents . . . to turn the rushing streams, the silent lake shores and the awe-abiding woodlands of this mysterious land into a true garden of Eden."

The "Eden" of Bartram's day remains the habitat for wild turkeys, bobcats, the endangered Florida panther, ospreys, herons, egrets, and bald eagles.

POSTBELLUM INDEED

As author Chris Monaco notes, the character of the Florida Railroad was markedly different from what former US senator David Yulee originally had in mind: "For a multitude of reasons, the road became an important regional carrier and sparked the development of numerous towns along its path, but failed to accomplish Yulee's more grandiose ambitions."

After the Union conquest, the Dickerson syndicate's decision-makers continued to operate the crippled Florida Railroad. The line, by then, was a bundle of war-wracked stations, rolling stock, and tracks.

The Internal Improvement Fund made note in its report in 1866 that the Florida Railroad Company had failed to make interest payments on the mortgage bonds issued before the war. Therefore, the IIF put the company up for auction. Dickerson and associates bought the line for $323,400, or one-fifth of the original value of the bonds.

By 1869 both Yulee and the syndicate shared interests in the railroad, which was financially stable. Its reconstructed route once again carried passengers and freight between Fernandina and Cedar Key. In 1870 at Fernandina, Yulee hosted President Ulysses S. Grant, who, as a Union general, had so ably interceded to expedite his release from a cell at Fort Pulaski, Georgia.

Two years later, the Dickerson syndicate reorganized the Florida Railroad as the Atlantic, Gulf & West India Transit Company. Often dubbed "the Transit Road," it enabled many more settlers to find the state's long-anonymous interior. The depot at Arredondo got the nickname "boss vegetable station"—a pivotal point where farmers, ranchers, and merchants brought livestock, naval stores, lumber, rice, cotton, fruits, and vegetables to be moved along to domestic and foreign markets.

The Transit outfit and some subsidiaries began that forgotten leg of the line into Tampa. The Peninsular Railroad connected with the former Florida Railroad at Waldo, going to Ocala and Silver Springs. The Tropical Florida Railroad operated from Ocala to Wildwood. Since then, the line changed hands many times and some routes were redirected. There are rusted relics of abandoned segments—and only whispers of many others.

The islands of the Cedar Keys prospered after the war, their economy fed by shipbuilding, sawmills, pencil factories, and the fishing industry. In 1865 the Eberhard Faber company based in Manhattan built a mill on Atsena Otie Key. Faber had been exporting eastern red cedar to Germany for more than a decade, and Cedar Key had plenty of it at the time. Meanwhile, the Eagle Pencil Company built a mill on Way Key, near the terminal for the Florida Railroad.

THE LAW ACCORDING TO JIM CROW

As referenced in earlier chapters, African-American slaves performed most of the hard labor needed to build railroads in Florida. In some instances, Irish and Dutch immigrants stood in, for $1 a day. In other cases, the state leased convicts, both black and white, to rail builders.

During the years of Reconstruction, Florida imposed more than a dozen segregation laws which spelled out harsh penalties for infractions. A statute dating to 1865 stated: "Negroes or mulattoes who intruded into any railroad car reserved for white persons would be found guilty of a misdemeanor and, upon conviction, sentenced to stand in the pillory for one hour, or to be whipped, not exceeding 39 stripes, or both, at the discretion of the jury." (Whites faced the same penalty for entering a car reserved for persons of color.)

Another statute in 1873 barred segregation of railroads and other forms of public transportation, as well as inns, theaters, and non-private schools.

In the previous era of slave labor, gangs of railroad workers had duties well after the tracks were laid and trains kept a schedule. When conditions on a route indicated a maintenance problem, these work gangs went from section to section to repair damaged track, clear fallen trees, and fill in washed-out roads.

Historians have called these workers "gandy dancers," while giving differing explanations for the term's origin. One is that a company named Gandy manufactured a tool that rail workers used to lift a tie so as to level the track. In practice, the "gandy" resembled a very long rod with a chisel end which was wedged under a rail tie. One worker then jumped on the outer end while another shovelled ballast under the tie.

One constant in the lore about gandy dancers was their practice of chanting in rhythm to pace the work and act in unison. "Down, now, uh . . . down, now, uh . . ." is one example of a call-and-response lyric, sometimes known as "lining" songs. These gangs consisted of eight workers and a boss who stayed in section houses spaced at 10-mile intervals along the rail route.

After the Civil War, there were similar jobs for section gangs, but with wages. Former slaves also worked in railroad repair shops, as cooks and porters on the trains, and as laborers who attended to the baggage and freight duties at each station.

Although there were separate waiting rooms and passenger cars for African Americans, they gained an appreciation for mobility that did not depend on blistering their own two feet. As Murray Laurie noted, "Church choirs, baseball teams, and Sunday School classes could travel to near and distant places to join other communities and meet friends and relatives. Many Black families bid farewell to their young men and women at railroad stations as they headed for a better life up North."

Some former slaves got jobs with the very planters who once paid for their bondage. But the era of wealthy plantations was in decline. Tenant farmers and sharecroppers, both black and white, replaced the old system.

Twelve Hours of Adventure for $11

Say you are boarding a Florida Railroad coach in Fernandina in 1869, heading to Cedar Key on the other side of the state.

Upon paying the fare of $11, you would commit to a twelve-hour ride over a largely uninhabited landscape, over a rough roadbed across swamps, and into the starkly wild thoracis of Florida. Waving good-bye to friends or relatives, taking in salty air from the Atlantic Ocean, you would head south to cross the trestle spanning Amelia Island and the mainland. Veering to the west, you'd travel 27 miles through remote pine forests to Callahan.

At Baldwin, the next station, you'd notice the commotion in this bustling junction with the Pensacola & Georgia Railroad—linking Jacksonville and Pensacola—where some fellow travelers might debark for a connecting train.

Next stop, Trail Ridge, a simple 17-mile hop, then 22 miles of either dense forests or swamp, as the train crossed the Santa Fe River. After a pause in Waldo to gather water and fuel, you'd go another 12 miles over ponds and lowlands into the busy hub of Gainesville. With a population of 1,500, it had enough hotels to give weary travelers a choice of respites.

Reboarding the train, you would travel 15 miles westward through rolling woodlands of pine, oak, and hickory stands, and arrive at Archer. Assuming there had been no rails washed out or accidents on the track, you'd continue through cypress hammocks and lowlands for 22 miles to Otter Creek.

From there you'd push westward the last 35 miles through coastal marshes to cross a string of small islands and arrive at Way Key in the Cedar Keys, the terminus of the Florida Railroad. Sunset would time-punch your arrival at the Gulf of Mexico, in this perky seaport with about 400 residents.

If you were traveling onward by sea, you could board a ship in the harbor bound for Key West, Havana, Pensacola, or New Orleans to make further connections.

TURPENTINE, TIMBER, AND HOT COFFEE

A few years after the Civil War, Confederate veteran George William Bryce used some inheritance money to buy 80 acres of land near the St. Marys River in Nassau County, along the route of the Florida Railroad. According to the *Florida Times-Union,* Bryce and his wife, the former Mary Louise Crichton, homesteaded in a log cabin for almost two decades, before building Homeplace for their family of twelve children.

Credited with founding the town of Bryceville, the family launched a lumber and turpentine business. Their home and office were part of the business complex, where a side track from the railroad led to a loading area. Bryceville became a stop on the route between Fernandina and Cedar Key.

Bryce's great-grandson, Murrell Mixon, worked to restore Homeplace in 2004, along with his wife, Patty. In the process, her sister, Nan Key, compiled some background: "The home's water tower, believed by some to be the state's oldest, stands nearby," a source for Homeplace, the business, and the steam locomotives.

Two of Bryce's sons, John and Crichton, were engineers for the Florida Railroad: "A pot of coffee was always on the kitchen stove [at Homeplace]. If the train stopped in the middle of the night, the engineer always knew the kitchen door was open for him to go get a hot cup of coffee."

George Bryce became the town's first postmaster in 1879. He also built a country store near the depot.

A CONNECTICUT YANKEE

Henry Shelton Sanford, born in Connecticut in 1823, bought a sugar plantation in Louisiana in 1869 and a cotton plantation off the coast of South Carolina. By 1870 he was ready to invest substantially in Florida real estate.

Well traveled, he began serving in the US diplomatic service in 1847, in a career that took him to Russia, Germany, France, Belgium, and Central and South America. In 1861 President Abraham Lincoln named Sanford the US minister to Belgium—from whence he lobbied against Belgian diplomatic recognition of the Confederacy. As the US fiscal agent during the war, he also coordinated the gathering of Union intelligence in Europe and funneled arms to Federal troops.

Sanford's interests in Florida revolved around citrus groves near Lake Monroe in the central part of the state. His land grant of 23 square miles, the St. Gertrude Grove, and later acquisitions spurred some early development in that industry. As a result, he became namesake of the city of Sanford. His solution to labor problems was to bring in a hundred immigrants from Sweden.

More about Henry Sanford and the city will appear in the next chapter.

A STEAMING HART

Hubbard L. Hart, born in Vermont in 1827, moved to Savannah in 1852 and opened a stagecoach line carrying US mail. About the time the Internal Improvement Fund was gearing up, he moved to Florida and opened a stagecoach mail route from Palatka to Tampa.

Within a few years, Hart had built a wharf and a general store at Palatka. In 1860 he bought the steamboat *James Burt* and then the *Silver Spring*. During the Civil War, Hart ferried supplies for the Confederacy.

After the war, Hart was able to clear obstacles hindering traffic on the Ocklawaha River and buy more boats to transport passengers and cargo. By the late 1860s, Florida destinations were a magnet for out-of-state visitors, many of them drawn to Silver Springs.

Hart's company, the Orange Grove and Ocklawaha River Steamers, prospered during the late 1800s. He also invested in railroad and canal development, hotels, and the citrus industry. Before the turn of the century, railroad competition dented Hart's steamer business, but it remained profitable as a winter enterprise.

"TERRA INCOGNITA"

In 1875, when US Representative William Darrah "Pig Iron" Kelley of Pennsylvania wintered in northeast Florida, he referred to the relative wilderness as "terra incognita," or unknown land.

The climate promptly spread on him a cloak of repose so heavy, Kelley said he languished in ennui for a while, came to his senses, and willed himself to return home early. Clearly, he was intoxicated by the tropics. But more than a decade later, Kelley penned his initial observation: "The controlling impression I recall was that at some period when, by the decay of successive growths of the luxurious vegetation, Florida should have lifted out of the water, she would probably be a safe and agreeable home for human beings."

An abolitionist and friend of Abraham Lincoln, Kelley had helped found the Republican Party in 1854. He was a judge and an author, including *The Old South and the New: A Series of Letters* published in 1888.

On a side trip while in Florida, Kelley visited botanist Dr. William Wittfeld, a German who, like many of his countrymen, had fled Europe after the revolution of 1848. Wittfeld's farm was at Georgiana, where the Indian and Banana Rivers converge. On his property Kelley found a vibrant array of pineapples, bananas, citrus, orchids, and "resurrection grass." Kelley admitted to being amazed that while Wittfeld had a healthy field of sugarcane, he had dug it up "because no sugar factories were established . . . and [Wittfeld] had no market for [his] cane or syrup."

According to Kelley, Wittfeld was confident that sugar, tobacco, indigo, and rice would become annual staples grown in Florida. Whenever capital materialized to build well-equipped sugarhouses, run by experienced superintendents, "Florida farmers will supply them with ample stores of cane richer in sugar that ever was cut in Louisiana."

In *The Old South*, Kelley opined at length about the laggard pace of Florida railroad development and population growth compared to other states—citing US Census statistics from 1840 and 1870 and Henry Varnum Poor's *Railroad Manual of the United States*. "The [federal] government had been 'specially' lavish in its grants of land to [Florida] directly, and to her railroad companies," he wrote.

Kelley also noted that Florida had but 416 miles of railroad at the close of the Civil War, and they were "badly located . . . and the extravagance and corruption which attended their construction had bankrupted the companies which owned the lines and the State."

Florida's population was 54,477 in 1840; three decades later, it was 187,740. According to Poor's 1874 manual, Florida had a paltry 484 miles of railroad, finished and unfinished, causing Kelley to conclude, "It was man and not nature that had inflicted bankruptcy upon the state, and stagnation and gnawing penury upon her people."

Kelley describes young Florida almost as an ingénue in the throes of oligarchs, at the mercy of their egocentric agenda to monopolize her abundance. He cites the "aristocratic dwellers" who built showy plantations north and west of the Suwannee River, whose primary aim was to hog the benefits of access to the Panhandle.

Once these self-chosen "rulers" controlled the taxable resources of the state, its credit, and the enormous federal land grants, they could "entrench themselves in the exercise of Florida's executive, legislative and judicial functions." Kelley cites their subsequent action, or inaction, in terms of abandoning all pretense of promoting settlement and developing resources.

The state guaranteed the bonds issued by railroad companies assisted by the Internal Improvement Fund, which actually became a guarantee of ruin. The state secured its payments of principal and interest by a mortgage pledging "all the land she had received from the [federal] government or might acquire." Therefore, Kelley wrote, "Her supreme power was thenceforth restricted to the further impoverishment of her people by taxing their uncultivated and unproductive land."

This hopeless cycle repeated itself over and over, until Florida experienced a form of post-Reconstruction deliverance—the machinations of which come to light in the next chapter.

"BAPTIZED" IN THE ST. JOHNS RIVER

During the last few years of Reconstruction, author Edward King took a St. Johns River steamer from Jacksonville to Tocoi Landing, then boarded a St. Johns Railway "horse-car" for the 18-mile journey to St. Augustine.

In 1875 King penned his observations in *The Great South: A Record of Journeys:* "The cattle, knee-deep in water, are feeding on the fresh herbage springing from the sand-bars; hundreds of little fish are leaping out of the current and falling back again, their shining bodies coquettishly bent as if they were making mock of the sun. Sometimes the boat enters a pleasant inlet, where the pines on the shores have cut across the 'hummock' and stand quaintly draped in Spanish moss, as if they had come to be baptized."

The riverbanks were lined with "a wealth of exquisite foliage to be seen nowhere else upon this continent," King wrote, citing "a grand forest of cypresses robed in moss and mistletoe; of palms towering gracefully." He noted the abundant tree variety—white and black ash, magnolia, water oak, poplar, buttonwood, sweet bay, olive, juniper, red cedar, sweet gum, and live oak; also shrubs of azalea, sumac, agave, poppy, mallow, and nettle. "The fox grape clambers along the branches, and the woodbine and bignonia escalade the haughtiest forest monarchs . . . the gleaming water out of which rise thousands of 'cypress-knees,' looking exactly like so many champagne bottles set into the current to cool."

The land portion of King's journey was part iron rail and part wooden, with occasional run-ins with a creature napping on the track. Alligators were caught dozing, and the conductor told King that once, he encountered two young bears, directly in the train's path and asleep.

DOWN AND OUT AT THE DEPOT

As discussed at length previously, cattle ranching was a Florida first in Colonial times, territorial times, and beyond. Where there are cows, of course, there will be rustlers, and the practice of rustling had been fairly democratic—as Europeans, Americans, and Indians poached from each other with impunity.

One colorful Florida rustler was M. B. "Bone" Mizell, born in 1863. His biographer, the late Jim Bob Tinsley, described a Florida cowman's lot in life as "a world of cattle wars, vigilante actions, hangings, lynchings, fence cuttings and cow-town duels . . . [Mizell] was a man who used his sense of humor and a bottle of booze to survive in the Florida cowman's world." The famous Western artist Frederic Remington painted Mizell in 1895 and dubbed the work *A Cracker Cowboy.*

In an article published in *Wild West* magazine in 1999, Jim Bennett summed up the link between this Florida cowhand and the way his bread was buttered: "On July 14, 1921, Morgan Bonaparte Mizell, 58, died with his boots on. When death came, he was waiting for a telegraphic money order . . . in the Fort Ogden, Florida, depot house."

Often that money order would have been sent by cattleman Ziba King, a former Confederate officer who walked to Florida after carpet-baggers took his family's plantation in Georgia.

King moved to Fort Ogden, up the Peace River, to homestead 160 acres. His dry-goods business helped pay the bills until he could build a cattle herd; records from Manatee County in 1885 show King had 40 acres of tilled land, 6,000 acres of wooded and pasture land, and $60,000 in livestock. By 1900 King had 50,000 head—10 percent of all cattle in Florida—and was called the "cattle king of South Florida." Besides his businesses, King won election to both houses of the Florida Legislature. He was an official in three banks and a judge in Arcadia.

As one historian tells the story, Bone Mizell often worked as Ziba King's ranch foreman. On a day in which he drove several "strays" to the railhead in Arcadia and sold them, Mizell walked to a saloon to quench his thirst. Arrested shortly thereafter, charged with rustling cows carrying the markings of King's ranch, Mizell found himself facing Judge King on the bench. In his defense, Mizell pointed out that he had often marked strays with King's brand, "and figured these cows were nothing more than payment for services rendered." Charges dropped, case dismissed.

"Height" partly explains the rapport between two cowmen who, literally, saw eye-to-eye: Mizell's daddy was said to admire the diminutive Napoleon Bonaparte, yet his son, Bone, at 6-foot-5, was one tall drink of water. A barefoot Ziba King stood 6-foot-6.

COWS AND DOGIES FOR DOUBLOONS

Despite the Civil War, wild "scrub cattle," or "Cracker cattle," descended from Spanish and British herds were plentiful in Florida. Ranchers who had supplied the Confederacy could now sell beef to the reunited nation. For decades, Florida's cattle trade grew and matured as drovers moved herds to railheads for shipments to Cuba and Nassau.

Partly because of its strategic port in Key West and later ones established on the Gulf coast, Florida became the nation's leading cattle exporter. According to the Florida Memory project, in the decade between 1868 and 1878, Florida ranchers received millions of dollars in gold doubloons, having sold more than 1.6 million head of cattle to Cuba.

This Caribbean commerce "provided income to cattlemen, merchants, and shippers, and contributed to the state's recovery from Reconstruction-era depression."

MATHESON-STEELE JUNCTION

As mentioned in Chapter 2, Augustus Steele had begun to turn Cedar Key into a civilized destination and thriving port in the mid-1840s. His only child, a daughter, was born in the islands and educated with private tutors.

By 1861 rounds of visitors were arriving at the new Florida Railroad depot on Way Key. On the return trip, departing citizens set off to shop in Gainesville and points east.

In a scenario posed by Murray Laurie of the Archer Historical Society, it's possible that Cupid rode one of the trains as well: "Would the pretty girl named Augusta Florida Steele . . . have met the dashing young Confederate veteran James Douglas Matheson, recently arrived in Gainesville to begin his career as a merchant, without the Florida Railroad? Was it the Reverend William McCormick, the Presbyterian minister who traveled by train from Gainesville to Arredondo to Cedar Key to preach to his far-flung congregation, who served as a matchmaker?"

The Archer journal directs one to the historic Matheson House in Gainesville, where the couple set up their household after a wedding in 1867. Matheson's relatives from South Carolina had built the house a decade earlier, but it was unoccupied during the Civil War.

The family had lots of visitors who arrived by train at a station just blocks from the house. The couple sometimes traveled by train to New York City to buy retail goods for Matheson's store. According to a diary that "Gussie" kept, they would dine that night "on fresh oysters sent by express train from Cedar Key."

High-Tech Training

Toward the end of the Civil War, George Pullman began to design and build comfortable, luxurious passenger cars that were as fine as many hotel suites.

George Westinghouse received a patent for his invention of air brakes for trains in 1869, and in 1875 Eli Janney got a patent for the automated "knuckle-design" train-car coupler.

In 1878 livestock dealer Gustavus Franklin Swift hired engineer Andrew Chase to design a refrigerated railcar. Swift had a logistics dilemma while trying to deliver live cattle to Eastern butcheries. He wanted to be able to slaughter cattle in Chicago and ship the edible parts chilled.

Chase designed a car with refillable bins at the top where air would circulate over ice. The cooler, heavier air descended, displacing lighter, warmer air which escaped through ventilators. These cold-rail compartments enabled Swift to ship nationally and internationally, and reset the meat industry.

Gavel to Gavel

When Florida celebrated its quadricentennial in 1965, the state published and reprinted numerous treatises on how that 400 years had treated society and industry. One such work was *Carpet-Bag Rule in Florida, The*

Inside Workings of the Reconstruction of Civil Government in Florida after the Close of the Civil War. It had been written in 1888 by John Wallace, a senator from Leon County.

A contemporary introduction, written in 1964 by noted historian Allan Nevins, opens with a dismal prelude to an unconscionable era: "The chapter entitled Reconstruction is one of the most grimly depressing in all American history: a chapter full of knavery, malice, blindness, brutality, and greed." Further indicting a level of epochal evil that lacked the sparks of heroism displayed during the war, Nevins said, "It is especially painful in that it seems to prove the national character held fundamental flaws."

CHAPTER 7

Pioneer of Portent

William Chipley Warms to Pensacola

AFTER THE AFORESAID LOSSES FROM THE CIVIL WAR AND THE YEARS OF Reconstruction, railroad tracks in Florida were in a state of 52 Pickup. Operations were in a financial shambles. Prospects to develop new lines were all but out of steam.

William Dudley Chipley, as mentioned earlier, was a Civil War veteran who languished in a Union army prison the last year of fighting. Afterward, he went home to Georgia and built a rail line connecting Columbus with Rome.

Busily improving other railroad outfits, Chipley headed south to Pensacola. Although blessed with a deepwater port, it was all the way west, essentially cut off from the rest of the Panhandle and the state. Eventually Chipley would become mayor of Pensacola, concurrently expanding his rail career and promoting all things Panhandle.

More than two decades before Chipley's arrival, Florida had granted a charter to the Alabama & Florida Railroad. In 1861 the company completed a 44-mile track from Pensacola north to Pollard, Alabama. Eight years later, in a foreclosure sale, the bankrupt company passed to the Pensacola & Louisville Railroad.

That entity was reorganized as the Pensacola Railroad in 1877, with Chipley running the show. Favorably connected with the mighty Louisville & Nashville, the line became one of its subsidiaries in 1880—thanks to Chipley's initiative and the judgment of his longtime associate Frederick R. deFuniak, general manager of the L & N. He had been born in Rome, Italy, in 1839 and emigrated to the United States during the Civil War. He enlisted in the Confederate army as captain in the engineering department and rose to the rank of lieutenant colonel. (As many Floridians realize, Chipley and deFuniak were namesakes for two cities in the Panhandle. Such settlements were the spawn of rail development, as well as the source for those early cross-ties—hewn from abundant local forests of yellow "longleaf" pine.)

BROKE AND LONELY

The state's Internal Improvement Fund had been bankrupt and effete since the Civil War, and remained that way until sawmill magnate Hamilton Disston of Philadelphia made Florida Governor William D. Bloxham an offer too good to refuse.

Disston's friend, Henry Shelton Sanford, had shown him the charms of Florida on various fishing trips around his namesake town. Disston was enchanted with the array of economic potential he saw across the peninsula.

Sanford had established the Florida Land and Colonization Company to boost regional growth. Foreigners controlled much of the company, with Scotsman Sir William Mackinnon, 1st Baronet, one of the two largest stockholders. (The investors had capital holdings of more than 100,000 acres in several counties: Brevard, Hernando, Hillsborough, Manatee, Marion, Monroe, Polk, and Sumter.)

Disston—having heard that Florida would give any developer half of whatever reclaimed swamp acreage he could drain—saw stars and dollar signs and immediately surveyed and examined the interior of central Florida. Only then did he learn of a serious obstacle to his quest—that some of the land he favored was in the hands of a federally appointed receiver to secure a debt ($1 million, erroneously downplayed as $125,000).

That's when Disston asked Bloxham how many cherry-picked acres he could buy for $1 million. Having already fielded lowball offers from parties both foreign and domestic, Bloxham readily came up with the round number of 4 million acres.

When the so-called Disston contract closed in June 1880, the *New York Times* described the deal as possibly "the largest purchase of land ever made by a single person in the world." At the very least, it made Disston the largest landowner in the United States. His purchase gave the IIF a financial transfusion, because new land deals in Florida could entice railroad developers in the same fashion as other places in America (notably, the Transcontinental Railroad, completed in 1869).

THE BRITISH ARE COMING

Disston and his associates were incorporated as the Atlantic and Gulf Canal and Okeechobee Land Company. They set out to drain the Kissimmee River floodplain as it flows into Lake Okeechobee, eliminate surface water in the Everglades, and build a network of canals to dry up parcels in the adjoining wetlands. Once he undertook the improbable project, he realized he needed to meet someone capable of turning reclaimed turf into viable settlements.

A year after the Disston purchase, Sir Edward Reed of England came to the United States to scout for some choice real estate for his British consortium. Disston approached Reed and agreed to sell him 2 million acres. Reed and crew set about creating some "flourishing" towns.

There is some indication that one was Runnymede, née Wharton, founded in 1885 on Lake Runnymede east of what is now St. Cloud. It had a three-story hotel, which the Disston Drainage Company used as its headquarters. The regional railroad, the Sugar Belt Railway, built a depot nearby.

Runnymede is now a ghost town, not unlike Disston's misguided vision for a fully drained Everglades. Nonetheless, he is credited with salvaging Florida's finances at a perilous point in its history. "Disston" place names include lakes in Flagler County and St. Petersburg; avenues in Clermont, Tavares, and Tarpon Springs; and a street in Tallahassee.

Aware that Tampa would be nearing a major growth spurt, Disston envisioned another city in the bay area. One of his land development companies—equipped with lumber from his northern sawmills—founded the town of Tarpon Springs, building a commercial pier and two hotels.

Disston then turned his attention to an area on the eastern shore of Boca Ciega Bay, opposite Long Key. There he established a new town called Disston City, building a wharf, a school, and a hotel and investing in a fleet of steamboats.

RUSSIAN ROULETTE

Enter Peter Demens, a Russian exile who had been a captain in the service of Tsar Alexander II and abandoned his homeland in 1881, ostensibly for political reasons.

Demens, who owned a sawmill in Longwood, acquired the fledgling Orange Belt Railway in 1885 from three would-be developers who had signed for rail ties from Demens's mill. Before failing to pay for the merchandise, their goal had been a 35-mile line from Lake Monroe on the St. Johns River to Lake Apopka.

Demens formed the Orange Belt Investment Company with some backers and issued $50,000 in bonds to complete the line to Clermont. He then decided to extend the railroad to a site near Tampa Bay, reaching Pinellas Point in 1888. From then until 1897, the 117-mile line was the longest narrow-gauge railroad in the country.

Disston approached Demens, offering him about 60,000 acres of land if he would make Disston City the western terminus for his railroad. Hungry for a sweeter deal, Demens upped the ante another 50,000 acres. Disston balked, expecting his city to flourish if Orange Belt trains stopped anywhere nearby.

Demens chose to terminate his railway at St. Petersburg (named after his hometown in Russia). Thus Disston City idled and today is known as Gulfport, a quaint tourist draw. St. Petersburg thrived with the arrival of the Orange Belt Railway, and grew into one of the state's major cities.

At one point Demens faced a financial crisis which he averted with help from meat-packer Philip Armour in Chicago and some financiers in Philadelphia. Nonetheless, the line went bankrupt in 1893. Chapter 8 will speak to the line's acquisition by Henry Plant and its new name: the Sanford & St. Petersburg Railway. (As for Demens, he moved to Los Angeles and took up literary commentary. His penname was P. A. Tverskoy.)

BEATEN BY THE PULSE OF A "LIQUID HEART"

Disston's dream was to replace the "river of grass" with an agricultural bonanza. Yet draining the gigantic swamp was a goal some called cock-eyed and others viewed as an unconscionable assault on Florida's ecological "liquid heart."

In *Seeing the Light, Wilderness and Salvation: A Photographer's Tale,* authors John Barry and Tom Shroder (in a tribute to photographer Clyde Butcher) posed the view that drying out the Everglades became a chief goal of government upon statehood. They refer to Disston as "the unlucky dreamer" who took on the challenge without understanding the consequences of tampering with ancient, vital, nonnegotiable food chains and decapitating the peninsula's supply of freshwater.

"The man who struck the first blow with his dredges blew his brains out afterward. Not because he regretted trying to destroy the Everglades, but because he failed . . . So he drew a bath one evening, lay in the warm water, and shot himself in the head," Shroder and Barry wrote. (Most obituaries omit suggestions of suicide, stating that Disston died in bed of heart disease after a bout of typhoid pneumonia. What isn't known for certain is whether he killed himself and was perhaps moved from the tub to the bed as a kindness.)

Disston wasn't the only visionary to consider disturbing the swamp. Chapter 11 will describe Henry Morrison Flagler's contemplation of extending his Florida East Coast Railway to Key West by an alternate route to the west, through the Everglades to Cape Sable, and his decision to follow the advice of engineers who vetoed the western route as perilous.

PANHANDLE PROMISES

The Florida Legislature granted a charter for the Pensacola & Atlantic Railroad in March 1881, granting permission to build a line from northwest Florida, near Flomaton, Alabama, to the Apalachicola River (after 70 miles, it would meet the tracks of what began as the Pensacola and Selma Railroad).

The new route excited people for hundreds of miles, and understandably so. Long hindered with river traffic as their sole transportation, Panhandle farmers and lumber merchants could practically taste the gravy flowing from a railroad network across the state.

A survey team headed east from Pensacola and arrived at what seemed an anomaly: a large circular lake in the midst of virgin forest. William Chipley and the rest of his party made camp and crafted a legacy. He deemed the spot so special that it needed a depot on the new rail line, and he decided that the lake and those surrounding trees needed a protector.

The principals of that early survey expedition led the way to forming the Lake DeFuniak Land Company in 1885. The namesake was Frederick deFuniak, president of the Pensacola & Atlantic Railroad. Later the town took the name DeFuniak Springs, and once it had reliable transportation, it became the winter home of the New York–based Chautauqua educational enterprise.

By agreeing to build a line from Pensacola to River Junction—where the Chattahoochee and Flint Rivers flowed into the Apalachicola River—the Pensacola & Atlantic Railroad received a boon of more than 2.8 million acres. The lands ranged from fertile cotton fields in what would become Escambia, Santa Rosa, Okaloosa, Walton, and Holmes Counties, to wild and rugged Washington and Jackson Counties.

The railroad company issued $3 million in stock and $3 million in bonds. Within a few months, the Louisville & Nashville—whose general manager was deFuniak—acquired a majority of the P & A stock and all the bonds. If that sounds bold, the L & N had considered the various profit streams inherent in all those existing and potential assets: revenue from land sales, plus a voluminous freight business from untouched forests, livestock, farm produce, and naval stores.

Just considering the footprint around Lake DeFuniak, the L & N noted a pair of major sawmills whirring out pristine yellow pine for a lumber-hungry market. In its fertile fields, which drew the interest of federal agricultural geeks, were blueberry orchards, stands of pear trees, and a growing list of commodities and farm produce in need of a ride.

Once the settlement had a rail depot, the rural idyll drew primarily Scottish settlers from Eucheeanna and Alaqua who built homes near the lake. About 1887 Lake DeFuniak had a population of perhaps a hundred; three years later, the number was eightfold. The L & N actively promoted the charms of Lake DeFuniak and of the Chautauqua winter campus—offering discounted round-trip fares from Cincinnati, St. Louis, Louisville, and Nashville.

Chipley also promoted the notion to deFuniak that L & N extend the line to Southport on St. Andrews Bay. Southport Lumber Company laid part of the track. The route was successful, but only as long as forests could feed the logging industry. Once the trees were depleted, the lumber outfit was reduced to kindling. Another entity reorganized the spur as the Alabama & Western Florida Railroad, which operated from 1926 to 1939.

Some historians have characterized Chipley as the most important player in the growth of west Florida. Whether superlatives are in order, he did have a good sense of timing when it came to buying up and turning around floundering railroad companies. He did so by upgrading the rolling stock and revising shipping systems so that farmers and other freight customers saved money.

PANAMA CALLING

In 1883 surveyors provided a plat for the town of Harrison on the Gulf of Mexico. Six years later, the *St. Andrews Messenger* told readers about the town's "cool summers—pleasant winters—plenty of deer and turkey—fine oysters in abundance—trout, mullet, redfish, pompano, snapper, grouper, tarpon and turtle . . . vegetables in winter."

In 1906 developer George M. West established the Gulf Coast Development Company on St. Andrews Bay, with the aim of spurring new settlements on the Gulf to complement the thriving fishing village of Harrison. The following year, construction began on two regional rail lines. One was the Atlanta & St. Andrews Bay Railway from Dothan, Alabama, to Harrison. A. B. Steele, president of the Enterprise Lumber Company of Atlanta, wanted the railroad to coincide with the coming of the Panama Canal, as he anticipated a huge trade business via ports on the Gulf.

Steele's lumber railroad already connected with the Central of Georgia Railway at Dothan and with the L & N at Cottondale. So why not extend the route another 55 miles to the coast and preempt competitors? According to author Gregg M. Turner, the lumberman was not alone out on that limb. He had borrowed $70,000 from Asa Griggs Candler, the onetime drugstore clerk who had bought the formula for Coca-Cola in 1888 and used his marketing acumen to create an iconic brand.

Concurrently, West changed the name of Harrison to Panama City, as it was geographically halfway between Chicago and the Panama Canal.

Steele's line reached the bay in 1908. After he died, Candler gained control of "the Bay Line." Turner's book *A Journey into Florida Railroad History* traces other turns in the track: Steele's son bought back the Bay Line, then sold it to Minor Keith of the United Fruit Company. When his plan did not materialize, Keith sold the Bay Line to a subsidiary of the International Paper Company, which had a mill near Panama City.

While rail traffic did not meet Steele's initial expectations, his Atlanta & St. Andrews Bay Railroad survived and became a reliable line (today, the current owner, Genesee & Wyoming, operates the Bay Line Railroad). Concurrently, the Birmingham, Columbus & St. Andrews Bay Railroad Company was under construction from Chipley to Southport, across the bay from Lynn Haven. That enabled it to connect with the Sale-Davis Lumber Company's logging railroad at Southport. Its first train to Chipley ran in 1912.

Meanwhile, the St. Andrews Bay Railroad, Land & Mining Company floated an early plan to build a line from Grassy Point on North Bay—by Southport—to Park Point. However, financial woes killed the project before the line was built.

SAWMILL SAGA

In 1894 the Yellow River Railroad opened between Crestview, Florida, and Florala, Alabama, as a 27-mile logging track backed by sawmill operator W. B. Wright. Despite its small size, the line drew the interest of the mighty L & N.

According to author Kincaid A. Herr *(The Louisville & Nashville Railroad, 1850–1963)*, the L & N had already taken over a project from the Alabama & Florida Railroad to build a 100-mile line from Georgiana, Alabama, southeast to Graceville, Florida. Having "advanced the steel through the pine woods slowly but surely," it wrapped up construction in July 1902.

Then the L & N chose to build a 22-mile line from Duvall, Alabama, to Florala, over the state line, so as to connect with the Yellow River Railroad. The job was done on July 1, 1903. Several months earlier, Herr wrote, the L & N acquired all of the small railroad's issues of stocks and bonds. Three years later, the Yellow River Railroad became part of the L & N.

The conglomerate acquired or leased portions of other railroads operating lines in Florida, including the Pensacola Railroad (1880), the Pensacola & Selma Railroad (1880), the Pensacola & Atlantic (1891), and the Alabama & Florida (1899).

"HERALD" OF HOPE

The Lake Monroe and Orlando Railroad was organized in 1875 and granted a state charter to build a line from Sanford to Orlando. This route would connect Orlando with a very strategic city—as Sanford was at Lake Monroe on the St. Johns River. Unfortunately the LM & O was too undercapitalized to begin construction. By fall 1879 the company faced a critical deadline: If it didn't show signs of being in business by 1880, it would lose its land grants from the state.

Meanwhile, the South Florida Railroad, incorporated in 1878, had no charter because its proposed route was too similar to the Lake Monroe outfit. With time running out for the latter, its directors agreed to accept a bold, even risky, solution. They allowed real estate promoter and hotel owner Edward Warren Henck, a pioneer settler of Longwood, to transfer the Lake Monroe rail charter and land grants to his South Florida Railroad Company. Henck and another backer, Frederic Rand—a land agent for Henry Sanford—would proceed with building the line from Sanford to Orlando and beyond.

The charter transfer was official in December 1879. According to *Taplines* editor Don Hensley, those who celebrated included Henck's associates from Orange County. One was Dr. C. C. Haskell. They hired an engineer and surveyor to map a line to Orlando and onward, southwest to Charlotte Harbor on the Gulf coast.

Fortuitously Haskell's brother, Edwin B. Haskell of Boston, was managing editor and part owner of the *Boston Herald*. His partner, the

South Florida Railroad employees on the job near Bartow. E. W. Henck had launched the company in 1878 and later got financing from the owners of the *Boston Herald*. Henck was attempting to build from Sanford to Tampa but ran out of money by the time the route reached Orlando. The venture—the first new railroad begun after the Civil War—got off the ground with great fanfare in 1880, when former president Ulysses Grant turned the first shovel for the groundbreaking of the South Florida Railroad. STATE ARCHIVES OF FLORIDA, FLORIDA MEMORY.

newspaper's business manager, Royal M. Pulsifer, was fond of speculative ventures in railroads and mining.

Henck, also from Boston, traveled north to confer with Haskell and Pulsifer, who agreed to invest in the South Florida Railroad's future. The two subscribed to a majority of the rail company's stock. As Hensley noted, this made the *Boston Herald* "the first and only newspaper to build and own a railroad."

Their venture—the first new railroad begun after the Civil War—got off the ground with great fanfare in 1880, when former president Ulysses Grant turned the first shovel for the groundbreaking of the South Florida

Railroad. The line made Sanford an important regional rail hub, running twenty-five trains a day.

By the 1880s Seminole County had sacrificed some citrus groves during successive freezes, and celery became the substitute crop. The railway made a 12-mile loop around numerous celery farms, which, according to a historic marker in town, made Sanford the first city in Florida with an integrated rail system. The company also operated the state's largest ice plant, the Rand Yard, enabling farmers to ship perishables nationwide.

More about the saga of the South Florida Railroad will surface in the next chapter.

BOSTON "SOUTHERN"

Conceived in 1878, the narrow-gauge Gainesville, Ocala & Charlotte Harbor Railroad was intended to connect central Florida counties with a port on the Gulf coast. Part of the plan was a branch from Rochelle to Palatka, which had access to steamboats on the St. Johns River and seaworthy vessels calling at ports on the Atlantic. A spur north from Gainesville to Lake City would connect it with other lines.

By spring 1879 the owners realized that traffic originating in Palatka was more promising than Gainesville. They designated Palatka the main line and Gainesville the branch. With grading well under way within a year, the company was ready to receive a shipment of iron rails.

In the winter of 1881, the directors changed the name of the company to the Florida Southern Railway (not to be confused with the South Florida Railroad mentioned above). Tracks were laid at Palatka and reached Gainesville by late summer. Train service for the 55 miles between Palatka and Gainesville opened in late August 1881.

The line made stops in Archer, Hawthorne, and Rochelle, where the route went on to Ocala. Three years later, the Savannah, Florida & Western Railroad linked to these tracks, providing service through Alachua to Waycross, Georgia.

The Florida Southern Railway arrived in the cattle settlement of Arcadia in March 1886 and remained the "end of the line" for several months. By the end of the year, the population had grown enough for the state to call it a town. By 1901 Arcadia became an incorporated city.

Three men in Boston were principals of the Florida Southern Railroad: John R. Hall, president; William L. Chandler, secretary and treasurer; and Edward Avery, corporate attorney. Charles Francis, vice president and general manager; Charles Boardman, land agent; and N. R. Gruelle, general superintendent and surveyor, managed operations from the home office in Palatka.

CALLAHAN, NÉE SHARON

First settled in the 1840s, the town of Sharon lay along the route of the Old Kings Road in what is now Flagler County—a road that actually dates to the pre–Revolutionary War era when Britain controlled Florida. Originally a mere footpath, it took travelers from the St. Marys River to Jacksonville.

Sharon was renamed for Daniel Callahan, a native of Ireland and a partner in Joseph Finegan's construction firm (the company which built the Florida Railroad in the 1850s). For several years Callahan operated a mill near the new depot in "Sharon."

By the 1880s the Savannah, Florida & Western Railroad crossed the route of the old Florida Railroad, making it possible for sixteen trains a day to run to Callahan. The town had separate depots for passengers and freight. Callahan's farmers and merchants were able to prosper from ready rail access to Fernandina and the ships there bound for Atlantic coastal markets.

Much earlier, Isaiah D. Hart had petitioned Congress for a better road for the territory, especially for mail delivery. And there is a reference to Hart's Road on early maps of northeast Florida. There was no town, however, until the tracks of the Florida Railroad crossed Hart's Road in 1858.

"FISH & OYSTERS FOR DINNER"

As mentioned in Chapter 3, Serena Haile and her family had chosen to live in the vicinity of Gainesville in the 1850s because the Florida Railroad Company's line was working its way there. In Serena's journal are entries from the 1880s. One mentioned that the train could not stop in Gainesville for a period of time, as Jacksonville had reported cases of yellow fever.

Three of Mrs. Haile's sons worked on the railroad, so she often went to the depot at Arredondo for a brief hello when the train stopped on its way to Cedar Key. She collected mail at the station, and rode the train into "the city" to visit friends and family.

The rail line ran parallel to what is now Archer Road. The Hailes and other farming families depended on David Yulee's railroad to get crops to market and bring in supplies. Another of Mrs. Haile's entries illustrates the back-and-forth process: "Sent 14 boxes Oranges to Baltimore . . . Fish & Oysters for Dinner by Freight."

BY THE NUMBERS

Florida's early railroads were chartered by the territory, the state, or under general laws of incorporation. More than 550 companies got railroad charters (build and/or operate) from 1831 until shortly before World War II. Of that number, it is said only 255 companies built all or some portion of the intended routes.

Mergers and other actions pared down the number to 22 railroads operating in Florida in 1939. Here is a recap of companies referred to previously, by the decade chartered:

> 1830s: Leon Rail-Way Company, re-chartered as Leon Railroad Company, then Tallahassee Railroad; Florida, Alabama & Georgia Railroad, operating as the Alabama, Florida & Georgia Railroad; Lake Wimico and St. Joseph Canal Company, re-chartered as the Lake Wimico and St. Joseph Canal and Railroad Company; Pond Creek and Blackwater River Canal Company, re-chartered as the Arcadia Railroad

> 1850s: Alabama & Florida Railroad, reorganized as the Pensacola Railroad; Florida, Atlantic & Gulf Central Railroad; Pensacola & Georgia Railroad; Florida Railroad; St. Johns Railway

> 1870s: Silver Springs, Ocala & Gulf Railroad

> 1880s: Pensacola & Atlantic Railroad; Tropical Peninsular Railroad

Later chapters will reveal the influence and footprints of two major railway visionaries who turned Florida in the 1880s and 1890s into grand central station.

CHAPTER 8

Firmly Planted

"Henry and Friends"

No one in Connecticut in the 1800s could have foreseen that a native son being nudged toward the life of a clergyman would reject Yale Divinity School, create a transportation empire, and extend his presence so far that southwest Florida would owe its destiny and reputation to his mindful choices.

That uneven saga began on October 27, 1819, when Henry Bradley Plant was born in Branford, a town near the shore of Long Island Sound, about 8 miles east of New Haven. The town had long roots dating to the early Colonial period, and ancestors on both sides of Henry's family had distinguished themselves in the Revolutionary War.

His father, Anderson Plant, was a successful farmer who died of typhus fever when Henry was six years old. His infant sister and an aunt died, too. Though the boy became ill, he recovered. His mother, Betsey, remarried and the family moved to Martinsburg, New York.

Henry spent a lot of time in Branford with his grandmother, Sarah Plant, who hoped he would become a minister. His father-figure for more than a decade was Father Timothy Gillette, the minister of the Congregational Church of Branford and the schoolmaster at Branford Academy. Author Kelly Reynolds described Gillette as "popular, warm-hearted, vigorous, articulate, reliable, and decisive." In *Henry Plant: Pioneer Empire Builder*, Reynolds said Plant would be known by these same characteristics all his life.

A portrait of Henry Bradley Plant (1819–1899), whose transportation empire of railroads and steamships forever changed central Florida and the west coast. Plant built a 9-mile spur from his downtown Tampa terminal to Black Point, a site closer to the Gulf of Mexico. With support from city leaders, Port Tampa opened in 1888 with a mile-long wharf into Tampa Bay to accommodate slips for 26 ships, railroad cars, and warehouses. Plant built two hotels on the wharf, as well as his signature lodging, the Tampa Bay Hotel on the west side of the Hillsborough River. STATE ARCHIVES OF FLORIDA, FLORIDA MEMORY.

Impatient to be productive, Henry eschewed the offer of a college education and took a job as a deckhand with the New Haven Steamboat Company. Its fleet—*New York, New Haven, The Splendid, The Superior,* and *The Bunker Hill*—ran between ports on Long Island Sound.

Much of his time on the job was aboard the *New York,* where deckhands took their meals standing up in the galley and slept in the forecastle—a small, cramped space Henry called "the eyes" of the boat: "Taken all in all, it was rather rough on a fellow that had just left a good home, and when some of my towns-people would come aboard and catch me with swab or broom in hand, I didn't feel altogether happy, but had too much pluck to quit."

With the promise of a captaincy upon completing his apprenticeship, Henry stuck with his menial chores. But his method on one assigned task would inform the course of his future.

The vessels carried mail and express parcels, with little care given to the way they were stowed in the cargo bays. Henry took it upon himself to carefully organize the materials. The captain was impressed enough to allocate a stateroom to store "rush" merchandise. He put Henry in charge of that duty, and allowed him to move his bedroll into the larger space.

In 1842, at age twenty-three, Henry married the former Ellen Elizabeth Blackstone, daughter of the Honorable James Blackstone of Branford.

When Alvin Adams, of the Adams Express Company, took over the steamboat line and branched into railroads, Henry stayed on. As noted in the *New York Times* in 1899, young Henry was such a valued employee, he was entrusted with valises suspended from a shoulder strap containing "large sums of foreign gold . . . millions of dollars . . . ordered from the New York Sub-Treasury to the Philadelphia Mint for recoinage."

Following a few years of promotions, Henry took charge of the Adams Express Company's New York office. In 1854 he became general superintendent of the firm's territory south of the Potomac and Ohio Rivers.

In 1852 the Plants welcomed a second son, Morton Freeman Plant. (They had lost their first-born child, George, in 1845.) Within a couple of years, Ellen was in poor health, so the couple spent a few months in Jacksonville. This experience planted the seeds for "what if" in the active imagination of someone who had come to favor travel and considered any outing a trigger for the mind and spirit. Whether Henry was alone or with others, in a Pullman car or a horse-drawn carriage, a journey was its own reward.

Plant was a widower by 1861. At the outset of the Civil War, the principals of Adams Express decided to split their Southern properties from the whole and transfer them to Plant. He and the affected stockholders formed the Southern Express Company and incorporated with a Georgia charter. During the war, the company transferred funds and collected tariffs for the Confederacy.

Again, his reputation preceded him. When General Robert E. Lee was based north of the Potomac River, awaiting large sums from his Confederate officers, "they shipped it through Mr. Plant's hands" rather than trust normal channels.

TESTING THE WATERS IN FLORIDA

As stated in an earlier chapter, Southern railroads were in a physical shambles after the war. Many faced bankruptcy during an economic depression in 1873, the year Plant remarried. He readily surmised that expertise and money could revive the railroad industry and reboot the South's entire economy.

In 1879 Plant bought the Savannah, Florida & Western Railroad, the Waycross & Florida Railroad, and the Atlantic & Gulf Railroad. The latter dated to 1866 and was a 237-mile line from Savannah to Bainbridge, Georgia, on the Flint River. Existing branches went north to Albany, Georgia, and south to Live Oak, Florida.

Henry Stevens Haines, who worked for the Atlantic & Gulf, agreed to stay on and manage the new owner's assets. A native of Massachusetts who grew up in the South, Haines was working as a railroad superintendent in South Carolina during the 1850s. When the Civil War began, he joined the Confederate army and was given the rank of colonel.

In charge of logistics throughout the Carolinas, Haines bent the railroad system to his will to coordinate troop transports and supply lines. His lengthy experience made him an authority on track construction and rail line management. Reynolds noted the extent of his abilities: Haines could "lay track, run an engine, mend a boiler, issue payroll, and balance the books—all in the same morning."

He would become Plant's trusted right hand, making significant contributions during the fourteen years he worked for the man. Plant was able to run his interests from New York City with confidence, because he had Haines working from an office in Savannah. These "Henrys" became the namesakes for Haines City and Plant City in Florida.

Purchasing steam engines and more rolling stock for the Savannah, Florida & Western, Plant bought more efficient gear, remodeled the passenger-car interiors, and switched the track to standard-gauge (a section later in this chapter will address his reasons for the latter move). He also bought the Savannah & Charleston Railroad, then renamed it the Charleston & Savannah Railway. This gave him a line from Charleston to Bainbridge, and into Florida on the Atlantic & Gulf branch to Live Oak. However, he kept the entity separate from the Savannah, Florida & Western; both lines operated on the same tracks, forming a spine for Plant's expansion.

By 1881 Florida's Internal Improvement Fund was giving away land again, but "Yankee" Plant was not welcome, as Florida had been badly scalded by carpetbaggers. Therefore, Plant took up the challenge of persuading the state of the overall advantage of a better railroad system for the South.

"There are two ways of getting to Jacksonville from Savannah, and whichever you choose, you will be sorry you had not taken the other," so wrote G. W. Nichols in *Harper's Magazine* in 1870. Plant's solution was a Georgia charter to build southeast from Waycross and a Florida charter to build northwest from Jacksonville. The route would replace the heretofore arduous journey Nichols cited, that of having to ride west to Live Oak, north to Lawton, Georgia, then east to Savannah near the coast.

To get his strategy off the ground, Plant bought the East Florida Railroad based in Jacksonville, which laid tracks north. His "Waycross Short Line" built tracks south. The East Florida line built a dock to the middle of the St. Marys River. From the Georgia side, his "Waycross" line built another dock to the middle of the river. Happily, the docks aligned.

The railroads involved in this finesse also were separate entities operating on common tracks. Thus, Plant's stepping-stone system opened Florida to the rest of the South, and gave the rest of America greater access to Florida.

WORKING UP A HEAD OF STEAM

In 1882 Plant created the Plant Investment Company (PICO) and invited several friends to join in his ventures. Carefully chosen members of the "club" were Morris K. Jesup, a banker in New York who owned a railroad supply house; William T. Walters of Baltimore, a merchant who bought bankrupt railroads; Benjamin Franklin Newcomer, a banker from Baltimore; Henry Shelton Sanford, former US ambassador and Florida land investor; and Henry Morrison Flagler, who still worked for Standard Oil Company and hadn't yet blinked in the direction of St. Augustine, Palm Beach, or Key West.

Plant System vice president Henry Haines described the altogether simpatico process whereby PICO members participated: "When it is decided to do a certain thing, build a piece of railroad for instance, they figure out what each is to pay and they send in their checks for that amount."

Plant then turned his focus to the Gulf of Mexico and pondered how he could get a rail line from Charleston to a port on Florida's west coast. First, he built railroad tracks from Live Oak to Rowland's Bluff. However, Rowland's Bluff (renamed Branford, after Plant's hometown) was on the Suwannee River, not nearly close enough to the Gulf.

So Plant, well-schooled from the deck up in the workings of steamboats, saw the value of buying his own Suwannee River vessels (as well as steamboats on the Flint, Chattahoochee, and Apalachicola Rivers). He called the fleet "the People's Line," and by 1883 a Plant System steamboat could connect with the railroad at Branford.

That meant the route from Charleston to the Gulf was practically sewn up. The Plant System of steamers and rail lines already carried products between Georgia and Florida, but Plant wanted his own Gulf port terminal connected to Plant-owned tracks. He considered three options: Cedar Key, Tampa, and Charlotte Harbor.

A Port of His Own

As mentioned earlier, David Yulee's Florida Railroad took a bashing during the Civil War. After rebuilding the damaged line as much as possible, the syndicate that owned a controlling interest still faced a dire outlook. The members had defaulted on interest payments on the railroad company's bonds, plus the 1 percent owed the state's sinking fund. Hence, trustees of the Internal Improvement Fund took over and auctioned the company. The buyer was an agent for Edward Dickerson's syndicate, and numerous creditors and European bondholders. Still, the group let Yulee retain a minor ownership interest.

Dickerson et al. operated the railroad until early 1872. Then the syndicate changed the railroad's name to the Atlantic, Gulf & West India Transit Company. It operated as such until 1881, when British investor Sir Edward James Reed reorganized it as the Florida Transit Railroad Company. By 1883 it had morphed into the Florida Transit & Peninsular Railroad Company.

At one time, Yulee and his associates had tried to interest Plant in buying the "Transit Road." And at one time, Plant had written to Yulee hoping he would see the benefit of having steamship service from his railhead at Cedar Key to Key West, Havana, and other ports. Alas, Plant got no reply. Even so, the two organizations had some amiable agreements to coexist and accommodate the flow of passengers and freight.

At one point, the Florida Transit & Peninsular Railroad Company submitted a lease to Plant that would have provided use of its tracks. At the time of that proposal, Henry Plant likely was unaware that the deal with the "Transit Road" did not include the western railhead on Way Key (Cedar Key). By this time, Yulee was winding down his business interests in Florida, but his family still owned the best land around the Gulf coast terminus.

Plant made several attempts to meet with Yulee and his associates about negotiating a deal to buy the terminus, but got nowhere. When he finally got them into a meeting, Yulee's group declined to sell the railhead at what Plant considered fair market value.

The outright greed wrenching victory from his grasp prompted the normally polite Plant to respond in words and tone not often associated with that gentleman: Vowing to wipe Cedar Key off the map, Plant predicted that "owls will hoot in your attics and pigs will wallow in your deserted streets!"

Writing about the incident in 1960, historian and journalist Hampton Dunn noted in a "Photouring Florida" essay that for years after that impasse, Cedar Key suffered under the "curse" slapped on her by the railroad magnate: "Back in the 1880s, when Cedar Key was a swingin' place, had a population of 5,000 and the second largest port in Florida, Plant wanted to build a railroad here. He was stopped cold by [Yulee]."

ASTOR FROM THE PAST

Cedar Key was not the only hamlet to feel the effects of a transportation shift. By 1885 the Plant System's expansion through central and western Florida left the St. Johns River town founded by New York visionary William Astor somewhat sidelined.

Following Astor's death in 1892, his holdings passed to his son, John Jacob "Jack" Astor IV. By then, though, the former "Manhattan," renamed Astor, was being eclipsed by the pace of changes throughout Florida. Steamboat traffic stalled, tourists found more enticing destinations, and many locals moved on.

The St. Johns Railway had changed hands in 1888, and with some upgrades, business perked up for a few more years. However, the brutal freeze in December 1894 and February 1895 was a death knell for area citrus, which also scuttled the St. Johns & Lake Eustis Railroad. Eventually the line from Tocoi Landing to St. Augustine became irrelevant and closed down in 1896.

Once train service fell off, the town of Astor was isolated, all but abandoned. Today the area is surrounded by the Ocala National Forest.

But, oh, what a heyday Astor had enjoyed—one that lives in the memories of pioneers' descendants. One early settler was J. G. Cade, whose family moved from Kentucky in 1884, when he was just eleven: "Astor was so crowded . . . it was impossible to find lodging for that night. It took the incoming boat several hours to unload and reload for its return trip."

Cade described general stores on both sides of the St. Johns River, where families could buy groceries and all manner of staples brought in on steamboats and rail lines: "tobacco, snuff, firearms, harnesses, calomel, quinine, calico and brogan shoes." In the rear of both stores sat three wooden barrels with faucets—a primitive sort of tap as one might see on a jeroboam of wine: "One contained liquor, one vinegar and one cane syrup—all sold by the gallon. You had to furnish your own container and, furthermore, drink your $1 per gallon liquor at home."

In many instances, no money changed hands for these tap-lines, Cade said, as the proprietors accepted almost anything in trade: a hen, some chicks, eggs, fruit—even hides from cattle, deer, and alligators.

As for Jack Astor—the businessman, inventor, writer, and colonel in the Spanish-American War—he perished in the North Atlantic when the *Titanic* sank in 1912.

A VOW MEANT TO WOW THEM

Henry Plant vowed to find another west coast port and build toward it. First he built the Live Oak, Tampa & Charlotte Harbor Railroad through dense forests from Branford toward Fort White and High Springs.

When the work got close to Newnansville in Alachua County, workers met another crew building tracks for the Florida Southern Railroad. Its mission was to build north to Lake City, and the crew had laid tracks from Palatka to Gainesville. Its charter also said the Florida Southern could build "to the waters of Tampa Bay and Charlotte Harbor."

Florida Southern president Franklin Quimby Brown needed a financial boost, which prompted Plant to suggest a multilayered win-win: If Brown would allow Plant to link his Live Oak, Tampa line with Brown's line where the two intersected, and give Plant the rights to the route to Tampa, Plant would buy a controlling interest in Brown's line and finance Florida Southern's route to Charlotte Harbor.

Meanwhile, the South Florida Railroad, attempting to build from Sanford to Tampa, had run out of money upon reaching Orlando and Kissimmee. (As noted in the previous chapter, E. W. Henck had launched the line in 1880, with financing by the owners of the *Boston Herald*.)

Early on, the South Florida Railroad owned only one engine, the Seminole. According to *Taplines*, the petite locomotive hauled the northbound morning train from Orlando and reached Sanford an hour and forty minutes later. The Seminole spent the day switching tracks and departed Sanford by 4 p.m. In early 1881 the railroad acquired an even smaller second engine and named it the Herald. The company then bought a used engine from a New York line and renamed it the Kissimmee.

Because of construction delays, corporate tempers flared, as they are wont to do. Within a few years, Henck lost his place "in line" and James E. Ingraham was running the company. Ingraham knew Henry Sanford, and the two happened to be walking one day on Bay Street in downtown Jacksonville. Sanford noticed that Henry Plant had paused on the opposite side of the street and encouraged Ingraham to make the gentleman's acquaintance.

Plant accepted Ingraham's invitation to experience a journey on the South Florida Railroad, along with as many guests as he wished to include. The party of eight or so—Mr. and Mrs. Plant, Mr. and Mrs. Henry Haines, and a few associates—arrived via the steamboat *Henry B. Plant*. Upon docking at Sanford, they rode the train to Kissimmee. The trip was a treat, especially the service, with a professional staff in uniform, wearing gloves.

Plant inquired whether Ingraham's shareholders might sell part of the South Florida Railroad. Ingraham suggested a three-fifths interest, plus a promise to extend the line to Tampa and combine the railroad operation with Plant's line of steamboats. In 1883 the Plant System acquired that three-fifths share; a decade later, PICO owned all of it.

Ingraham also joined the Plant System. And like Henry Haines, he became a trusted advisor in Plant's inner circle.

Author Sandra Wallus Sammons relates Plant's sense of urgency about this time, as he was competing with efforts by the Florida Transit Railroad to reach Tampa first. To improve his system, Plant retooled the Florida Southern's track to Gainesville and built a spur from Fort White to Lake City.

HIGH TIME FOR TAMPA

Considering the size of Tampa, its national profile as a major port, its Gulf coast proximity, and its contributions to the state's economy and culture, it might seem curious that it lagged behind other Florida settlements in the Colonial and territorial eras.

That is partly because the Tocobaga tribe were able to repel intruders when the first Europeans came calling. New Spain in the 1500s did not bother to mark Tampa with a permanent outpost. Toward the end of the 18th century, some wanderers started a settlement called Spanish Creek, which took hold.

Based on scientific evidence about pottery-making cultures, villages of Tocobaga people were well established along Tampa Bay long before European explorers. Each village had a distinctive central common area. Ceramic fossils by the burial mounds were decorated, while those at the shell middens were plain.

After 1824, when the US Army built Fort Brooke at the mouth of the Hillsborough River, Tampa toyed with getting in gear. The area then had a few families descended from generations of Cuban fishermen and some feisty bands of Indians who eked out a living in the wild. Among those who had drifted south, a motley crew of locals were OK with the presence of American soldiers.

By the end of the Civil War, Tampa was a ghost town with an empty treasury. During Reconstruction a few settlers returned, primarily to cultivate citrus groves. At the time Henry Plant took notice, more homesteaders had arrived, and anyone who wished to cross the Hillsborough River did so by ferry.

BONE VALLEY BONANZA

Bone Valley squats 20 to 40 feet under stretches of Polk, Hardee, DeSoto, and Manatee Counties in the Hawthorne Formation, a geologic mix of clay, sand, and limestone. Scientists believe mineral deposits there formed from a blend of dissolved phosphorus and the remains of sea life and animals: say sharks, whales, three-toed horses, and giant sloths out for a Sunday sashay across the Bering Strait—as if *Jurassic Park* creatures munched on dragon-size Prozac.

Before the early 1880s, the languid hamlets around Tampa Bay had stagecoach service to Tuckertown (later named Dade City) and Sanford. Except for water transport, the city was adrift from the rest of the state.

Decades after the Civil War, however, Tampa would have a new reason to flex some economic muscle—thanks to the discovery of phosphate deposits throughout Bone Valley. Mining and transporting phosphate gave Tampa's economy a major boon, as phosphate is an essential ingredient in fertilizer. (Florida provides about three-quarters of phosphate in the United States and about 25 percent of the world's supply.)

A THOUSAND ACRES PER MILE

The state had already approved charters for rail lines to Tampa. One company, the Jacksonville, Tampa & Key West Railway, could build from the St. Johns River to the Gulf. Its charter granted a mileage bonus as well— 1,000 acres per mile of laid track more than the South Florida Railroad would receive.

Time was not on its side, however, as the charter had a seven-month window to build 75 miles of track through thick forests and wetlands. Undeterred, PICO bought the J, T & KW and began construction. Haines's expertise was invaluable, as he persuaded Plant to build concurrently from both termini.

Haines supervised the work, which began in June 1883—a muggy, scorching time to be laboring outdoors in Florida. As tracks stretched onward, entrepreneurs examined the route and scooped up land near the line. The work was completed just prior to the January 1884 deadline.

In February 1886 the Jacksonville, Tampa & Key West Railway reached Sanford. Plant's South Florida Railroad also ran from Sanford east to Jacksonville. He was clearly ramping up preparations for his rail lines and steamships to provide through-traffic to Cuba, the Caribbean, and ports along the Atlantic.

Between 1890 and 1893 the People's Line of steamships added more ports of call for the Plant System, expanding a network between New England and the Maritimes of Canada, with stops in Boston, Halifax, Cape Breton, and Prince Edward Island.

PICO had tried to buy Franklin Brown's Florida Southern Railway, but was unable to close the deal. Plant's response was to buy some of the Southern's corporate bonds.

Plant had promised Brown he would not build the Savannah, Florida & Western south of either Gainesville or Palatka, as they were the northern boundary for the Florida Southern. However, the South Florida Railroad was exempt from that understanding. Plant then made agreements with every company building a route to Tampa, with one exception—Sir Edward Reed's Florida Transit Railroad (successor to Yulee's company).

As stated in Plant's agreement with Brown, the Florida Southern would not build a line south of Pemberton Ferry and Brooksville or north of Bartow. The South Florida Railroad would build a branch between Pemberton Ferry and Bartow, and give Florida Southern permission to use the tracks.

The deal with the Jacksonville, Tampa & Key West Railway spelled out its agreement to not build south of Sanford, and the South Florida Railroad would abdicate its rights to routes given to other companies. In addition, the J, T & KW sold some already-completed grading work at Tampa and Bartow to the Plant System's line.

A PORT IN PLAY

Two companies were now grinding their wheels to reach Tampa first, and the winner would not be the other guy.

The South Florida Railroad's tracks hit the mark, giving Plant dibs on the best sites. His terminal in Tampa opened on December 10, 1883. Within several weeks, the full route was open. (The arrival of the Plant System in Tampa broke up Cedar Key's grip on the Gulf shipping trade, something of a coup. Hard to believe now, but at the time, big-dog Cedar Key had a much larger population of 2,000. By comparison, about 700 souls inhabited tiny little Tampa.)

In 1893 the Savannah, Florida & Western Railway acquired the remaining two-fifths ownership interest in the South Florida Railroad. Afterward, Plant built the extension from Pemberton Ferry north to Inverness. From there his Silver Springs, Ocala & Gulf Railroad continued farther north. The network also had plenty of regional branches:

> The Sanford & Indian River Railroad ran from Sanford southeast to Oviedo and Lake Charm. In 1883 the South Florida leased its tracks.

> The St. Cloud & Sugar Belt Railway dated to 1888 and connected Kissimmee with St. Cloud via Narcoossee. The South Florida op-

erated it from the beginning, and it merged with the Plant System in 1893.

Bartow was guaranteed a station in the South Florida charter, and a branch was built from the main line at Lake Alfred to Bartow, opening in 1884.

Plant also kept his promise to Franklin Brown to extend the Florida Southern line to Charlotte Harbor on the Gulf coast. Tracks reached Trabue in 1886.

Punta Gorda, once a minor cattle port, is where the Peace River flows into Charlotte Harbor (also Ponce de Leon's port of call). In 1885 Isaac Trabue, a Kentucky lawyer who had supported the Union, intuited the economic importance of the coming Florida Southern Railway. Accordingly, he bought hundreds of waterfront acres in the area.

Author Gregg Turner reminds us that Trabue gave Plant some sizable tracts for his South Florida Railroad, and the rail company built a 4,200-foot dock into the harbor so his trains could meet steamboats. Thus, Bartow had a link to the harbor, and the town of Trabue was renamed Punta Gorda. Ever attentive to loose ends, Plant built the three-story Hotel Punta Gorda there.

The Plant System published a "Gate City" brochure which reflects the South Florida Railroad's notions about influencing social behavior on its various lines: "It is at this point the great transportation of the South, the Plant System, takes charge of the tourist and makes all his ways the ways of pleasantness and all his paths of peace . . . There is an intuitive lesson in good breeding in the elegantly furnished parlor cars . . . The coarsest nature is rebuked . . . To be rude, boisterous or vulgar, where the exquisite modeling and furniture are a constant lesson in harmony, is impossible."

Fully saturated in his own seductive hyperbole at this point, the breathless publicist pushed past the accoutrements—conveying "such a delicious sense of ease and luxury as to seem incompatible with travel"—so as to address his thrall with the iron steed: "The quiet ardor of the strong, complicated, yet almost noiseless machine, with an imperceptible, bird-like vibration of its muscular phalanges, is a flight beyond capricious imagination."

About 1893 the Plant System acquired the Orange Belt Railway and renamed it the Sanford & St. Petersburg Railway. It ran southwest for about 135 miles from Sanford to the Pinellas peninsula, at the western edge of Tampa Bay.

A stop on that line was the town of Juliette, a couple miles north of Dunnellon. But what about Romeo? *"Wherefore art thou?"* Romeo would be 2 miles north of Juliette—and both are now considered the next best thing to a ghost town.

Plant's Savannah, Florida & Western also opened a branch between Thomasville, Georgia, and Monticello, Florida.

Another acquisition related to a Northern investor with a yen for Florida, Robert Habersham Coleman. An industrialist from Lebanon County, Pennsylvania, he established the Cornwall-Lebanon Railroad in the 1880s as a passenger line for Mount Gretna, a summer colony he founded.

The wealthy descendant of a family whose investments helped grow the Cornwall Iron Furnace, Coleman bought land in Jacksonville and Mount Dora, Florida; purchased a railroad construction company; and controlled 50 miles of a line from Jacksonville to Palatka.

By 1889 he was worth about $30 million. Within two years, however, Coleman's fortune was all but erased after a winter freeze and another yellow fever scare—compounded by the capital markets quivering from low gold reserves. After losing two lawsuits, his railroad shuttled off to receivership. Henry Plant acquired the line and renamed it the Jacksonville & St. John's River Railroad.

MATCHLESS POSSIBILITIES

As mentioned in an earlier chapter, Vicente Ybor, a native of Spain, had relocated his cigar-making enterprise from Havana to Key West in the late 1860s. The potential for Tampa got Ybor's attention. He moved his cigar business there and built a "company town" for the families of his immigrant workers from Cuba and Spain. (Tampa later annexed the Ybor City neighborhood.)

Ybor's business partner was Cuban-born banker Eduardo Manrara, who established the Ybor City Land & Improvement Company.

According to the Gonzalez Habano Cigar Company in Tampa, which dates to 1918, Manrara was among those who lived during "the time of the titans . . . a period at the close of the century when business buccaneering spawned by the post–Civil War years was being replaced by the ascendance of responsible business leaders who believed that business and industry had larger purposes than accumulating wealth."

The seller of the tract that would become Ybor City was prominent landowner John T. Lesley. The real estate he discarded was "nothing but a series of alligator holes, a little high ground, and dense growth of pine, oak, palmetto and underbrush."

But not for long.

Working with Ybor and Manrara, Plant built a small rail line from the cigar factories in town to a point in Ybor City. By 1887 Tampa had its own US Customs House. After a yellow fever panic gripped Tampa that same year, Plant traveled from his home in New York City to support city leaders and allay their fears about the economy.

Asked later in life why Tampa was the hook for his big gamble, Plant referred to his first journey across the state from Sanford: "I found Tampa slumbering as it had been for years . . . It seemed to me that all South Florida needed for a successful future was a little spirit and energy, which could be fostered by transportation facilities . . . I made a careful survey of the situation, calculated upon its prospects and concluded to take advantage of the opportunity."

Lucy D. Jones, a scholar at the University of South Florida, has written extensively about Tampa. In one essay, she quoted a visitor's reaction in 1879: "This place looks discouraged from sheer weariness in trying to be a town."

Jones noted that three years later, a visiting journalist called Tampa "a sleepy, shabby Southern town," but one redeemed by an "implicit confidence in its own prosperous future."

Henry Plant's devotion to his vision changed Tampa overnight. Once his railroad reached the city, the stage was set for new businesses to start up and others to thrive.

Atlantic Casts a Long Shadow

As noted earlier, this era was mad about "Henry" as a given name, and a few of those Henrys were fond of each other. In addition to Plant's relationship with PICO members Henry Sanford and Henry Flagler, he collaborated with Henry Walters, who became chairman of the Atlantic Coast Line Railroad in 1884.

Walters's father, William Thompson Walters, a Baltimore produce and grain merchant, had been an original member of PICO. William appreciated the commercial advantages inherent in a network of railroads to carry farm products and passengers north and south. He and some associates collected such lines—anticipating that their system could kick-start the South's postwar economy. From these origins emerged dozens of pretzel-shaped regional lines and spurs south of Richmond, Virginia.

One of Henry Walters's contributions to the Atlantic Coast Line was to nudge George Pullman into thinking it was his idea to produce two sets of superb express trains to link Florida with the Northeast. In short order, the Pullman Palace Car Company began to produce tricked-out passenger cars for the New York and Florida Special—with electric lights in the drawing room, stateroom-style sleeping cars, a dining car, steam heat and hot water for a bath, refined interiors of mahogany and bird's-eye maple, and air-lock vestibules to shield passengers from flying cinders and engine sparks. The Florida Special was touted in advertisements as "the Aristocrat of Winter Trains."

During the 1880s and 1890s, the slogan "vestibuled train" was gold to be mined by railroad publicity staffs. One out-of-state carrier even called one of its trains The Vestibule. "More importantly, this development brought into existence the 'train' in the sense we know it today . . . a continuous unit for human uses . . . You could eat and sleep on trains and [arrive] in a fraction of the previous time," wrote railroad historian George H. Douglas in 1992.

A booklet printed by the South Florida Railroad described the Pullman experience: "Soft cushioned divans receive his body; a delicate luncheon is served at any hour; an airy 'smoker' invites him to gossip with his fellow guests—they cannot be travelers. No, he is the guest of a hotel on wings."

The first through-train known as the Florida Special left New Jersey on January 9, 1888, and made the 1,075-mile trip to Jacksonville in twenty-nine hours and fifty minutes. From there, Tampa must have seemed to be right around the corner.

BRIDGING THE DIVIDE

Plant's mainline Savannah Florida & Western Railway built its depot in downtown Tampa, at the mouth of the Hillsborough River, and initially there were no plans to extend it farther west. The city's existing port on Hillsborough Bay was too shallow to be commercially viable, so Plant discounted the idea of incurring the extra expense of a railroad bridge.

However, there was talk around town that the Army Corps of Engineers wanted to dredge a 27-foot ship channel in Old Tampa Bay, on the west side of what is now the Interbay Peninsula. Plant could see that the existing port was inadequate. A larger, deeper-water port and proximity to the Gulf could enable a world-class shipping facility.

At what would become the new deepwater Port Tampa, Plant built a depot, rail yards, an engine repair shop, and a power plant. He built a 9-mile spur from his terminal to Black Point, a site closer to the Gulf of Mexico. With support from Ybor and other city leaders, Port Tampa opened in 1888 with a mile-long wharf into Tampa Bay to accommodate slips for twenty-six ships, railroad cars, and warehouses.

As mentioned in an earlier chapter, Captain James McKay Sr. had helped rancher Jake Summerlin smuggle Florida cattle to Cuba during the Civil War. McKay had leased a Morgan Line vessel, the USS *Magnolia*, to make bimonthly voyages to Havana, selling cattle for Spanish gold. Before the war McKay, a native of Scotland, was mayor of Tampa. (One of his sons, James McKay Jr., and a grandson, Donald Brenhan McKay, also became mayors of Tampa.)

Two of James McKay's sons followed in the family shipping business. One of them, Captain John McKay, worked for the Plant System. He built a swing-style drawbridge over the Hillsborough River at Cass Street for Plant's railroad.

Plant's new spur opened on February 5, 1888; within four months, passengers on Plant's railroad were boarding a Plant steamer docked at the wharf. Cargo transferred from boxcars to the vessel's hold was making its way toward payday. Two new Plant System vessels, the *Mascotte* and the *Olivette*, traveled from Port Tampa to Mobile, New Orleans, Key West, Havana, Jamaica, Nassau, and Bermuda. Later routes took them to the Maritimes in Canada.

Plant believed the site called for a destination hotel, so he built The Inn at Port Tampa on the wharf, over water. With eighty-five rooms, it drew passengers cruising to the Caribbean or taking a train into Tampa and points east. A smaller lodging, the St. Elmo Hotel, had room for fourteen guests. Having extended the railroad to connect with his steamers, "hotels were a logical extension," according to scholar Lucy Jones.

The arrival of the railroad also generated interest in a bridge over the river. James Ingraham suggested the South Florida Railroad be the city's partner. So the city issued municipal bonds for part of the cost to build a bridge over the river at Lafayette Street, and Plant's railroad ponied up the rest. The modern iron-truss swing bridge opened in spring 1889.

By 1886 Plant's reach in central and southwest Florida amounted to a monopoly on the freight and passenger business. Tampa's economy revolved around Plant's railroad. As author Gregg Turner notes, the Savannah, Florida & Western bought Winston Lumber Company's rail line. Plant's aim was to extend the line to Bone Valley, with mines at Pebbledale, Phosphoria, and Tiger Bay.

Undeniably, rail service to move the abundant phosphate was a key reason Tampa became an important port and seat of industry (today Port Tampa remains the world's largest phosphate-shipping terminal).

While arriving second in line, the Florida Central & Peninsular Railway completed its route from Plant City to Tampa in 1890. The company built a depot near the Hillsborough River and extended its rails along the wharves.

PALACE IN THE WILDERNESS
PICO members usually deferred to Plant's ideas, with the exception of his dream for a magnificent resort hotel in Tampa to rival European palaces. In 1887, when skeptical investors vetoed the scope of the project he described, Plant was unfazed: "Very well, gentlemen, if you do not agree

with me that the hotel will benefit the railroad and the community, I will build it as a personal investment."

And build it he did. Opening in 1891, the five-story Tampa Bay Hotel was a $3 million *Arabian Nights* fantasy. Designed in a fanciful interpretation of the Moorish style trend, its silver minarets pierced the sky. Plant's "palace in the wilderness" had 511 rooms, many of them suites with five or more rooms. He and his wife selected the furnishings, which came to $500,000 of the total cost.

Located on the west side of the Hillsborough River, the "palace" needed a railroad bridge and got one. A rail spur brought a train up to the hotel's front entrance, where passengers could disembark and walk into the lobby.

Plant extended his rail line north to Clearwater, where he built the Hotel Belleview. At the time, Cubans were rebelling against Spain, and cigar makers in Tampa were sympathetic. Spain set up an embargo on Cuban tobacco, but Plant sent the *Mascotte* and *Olivette* on a quiet mission to Cuba to load up the two ships with all the tobacco they could hold. Therefore, the embargo failed. (Chapter 10 will address Tampa's role in the Spanish-American War.)

Lucy Jones described the relationship between Tampa and Henry B. Plant: "This spark of optimism arose from the rumored arrival of a railroad. Northerners coming to Tampa to plant citrus groves brought small amounts of capital, and gradually increasing land values, but the light at the end of the tunnel was truly a train . . . When Plant asked for a bridge over the Hillsborough River, Tampa built it."

A WOMAN OF WILL, GRIT, AND "FIRE"

Had Henry Plant taken a shine to Miami the way he doted on Tampa, Florida railroad history might read quite differently. And at one time, he did aspire to extend his railroad system southeast to the settlement carrying the Seminole word for "sweet water."

Rewind to 1875, the first time Julia DeForest Sturtevant Tuttle visited what is now Miami Shores. Married to a Cleveland industrialist, she had brought her two children south to visit their grandfather, Ephraim T. Sturtevant (a few years earlier, he and his wife had relocated from Cleveland, along with William B. Brickell and his wife, Mary).

Mrs. Tuttle encountered little more than a jungle, an abandoned fort, and a river flowing into pristine Biscayne Bay. Most of the colony of about 500 settlers had been saddled with land they bought from Reconstruction-era speculators.

Julia's husband, Frederick Leonard Tuttle, owned an iron-ore foundry in Cleveland. Her father-in-law, Henry B. Tuttle, was a merchant who had given a rookie named John Davison Rockefeller a job as assistant bookkeeper in 1855. (She and Rockefeller had attended the same Baptist church on Euclid Avenue for years. Julia also was acquainted with Rockefeller's friend, business associate, and Cleveland neighbor, Henry M. Flagler.)

Chronically ill from tuberculosis for many years, Frederick Tuttle died in 1886, having already sold the foundry and leaving a paltry estate. To create a new livelihood, Julia turned their family home into a boardinghouse. According to author Les Standiford, Julia wrote to Rockefeller in 1888 about needing to grow her income and perhaps move to a warmer climate: "I think Florida will become my new headquarters."

Julia arrived in Miami by barge with her grown children, a housekeeper, goods needed to set up a household, and two cows. She converted the two-story officers' quarters at old Fort Dallas into her home, notes author E. Lynne Wright, and stashed the cows in the barracks.

Not at all nonplussed by her lonely perch in a mosquito-blanketed wilderness cut off from the rest of the state, Julia was captivated by its possibilities as a permanent and viable destination. Soon after moving to Biscayne Bay, she began to lobby Henry Plant, urging him to build a railroad from Tampa to Miami.

Plant directed James Ingraham to examine the turf involved. When he received a dismal report about what might be involved in building a route of 250 miles—partly through the Everglades—Plant declined. (The next chapter will address Julia Tuttle's response to Plant's refusal, and what it meant for Miami and points south.)

PLANTING SEEDS, LEGACY IN LIMBO

On October 28, 1895, the *Atlanta Constitution* devoted some lavender prose to the railroad magnate: "Mr. Plant is one of those remarkable men who master all conditions and create environment. He is a builder—a creator. A whole State blossoms at the touch of his magic wand."

In 1896 *Harper's Magazine* opined at length on Plant's rail empire, citing the Savannah, Florida & Western main line's reach of more than 800 miles of track "under the single masterly administration of Mr. Plant. The policy of the management has been comprehensive, far seeing and sagacious. [The Plant System] has made new connections, opened up new industries, tapped fresh regions of trade, and created remunerative businesses. Its iron tentacles have penetrated and gleaned the orange-laden realm of Florida." Two years later, *Success* magazine was ready to crown Plant "the King of Florida."

Henry Bradley Plant died on June 23, 1899, four months before his eightieth birthday, with a personal net worth of more than $17 million. Only his physician was in attendance, and Plant had the misfortune to expire in New York instead of Connecticut.

He had put a provision in his will to keep the Plant-scape the way he wanted it. To prevent the Plant System from breaking up his assets, he created a trust leaving the bulk of his estate to his four-year-old grandson, Henry Bradley Plant II, with an edict that the trust be in force until the heir's youngest child turned twenty-one. He put in place a generous annuity to ensure his wife could continue to enjoy her current lifestyle, with a similar award for his son Morton.

Alas, Plant's family lacked the integrity to respect his judgment about the future.

Certainly Morton was not his father's son when it came to business. He had been given a job at Southern Express Company as a youth and eventually received the title of chairman of the board. Moving up, on cue, he became vice president of Plant Investment Company in 1884. More interested in yachting and the social aspects of philanthropy, he was not especially effective at taking a stand to fight for his father's final wishes.

Henry Plant's widow and Morton's stepmother, the former Margaret Josephine Loughman, contested her husband's will, and the courts of New York sided with her. As a result, Henry B. Plant's well-assembled empire of railroads, steamships, land improvements, and hotels became a pawn. Holdings in timberlands, mining properties, budding towns, and abundant farms became fodder for the accountants.

According to an essay penned in 1925 by F. H. Glover, all of the above—plus port terminals and wharves—"passed into other hands, controlled by minds that were keener for the immediate dollar."

As Gregg Turner explains in one of his books, the Plant System's legal advisor, Robert Erwin, initiated negotiations for the rail properties with Henry Walters of the Atlantic Coast Line Railroad. Mrs. Plant accepted Walters's terms, but specified cash instead of corporate securities (perhaps Plant's long rapport with Walters would have softened that particular blow).

When the deal closed on July 1, 1902, the Atlantic Coast Line bought 2,235 miles of railway lines for $46.5 million. Apart from the Plant System debt, which the ACL assumed, Mrs. Plant received the proceeds in Atlantic Coast Line stock. In the time it takes to sneeze, she exchanged the stock for a check.

The *New York Times* spoke eloquently about the transportation titan in an obituary published the day after his death: "Politics and speculation alike were shunned by the great developer. Often he quoted, 'It is easier to promise than it is to perform,' and he was scrupulously careful of his promises, but once he had committed himself he was extremely exact in keeping his engagements."

In addition to his Florida glorifications, Plant was a director of the Northeastern Railroad and president of the Alabama Midland Railway, the Brunswick & Western Railroad, and the Charleston & Savannah Railway. At the time of his death, the majority of the Plant System's railway assets were in Florida. His Southern Express Company was renamed American Railway Express, then Railway Express Agency.

Plant also was president of the Tampa & Thonotosassa Railroad Company. And employees of the T & T, like any other line in the Plant System, knew full well to expect, on absolutely no prior notice, the arrival of "No. 100," Henry Plant's private railcar. He lived aboard "100" every bit as often as he stayed at home on Fifth Avenue in Manhattan or in any of his luxury hotels in Florida.

Yes, Plant loved to travel. He also knew the promising results when one drops into town unannounced, for a hands-on, walking-around peek at what one had built.

F. H. Glover's essay, "Henry B. Plant—Genius of the West Coast," looks at Plant's rail empire, from Palatka to Port Tampa, from Orlando to Fort Myers: "Of all those whose money and thought and labor have entered into the making of this section of Florida, none has done more than Plant the builder, Plant the dreamer, Plant the man who knew how to turn vision into abiding fact."

Across such a raw and emboldened landscape, HBP was a monogram writ large.

GAUGING THE FUTURE

A railroading trend in place elsewhere had made its way to Florida. It reflected the rationale of consistency, so that one train operator could run its rolling stock on another's tracks without having to reset its wheels and axles.

Before the 1880s most developers built tracks with either a narrow gauge (3 feet between rails) or a standard gauge (5 feet, 2 inches). A new national "standard" gauge was determined to be 4 feet, 8½ inches between rails, and it applied to all rail lines in the territory south of the Ohio River and east of the Mississippi River.

In addition to demi-tracks, narrow-gauge systems operated with smaller locomotives, coaches, roadbeds, and bridges. Initially developers assumed smaller to be cheaper, but concluded that was a fallacy because labor costs were the bugaboo.

The *Orlando Sentinel* described a journey on such a line as "cramped, hot, smoky and slow . . . The diminutive trains only moved at about 25 mph. In 1884 a trip from Orlando to Tampa [a mere 85 miles] by narrow-gauge took five hours."

The South Florida Railroad had been built as a narrow-gauge track. In the summer of 1884, Plant converted its tracks to standard-gauge. In due time he switched the tracks of all his railroads to the new standard-gauge. Henry Haines was instrumental in guiding that decision.

"Haines was never a fan of what he saw as the inferior narrow-gauge railroad. The less-durable trains were ill-suited for the sandy rail beds and high humidity of Florida . . . By 1892, Haines had converted everything under his control," Christopher Sherman wrote in the *Sentinel*.

As a result of Plant's expansions, and others, Florida was drawing more of the curious who could finally experience its interior. And after the Transcontinental Railroad joined the two coasts of America in 1869, those numbers mushroomed.

The coming of the next century put the 1890s into tilt mode, and the world was abuzz with all manner of newness at hand, on the horizon, heralding the Gilded Age. Blessed with a new treaty, the Panama Canal was coming, with or without the original dream team. Alexander Graham Bell had patented the first telephone, and Thomas Alva Edison had created the means of electric illumination. Frenchman Joseph Monier had invented reinforced concrete for constructing bridges and roofing beams. German-born civil engineer John Augustus Roebling had perfected the use of twisted-metal ropes in the design of suspension bridges.

"Just when the railroad was ready for America, America was ready for the railroad," so said Sandra Sammons, in *The Two Henrys: Henry Plant and Henry Flagler and Their Railroads*.

These watershed moments made America itchy, anticipating the possibilities. And that restlessness was right on time for Florida's next railroad baron, waiting in the wings.

CHAPTER 9

A Decisive Detour

St. Augustine Beguiles Henry M. Flagler

WHERE DOES DRIVE GET ITS GRIT, THEN A STEADY SUPPLY OF FRESH GRIT? And from whence the seeds of courage and unwavering determination?

A later reference will make the case that ancestry comes into play for all of the above. Thus, it seems prudent to make the acquaintance of a few forebears of Henry M. Flagler, a visionary industrialist enchanted with reinventing Florida.

In a certain epoch identified as "the age of Louis XIV," France got to tell much of Europe what to do. Other monarchs mimicked the Sun King, even competing with strategies that framed his legacy of great power over the Continent. Not everyone was cool with the drill, however, especially the brawling states of Germany—many of them juggling Protestant squabbles with the secular tedium of how things work.

The third Bourbon monarch may have been christened Louis Dieudonné ("gift from God") and he may have floated above the fray of those not remotely on board with an absolute monarchy, but a Germanic temperament isn't that well suited to being pushed around. That would include some farmers in Franconia in the Rhineland Palatinate, a "state" in southwest Germany (if one were to gaze at a tic-tac-toe box, the lower right square would be southeast in a diagonal line from Alsace-Lorraine).

Weary after the so-called alliance wars of Louis XIV, a group of Palatines fled to Britain. Zacharra Flegler went to Walworth, England,

Henry M. Flagler, founder of the Florida East Coast Railway, developer of fine hotels in many east coast cities, and the person credited with putting the east coast of Florida on the map. PHOTO FROM THE DONALD MABRY COLLECTION.

to work as a carpenter. In January 1710 he set out for America with a wife and three children. Zacharra's wife was among the casualties of the wretched six-month voyage.

The refugees settled on the Hudson River, with settlements called East Camp and West Camp. Zacharra remarried and moved to Dutchess County, New York. Widowed again, he remarried in May 1711. Zacharra had three sons, and the youngest, Zachariah, also would wed three times.

Solomon Flegler, Zachariah's eighth child, changed the family name to "Flagler."

Solomon and his wife, Esther Ostron, had eleven children. One son, Isaac Flagler, born in 1789, became a Presbyterian minister and married Jane B. Ward. He supplemented his income with farming. After his wife died, Isaac went to live in Milton and married Ruth Deyo Smith in 1824. They had a daughter, Ann Caroline, known as "Carrie."

After Ruth died, Isaac met the twice-widowed Elizabeth Caldwell Morrison Harkness, and they married in 1828. Her first husband was Hugh Morrison. The second was Dr. David Harkness of Bellevue, Ohio. (David's son by his first wife, Stephen Vanderburgh Harkness, would be material to later events in the family's life.)

When David Harkness died, his widow and their son, Daniel Harkness, went to live with relatives in Salem, New York. Elizabeth met Isaac Flagler, a pastor in Seneca County, and they married. Their son, Henry Morrison Flagler, was born on January 2, 1830. He was named Henry after one of Isaac's brothers, and Morrison after Elizabeth's first husband. His birthplace was in Hopewell, New York, near Canandaigua in the Finger Lakes (although Flagler himself later said his hometown was Hope).

In 1837 Isaac accepted a post near Toledo, Ohio. Despite an age difference of eight years, half-brothers Daniel Harkness and Henry Flagler were close. Daniel, age fifteen, left home to work for L.G. Harkness & Company in Republic, Ohio.

Within two years, it was time to move again. Isaac and Elizabeth, with Carrie and Henry, went to a community near Medina, New York. Daniel stayed in Ohio, and his letters magnified Henry's angst about being uprooted from his half-brother.

Henry got along well with his half-sister Carrie, and he had no conflict with his parents. But he was restless and neglected his studies as he chafed at what he might be missing in Ohio. He also resented the effects of poverty on his father, whose dedicated preaching and hopeful farming fell short of breaking even.

POVERTY'S "PINCH"

As author Sidney Walter Martin described the feeling in *Florida's Flagler,* "The pinch of poverty at home spurred him on in his determination." Determined to make money, Henry dropped out of school after eighth grade and got a job as a deckhand on a boat running out of Medina on the Erie Canal. (If the details sound familiar, consider the previous chapter's description of Henry Bradley Plant's decision to make his way in the world at a young age as a captain's boy on a steamboat line. Both Henrys left good, loving homes to find a productive outlet.)

Henry Flagler chafed at the job on the canal boat—it just was not his thing, as it didn't hold any promising clues about actually getting ahead. Ambitious to advance, he wanted to go to Ohio, and his mother was confident that Daniel would help Henry get settled.

On the day Henry said good-bye to Isaac, Elizabeth, and Carrie—and then walked 9 miles into Medina to begin life on his own—Martin suggests the portent of the moment: "Of all his qualities, ambition and energy were the most outstanding . . . His heart must certainly have pounded rapturously on that October day when he tramped onto a dirt road and into an adventurous future. Whether this day or the day 68 years later when he completed his life's greatest achievement gave the biggest thrill was never known."

The trip from Medina to Buffalo was 40 miles, and Henry scored a free ride by offering to help with freight. Arriving late at night, he unloaded the cargo and stayed put for two days. Then, it was a rocky boat ride on Lake Erie to Sandusky, Ohio, during which he picked at a stale lunch his mother had packed. Seasickness was in the cards, of course, and that meant another day or so in Sandusky. He then set off walking the 30 miles to Republic. When Henry arrived there in 1844, his entire fortune included a nickel, four pennies, and a French coin. It is said that he would hold onto that coin for the rest of his life (as a nod to the biblical character who had but one talent).

Daniel worked in a store owned by his uncle, Lamon G. Harkness (who, like his brother, David, was a physician). Daniel showed great aptitude for sales and gave young Henry a good foundation in commerce. Eager to do well, and hoping his attitude would impress the Harknesses, Henry worked six days a week. He earned $5 a month plus room and board, and despite his youth, he was focused on success. A 1906 article in the *New York Tribune* described Henry's comprehension of salesmanship, thrift, ingenuity, and good judgment.

He learned the merits of what is offered for sale (candles, calico, and coffee), especially the rationale for selling brandy from the same keg at different prices for different groups of customers. Per the *Tribune*, the English paid $4 a gallon, the Germans paid $1.50 a gallon, and Native Americans paid "whatever Henry could get." Even at age fifteen, he was never complacent or thoroughly contented: Henry "wanted to do things . . . so that he might be useful and take a part in the work of the world."

As Daniel moved up, he went to work for F. A. Chapman and L. G. Harkness in their general store in Bellevue. He became a partner and the company changed its name to Chapman and Harkness. This left the manager position in Republic vacant, which is how Henry got his first promotion.

BROKERING CORN, REAPING A FRIEND

By the time he was nineteen, Henry advanced again with a job in the main store in Bellevue. His salary was $400 a year. Within a year, he had saved enough money to become a partner. In addition to general merchandise, the company operated a wholesale grain business, and by then Henry was brokering corn to shipping agents in Cleveland. (One of them, John Davison Rockefeller, was several years younger. Their relationship would shape the second, more famous phase of Henry's career.)

A sideline of the Chapman and Harkness grain concern was distilling liquor. Although Henry and previous generations of Flaglers loathed "the demon drink," he made peace with its monetary properties.

In 1839 the Mad River & Lake Erie Railroad arrived in Republic and later Bellevue. In anticipation, Lamon Harkness and F. A. Chapman bought up land around Huron County and sold it at high prices (a practice Flagler would fume over much later in life while choosing the routes for his railroad).

In Bellevue, Henry courted Lamon's daughter, Mary Harkness, and the pair must have turned a few heads on carriage rides around town. Mary was a slender, elegant brunette with luminous dark eyes. Henry was tall, handsome, with the rouge of ardor coloring his cheeks and a tinge of dawn's violet in sea-blue eyes. The striking couple were wed on November 9, 1853. Their first child was a daughter, Jennie Louise. Their second daughter, Carrie, died at age three.

As it became clear the country was girding for war, Henry opposed slavery but thought there had to be alternatives to conflict. As author Les Standiford noted in *Last Train to Paradise,* Henry and others in his circle believed the Civil War was "a distant and wasteful distraction." It also posed opportunities to make money, which intrigued Henry, who by now was getting restless. The grain and liquor trade had become too predictable. Henry needed a bigger challenge than running a business, and what better stimulus than starting something new?

In 1862, with money he had saved, Henry and his brother-in-law, Barney York, formed a salt-producing company in the mines of Saginaw, Michigan. Salt was in huge demand during the Civil War, and they prospered. Afterward, however, commodity prices went south. The Flagler and York Salt Company was bankrupt by 1866, and Flagler was $50,000 in debt (this was his only misstep in business, but it was a bitter pill).

Being penniless was like an angry stinging rash for Henry, and the lesson drilled home how much he hated failure and indebtedness. Mary's family helped Henry stabilize his finances, and the family returned to the Harkness enterprises. This time, they landed in Cleveland, where Flagler got another job in the grain business, with Maurice B. Clark, who was British. (Clark and John D. Rockefeller had been partners since the 1850s.)

Flagler and Rockefeller resumed their association. They were neighbors on Euclid Avenue, and often exchanged ideas while walking to work. Soon they were speaking less about ho-hum grain and more about a new endeavor.

WELL, WELL—TIME FOR REFINEMENT

Rockefeller and Clark were getting ready to invest in a fledgling but exciting industry, the petroleum business. Edwin Drake's successful oil drilling in western Pennsylvania was hogging headlines, and Cleveland had access via Lake Erie as well as a railroad connecting the city to the oil regions. A chemist, Samuel Andrews, also British, persuaded Clark and Rockefeller to join him in taking over a refinery.

While Rockefeller's forte was management and efficiency, Andrews was the science guy; while John scribbled in his sacred ledgers, Samuel tinkered with the ratio of costly sulfuric acid necessary to distill kerosene. In this new business giddy over the uses for raw petroleum, their refinery was soon producing more than 500 barrels a day. (Hard to comprehend today, but the world's known oil supply in the 1860s, and for the following few decades, was limited to America.)

Wanting to expand, Rockefeller invited Flagler to join the team. When Henry talked it over with his wife, Mary suggested that her cousin, Stephen Harkness, one of the wealthiest men in Ohio, might be interested in the enterprise. Harkness kicked in an initial $100,000—and more on other occasions—stipulating he was happy to be a silent partner and banker as long as Flagler spoke for his interests.

By 1867 Flagler was on board, forming the Rockefeller, Andrews and Flagler Oil Refinery. Soon they had a second refinery, headed by

William A. Rockefeller, John's younger brother. John D. Rockefeller had been shrewd from the beginning, buying land for the refinery with access to shipping by rail and water. This meant he could pit shippers against each other as they bargained for his business. According to business scholar Alex Epstein, less farsighted competitors chose sites near the Cleveland rail line "and took for granted that it would be their means of transportation."

Barrels were a basic cost for the refinery, whether one bought them or bought the staves to build them in-house. In another bit of foresight, Rockefeller decided to buy a relatively new invention, the tank car. Within a few years, the refinery owned more than seventy-five tank cars (railroad cars with holding tanks). The business was becoming far more efficient than the competition, producing more than 1,500 barrels a day.

The team welcomed Henry Flagler's abilities in sales, marketing, and negotiating. Rockefeller, in fact, credited Flagler with realizing they stood to gain from getting a lower freight rate on oil coming to their refinery. He did this by negotiating rebates and by guaranteeing daily shipments to the railroads.

Flagler also persuaded a skeptical Rockefeller that the company should incorporate to raise capital it needed to expand. Initially it wasn't an easy sell. Rockefeller discounted the idea, predicting it wouldn't work. Flagler pointed out certain advantages, such as being able to buy out less-productive competitors. They could offer these outfits a choice: go on as you are and keep losing money, sell to us for cash, or sell to us in exchange for stock in our corporation. Rockefeller acquiesced on taking the company public in 1870. (The same year, the Flaglers had a son and named him Harry Harkness Flagler.)

The new firm became the Standard Oil Company of Ohio, a joint-stock company capitalized at $1 million, divided into 10,000 shares at a par value of $100 each. Rockefeller held 2,667 shares; Flagler and Andrews held 1,333 shares each; the former partnership of Rockefeller, Andrews and Flagler held 1,000 shares. Stephen Harkness, William Rockefeller, and a new investor, Oliver B. Jennings, held most of the rest. Intent from the outset that stockholder interests were a priority, none of the shareholders in management drew a salary. They received only dividends, which was "not much of a sacrifice," wrote John Steele Gordon, as Standard Oil paid $105 per share in dividends the first year.

By now, Rockefeller said Flagler was his most trusted associate in business: "For years, this early partner and I worked shoulder to shoulder. Our desks were in the same room. We walked to the office together, walked home to luncheon, and home again at night. On these walks . . . we did our thinking, talking and planning together."

And plan they did. Gordon said they were so close, "they functioned virtually as a single entity as they designed and executed the strategy that allowed Standard Oil to dominate the oil industry." Calling attention to a future phase in his brilliant career, Gordon said: "Few entrepreneurs in the history of capitalism accomplished as much as Henry Flagler."

Reflecting the status quo that grew from the combined zeal of Rockefeller and Flagler, the company would soon declare assets of two refineries, 60 acres of Cleveland real estate, a barrel-making plant, shipping facilities on Lake Erie, dozens of tank cars, sidings and warehouses in the oil fields, timberlands to harvest the lumber for staves, warehouses in the New York area, and vessels in its harbor.

As put forth in a 2010 article, "John D. Rockefeller" on History.com, Standard Oil of Ohio achieved its lofty perch of controlling 90 percent of the country's refining capacity through secret alliances with railroads, accumulating segments of the supply chain to achieve economies of scale, buying out and intimidating rivals, and serving the growing demand for quality kerosene. Flagler easily persuaded Rockefeller that the company should be aggressive in buying up smaller competitors, or those with weaker operations. The logic was, Standard Oil would gain market share and have a louder voice. Flagler created an industry-specific formula for evaluating a fair price for other refineries.

Les Standiford describes Standard Oil's epic rise in light of Flagler's "remorseless goal" of controlling the oil refining business in Cleveland— by persuading oil-region producers to limit production and rein in price fluctuations. Flagler was criticized as "high-handed," using tactics to squeeze competitors. (If he did, in fact, force rate concessions from rail carriers, it likely pinched him a little later on, when he was the owner of a railroad empire in Florida.)

Historians and business scholars point to railroad rebates as the most controversial form of cost savings. They usually lay that in Rockefeller's lap, but if there is blame to go around, it should not be overlooked that he often cited Flagler's acumen on that score.

JOHN AND HENRY: BOOKENDS IN BUSINESS

It would be tough to place a sensible bet on which of these capitalists was more ambitious, but they exercised the energy in ways that complemented each other. It is likely that the younger man (Rockefeller) trusted his sharp sense of focus on details, while the other (Flagler) flew higher to take in the evolving picture. That they spoke with each other all day certainly reinforced the synergy between the two. Besides business, the two were close friends, as Rockefeller would describe it: "It was a friendship founded on business . . . which Mr. Flagler used to say was a good deal better than a business founded on friendship."

In an interview with Rockefeller some decades later, writer William O. Inglis quoted the most famous face of Standard Oil: "We had vision. We saw the vast possibilities of the oil industry, stood at the center of it, and brought our knowledge and imagination and business experience to bear in . . . thirty directions."

Despite his lack of formal education, and certainly well shy of a law degree, Flagler was the one who created most of Standard Oil's contracts (including the act of incorporation). The reason, Rockefeller would point out, was the kind of know-how that could benefit some lawyers: "Mr. Flagler drew practically all [of them]. He always had the faculty of being able to clearly express the intent and purpose of a contract so well and accurately that there could be no misunderstanding. I can remember his saying often . . . you must measure the rights and properties of both sides with the same yardstick."

Often noted is that Flagler, unlike Standard Oil's competitors, insisted on building only state-of-the-art refineries. As Gordon noted, "This was a brave financial decision but it made them the low-cost producers with all the advantages of that position." The trend was to put up cheap facilities, based on the reasoning that oil was a volatile business, so who needed a high-end refinery?

Rockefeller credited his colleague's commitment to quality with much of their success. He said Flagler believed that being in the business itself dictated a resolve to build solid and substantial facilities, and the promise to not overlook any aspect of producing superior results. (This personal mandate would show up in Flagler's railroad building, hotel building, and related projects in Florida.)

After all his experience in unrelated businesses, Flagler could readily appreciate that crude oil has its own antenna for price—with a little help from manipulation. Then and now, the price of oil can be roiled. Demand pushes one button, while supply grips a fickle fistful.

As Gordon explains the reasons, drilling and exploring (drill-ex) are highly expensive gambles, with as many dry holes as there are coquinas burrowing into the receding tide. Therefore, the only time drill-ex ramps up is when oil prices are high. New fields or offshore wells can blow in a hurry, with new sources of supply knocking the wind out of prices. That occurred in 1870, the year Standard Oil incorporated (when annual oil production was not even five million barrels).

But where might transportation come into play? Aside from the cost of crude oil itself, the profit margin on a barrel of refined oil depended most of all on the cost of transporting the commodity. Flagler knew the company could influence, if not control, that cost. That was largely because Standard Oil was based in Cleveland—which had competing carriers— whereas Pittsburgh, another major hub, had to accept the terms of the Pennsylvania Railroad. With its monopoly, Penn R could play highway robbery with Pittsburgh refineries.

The Pennsylvania Railroad had a line into Cleveland, too. But so did the Erie Railroad and the Lake Shore & Michigan Railroad (which answered, after 1869, to Cornelius Vanderbilt's New York Central Rail-road). Cleveland refineries also shipped goods by boat through the Erie Canal to New York.

"Flagler and Rockefeller would play the railroads like a fiddle," says Gordon. "They not only negotiated secret rebates for their own ship-ments, but also were able to extract a rebate on the shipments of other refiners . . . Their competitors, unknowingly, were paying a tax to Standard Oil." As cutthroat as it sounds, it was not illegal for the time. "Indeed, it can be argued that the capitalists of that era helped mightily to show what rules were needed."

While making up the rules, bending them, and/or otherwise causing a stir, Standard Oil had the upper hand. Flagler's blueprint for handling rivals became the stuff of legend. Of course, the company always paid a price that it considered fair, even if the seller did not concur. As historian Allan Nevins has noted, Standard Oil at the time often paid prices more generous than those involved in the Roosevelt administration's "monopoly" known as the Tennessee Valley Authority in the 1930s.

Writing about the Standard Oil Company in 1903, activist Ida M. Tarbell targeted Rockefeller with articles deemed "muckraking" at the time. Perhaps they were merely a tendentious attempt to open the public's eyes to a need for reform. Tarbell wrote for magazines such as *Collier's* and *McClure's*, which carried installments of her chronological indictment, "The History of the Standard Oil Company."

Tarbell claimed that Standard Oil was able to set the price of crude oil and refined oil by dictating output and by directing the way the commodities were distributed. Had her pen been a sword, Rockefeller would have been hoisted on his own petard. Tarbell believed Standard Oil's goal was to ruin its competitors and gain a monopoly. It would seem her muse might have been William of Ockham: "Where was [Rockefeller's] advantage? There was but one place where it could be, and that was in transportation. He must be getting better rates from the railroads than they were."

Begging your pardon, Miss Tarbell, but at least one economic historian of the current era does not agree. In *Vindicating Capitalism: The Real History of the Standard Oil Company,* Alex Epstein brands the success-by-rebates story "absurd . . . that railroads arbitrarily gifted Rockefeller with rebates so enormous he was able to bankrupt the competition . . . [He] did not achieve his success through the destructive, 'anticompetitive' tactics attributed to him . . . [He] had no coercive power to banish competition or to dictate consumer prices. His sole power was his earned *economic* power—which was no more and no less than his ability to refine crude oil to produce kerosene and other products better, cheaper, and in greater quantity than anyone thought possible."

Epstein cites Flagler's role in negotiating shipping agreements in 1867, when the Lake Shore & Michigan Railroad had extended its line into Cleveland. The open shipping rate of the day was 40 cents a barrel of crude from Pennsylvania and $2 a barrel of refined oil from Cleveland to New York. Flagler approached the line's vice president, General James H. Devereux, and proposed a special rate of 35 cents a barrel of crude oil and $1.30 a barrel of kerosene. In exchange, Flagler guaranteed the railroad sixty carloads a day—which today would be called a "quantity discount." The refinery also would pay to load and unload its freight, and pay for its own fire insurance.

The incentive worked, and Devereux took the deal. As he would later testify, the railroad offered the competing refineries the same special rates, if they could guarantee large, regular shipments. But Flagler's company was the only one that could make good on that promise. "Mr. Flagler's proposition offered to the railroad company a larger measure of profit than would or could ensue from any business to be carried under the old arrangements," Devereux said.

Indeed, Epstein said, a guarantee of regular sizable shipments was "a landmark, cost-cutting innovation in oil transportation," and the rebates given the refinery stemmed from its obsessive culture of efficiency.

In short, Flagler's dealings with the railroads produced "earned" cost savings: "To say that Rockefeller—by cutting his costs, thus enabling himself to sell profitably for lower prices and win over more customers—was rendering competitors 'unfree' is like saying that Google is rendering its competitors unfree by building the most appealing search engine."

Within time, the incorporation laws in Ohio created a new headache for Standard Oil of Ohio, which had established subsidiaries nationwide. The law was simple: A corporation could not own stock in another company, and it could not own property in another state. Before railroads and telegraph communications created a coast-to-coast common market, such rules had not intruded on commerce. Now, the law was out of touch.

Initially Flagler had named himself trustee to hold the stock of the subsidiaries for the benefit of the stockholders of Standard Oil. By 1879, however, the table was getting crowded with trustees. To comply with Ohio's unwieldy edict, Flagler crafted a structure whereby three people were named trustees for all the subsidiaries. On paper, these forerunners of the "middle manager" position controlled all of Standard Oil's property outside of Ohio. In fact, says Gordon, they did exactly as they were told: "This was the beginning of the trust form of organization, a term that has echoed down American economic history ever since."

By 1878 the scope of current and potential business prompted Standard Oil of Ohio to plan a move of headquarters to New York City. Flagler and Rockefeller bought homes in New York as well. In 1882 Standard Oil was worth $82 million (within six years, that figure would be almost double).

Also that year, Flagler collaborated with Samuel C. T. Dodd, a lawyer, to tweak the arrangement. They wrote a new document defining the Standard Oil Trust, setting up separate corporations in each state where Standard Oil owned major properties. Each corporation had a board of directors, but their stock was in the hands of trustees. The trustees issued "certificates of interest" to the stockholders of Standard Oil of Ohio, protecting the dividends.

In 1889 the state of New Jersey passed a progressive law, one that allowed corporations to own property out of state and to hold stock in other corporations. In 1892 a court ruling in Ohio deemed the Standard Oil Trust at odds with state law and said it had to be dissolved. When asked about the Ohio Supreme Court's ruling, Dodd shrugged off the event as if raindrops had temporarily spotted his shoes: "The only effect will be to inconvenience us a little." In fact, Standard Oil of New Jersey began to function as a holding company.

FLAGLER REDISCOVERS FLORIDA

"Railroads did exist in Florida prior to Flagler's arrival, yet they were small, unreliable, and often operated on different gauges, making for a disjointed trip," said Ben Dibiase, archivist of the Florida Historical Society.

Throughout their marriage, Mary Harkness Flagler had been ill. Her condition held all of Henry's attention outside of business and Standard Oil's legal drama playing out in public. Diagnosed with tuberculosis and in declining health, she was advised to avoid the brutal winters in New

York. Her husband decided to take her to Florida for the winter of 1878, and they set out for Jacksonville.

The couple arrived in something of a backwater burg and found little to tempt a visitor except for the climate. Henry was bored with the languid pace, and frustrated at the news from home about investigations and lawsuits. The Flaglers returned to New York after several weeks, because Mary refused to stay alone in Jacksonville. Another time, they visited St. Augustine, but pressing business called them back to New York.

Mary's condition declined further over the next few years, and she died in New York on May 18, 1881. Their daughter, Jennie Louise, was married and living out of state, so Henry asked his half-sister, Carrie, to move in to help with his son, Harry, who was eleven.

It was during this time that Flagler became president of Standard Oil Company of New Jersey. Even so, he began to spend less time at the office in New York. He had bought a large estate on 33 acres at Mamaroneck on Long Island Sound (known as Satan's Toe), and the quietude of the countryside seemed to energize him after the numbing loss of Mary. Henry decided that restoring the forty-two-room manor home would be a fresh challenge—one that would reward him for creating something versus accumulating wealth. He handpicked the materials and fixtures, put in a lengthy breakwater, and built a beach.

Widowed at fifty-one, wildly wealthy, and still the picture of health himself, Henry found himself vulnerable to the attentions of Ida Alice Shourds, a thirty-five-year-old, fiery-tempered redhead who had been one of Mary's caregivers. Uneducated, unrefined, irrational, reckless with money, and the life of any party, she also was the daughter of an Episcopal priest.

Against the advice of friends and family, Henry married Ida Alice on June 5, 1883. Some historians suggest that the match angered thirteen-year-old Harry for a few reasons—he resented anyone assuming his mother's place; he found Henry's choice of a mate embarrassing; and he was a teenager with an involuntary crush on Ida. Regardless, the relationship between Harry and his father became strained and grew more so, to the point of total estrangement in later years.

Flagler was too engrossed in business to take a honeymoon at the time, so the couple waited until December. Riding the train to Jacksonville, they stayed a few days, then traveled by boat down the St. Johns River. Landing at Tocoi, they rode the last several miles on the St. Johns Railway (a horse-drawn line discussed in earlier chapters).

St. Augustine captivated Flagler, and he began to notice the ancient city in ways that hadn't fully registered on his first visit—perhaps because he had then been focused on attending to his chronically ill wife. This time, Flagler became totally smitten with St. Augustine and began making plans to rescue the object of his affections from such ignoble obscurity. He would dress St. Augustine to the nines, reinventing her as no one had.

Author Edwin Lefèvre wrote about Flagler's passion for the city in "Flagler and Florida," a 1910 article for *Everybody's Magazine:* "He saw what you and I saw when we went to Pompeii or first gazed on the Pyramids. He saw palms—palms!—this man who had grown up in Ohio amid the wheat." An enthralled Flagler saw St. Augustine "as a magic pool; he steeped his soul in the glamour and romance of antiquity."

With his creative impulse fully engaged, Flagler went back to New York, abdicated his role at Standard Oil, and put his brains and wherewithal toward this fascinating challenge. Step 1 would be building a luxury hotel and a winter home in St. Augustine. Step 2 would be overhauling a railroad to provide adequate transportation for visitors. This, of course, would be child's play for Flagler, the expert organizer who had handily toyed with railroad owners on behalf of Standard Oil for more than a dozen years.

Writing in 2010 in *The New York Social Diary,* historian Augustus Mayhew put his inimitable stamp on Flagler's second career: "As yesterday's tightfisted corporate villains transformed themselves into charitable philanthropists and reviled robber barons were newly-christened as revered patrons, Henry Flagler reinvented himself from one of the nation's oil slicks into Florida's patron saint. With no experience as a real estate developer but with a Ph.D. in creating oil and railroad monopolies, Flagler converted Florida's East Coast into a packaged resort network."

In 2007 author and journalist Michael Grunwald offered his own take on Flagler's motivation in one of his books: "He wanted to step outside of Rockefeller's shadow, and develop a wild territory that Spaniards, Frenchmen, and Englishmen had been unable to tame."

Rockefeller, meanwhile, was "appalled" at Flagler's "gauche new wife" and increasingly extravagant lifestyle. Flagler's former partner had a winter home in Ormond Beach, yet most sources say he never visited his longtime friend in Florida.

PLACE = PURPOSE

Looking over Henry Flagler's life up to this point, it is easy to see a pattern of endeavor, success, failure, increased endeavor, more success, riches unimaginable to someone of his background, and no end of good fortune in sight. What there never had been in his life was a place that grabbed him. Not Canandaigua or Republic or Bellevue or Cleveland—not even New York, which grabs everyone sooner or later. He had homes in all those places of varying degrees of comfort, even luxury, but "place" didn't call him until St. Augustine set her hook.

The reasons are open to discussion, but perhaps timing was everything. Elsewhere, for almost four decades, he'd been preoccupied with digging his way out of poverty, getting ahead, providing for a family, making his way in business, building an empire. All of a sudden, without the duress of a long-invalid, albeit beloved spouse—and with the infantile demands of a saucy new one—it was easier to open his eyes to "place" and how he could make it his own.

On their next trip in 1885, riding in a private railcar, Henry and Ida Alice arrived in Jacksonville and took a ferry to South Jacksonville. From there they boarded the 36-mile Jacksonville, St. Augustine & Halifax River Railroad. Later that year, Flagler joined the company's board of directors and bought a controlling interest in the short line. He promptly converted the tracks to standard gauge and replaced all the rolling stock—setting his own "standard" for this opening gambit in his transportation empire.

When granted a charter to build the Florida Coast & Gulf Railroad, he renamed the company the Jacksonville, St. Augustine & Indian River Railway in 1893. As Gregg Turner noted, Flagler raided the executive staff of friend Henry Plant, recruiting Joseph Parrott to oversee building a new railroad and James Ingraham for his land agent.

Flagler happened to meet Dr. Andrew Anderson, and bought several acres of land from him for his first big real estate venture in Florida. The

Portrait of Joseph R. Parrott, who spent many years on Henry Plant's executive staff. In the 1890s, Henry Flagler recruited Parrott to oversee the building of his Florida East Coast Railway—starting with the Jacksonville, St. Augustine & Indian River Railway. It was Parrott who assured Flagler that the Key West Extension was possible. When he told Flagler there was "no more dry land" in Key West to build a terminal, the Chief said "then make some." STATE ARCHIVES OF FLORIDA, FLORIDA MEMORY.

men became fast friends, with Anderson providing some highlights on local lore—inspiring a vision balanced on historic values.

Ingraham provided a glowing assessment of their friendship: "Perhaps no one possessed Mr. Flagler's entire confidence and esteem to a greater extent than Dr. Andrew Anderson. Mr. Flagler talked over with Dr. Anderson, perhaps more fully than anyone else, his vision for St. Augustine, beautified on lines that would not materially interfere with the ancient landmarks of the city, but would, as it were, combine the utmost degree of advanced ideas for the comfort and pleasure of the American people with that charm that the individuality of the old town possessed in itself."

In 1888 Flagler purchased the St. Johns Railway and the St. Augustine & Palatka Railway from fellow New Yorker William Astor and his son, Jack (the Astors had built the latter line from Tocoi Junction to East Palatka). Soon enough, Flagler acquired the St. Johns & Halifax Railroad, a 51-mile logging line from East Palatka to Daytona; a branch to Ormond Beach; and a petite 3-mile branch to San Mateo. He also bought and remodeled an inn and called it the Ormond Beach Hotel. Shortly, Flagler added a golf course to the amenities.

He also did away with that primitive ferry ride in Jacksonville by erecting a steel drawbridge over the St. Johns River. He gave orders for its construction after establishing the Jacksonville Bridge Company. Of course, his engineers said the St. Johns was too deep for piers, and, yes, 90 feet was a challenge. As Turner noted, the resulting bridge made railroad history.

The Jacksonville, St. Augustine & Indian River Railway became Flagler's holding company. The carrot, in this case, was the potentially lucrative freight business from a region brimming with citrus, pineapple, and lumber. The real boon was a state land grant of 8,000 acres per mile of laid track.

SAINTS AND SINNERS

By the time St. Augustine became their permanent winter home, Ida Alice was coasting toward a mental derailment. She had begun to exhibit mood swings and a shrewish temper. During her ascent—but lack of acceptance—in society, she spiraled downward into a degree of madness on full display. She heard from and replied to ghosts. Per the advice from her Ouija board, she carried on an imaginary affair with the czar of Russia and threatened to kill Henry over his adultery.

As Grunwald put it, the latter assumption was not a fitful figment: "While Ida Alice was delusional, she was right about her husband's cheating. Flagler gave one mistress $400,000 and a Manhattan town house . . . He also became depressed"—telling a friend he feared his friends would find that an "unmanly weakness."

Meanwhile, the real mistress of Flagler's heart, the city of St. Augustine, was abuzz with the construction progress of his first hotel, the Hotel Ponce de Leon. With 540 rooms, it was designed in the Spanish Renaissance genre with Revival vernacular by two New York architects who would become quite famous—John Carrère and Thomas Hastings. Their client let people do their jobs, as long as they did them to his precise specifications. Constructed of poured concrete and coquina-shell aggregate, the hotel had the added luxury of electric lighting—all the easier to appreciate the stained-glass work of fledgling artist Louis Comfort Tiffany.

"The Ponce" opened to great national fanfare, crowds of boldfaced names from all corners, and a salivating press corps. In time, notables such as Teddy Roosevelt and Mark Twain would sign their names in the hotel registry. When comments flowed about the expense of the project, Flagler intoned that the amount would not matter to him in a hundred years, but "the building will be better because of my extravagance."

Mayhew described the fishbowl scene on opening night in light of national events: "During the winter of 1888, as private Pullman cars pulled out of New York heading to St. Augustine for the opening of Henry Flagler's Hotel Ponce de Leon, Albany legislators and Washington congressional committees launched investigations into the Standard Oil Trust . . . Despite pesky subpoenas and warrants, annoying court and congressional hearings, the Standard Oil cartel's most prominent trustees escaped the glare from headlines and indictments within several socially-exclusive Gibraltars . . . Rather than being probed and questioned about the inner sanctum of the world's most powerful syndicate or denounced by muckrakers, Euclid Avenue and Fifth Avenue moguls engaged in quail hunts and golf games."

As *Harper's* was writing about "Our Own Riviera," Flagler was thinking beyond the class of guests at ease in such a Gilded Age palace and toward the market of tourists seeking a more affordable lodging. He next built the Alcazar, in the Moorish style, then bought and remodeled the Casa Monica hotel and renamed it the Cordova. He built a house for him and Ida Alice near the flagship hotel and named it Kirkside. Soon he was building some affordable houses for workers.

Flagler had known from the beginning that the success of his hotels would depend on efficient and comfortable passenger transportation. Same song, second verse from building that first refinery by greasing the wheels of the railroads.

Except that northeastern railroads weren't as primitive and disjointed as the ones he found in Florida. Besides the physical assaults on railroads during the Civil War, financial chaos, and litigation, the system Flagler found in Jacksonville and environs had been built with crazy-quilt tracks, stopgap equipment, and assorted gauges (as mentioned previously, a train of one gauge couldn't proceed on a nonconforming track without switching out the wheels). For passengers, it was a matter of stop, hurry up, and wait, then start again. For a man of Flagler's bent, crossed wires were an unacceptable concept.

Many biographers have delved into what made the railroad baron tick. Edwin Akin's assessment was that Flagler "was not so much a businessman as a visionary in businessman's clothing." Although he had never crossed the pond or ridden the Transcontinental Railroad to the Pacific, "he arrived in St. Augustine and was transformed."

Personal tragedy occurred again in March 1889. Henry was devastated when his daughter, Jennie Louise Benedict, died after complications from childbirth. As a memorial, her father built the First Presbyterian Church of St. Augustine (Memorial Presbyterian Church), with a mausoleum for the remains of Jennie, baby Margery, and his first wife, Mary. Flagler also put up money for two other Protestant churches and restored the city's Catholic cathedral, which had been destroyed in a fire.

East Coast Railway Station, New Smyrna, Florida, c1904. LIBRARY OF CONGRESS

A Florida statute had decreed segregated education, so Flagler built a school for black children, in addition to a hospital, a jail, and a new city hall. He also financed paved roads, streetlights, public waterworks, and a sewer system. Called out again for what seemed a self-aggrandizing level of investment, Flagler was bemused—noting that he could make more money in New York in a month than he could in St. Augustine in a lifetime. However, the improvements he created would continue to be to him, "a source of great satisfaction."

Still working on the strained relationship with his son, Harry, Flagler put him in charge of hotel operations. Harry kept the position about a year, then returned to New York and his cultural interests. When Harry married socialite Anne Louise "Annie" Lamont, his father did not attend.

On the railroad front, Flagler's holding company extended lines from Daytona southward to New Smyrna, Titusville, and Rockledge—on the west side of the Indian River—by 1893. Next stop, Fort Pierce, which was an Atlantic port and fishing village about 240 miles south of Jacksonville. (State records indicate that between 1888 and 1910, Flagler received more than 2 million acres of land from the state for promoting railroad development.)

In addition to railroads and hotels up and down the state's east coast, Flagler bought some newspapers: the *Florida Times-Union* in Jacksonville and the *St. Augustine Daily Herald*, which he merged with the *St. Augustine Record* in 1899.

PALM BEACH POSSIBILITIES

As Les Standiford noted, Flagler often scouted for good sites to buy and develop, riding his train "incognito" to keep property owners from denting his wallet more than necessary. Such was the case in 1892, when he first laid eyes on the barrier island of Palm Beach, lying between the ocean and the Lake Worth Lagoon.

He noticed about a dozen houses with an "Old Florida" aesthetic and a junglelike abundance of natural landscape. Perhaps he heard a siren lamenting the lack of a resort hotel to dress up the pristine nothingness. Or maybe he just liked the place and wanted a hotel that would suit his own expectations and those of his wealthy clientele.

Choosing to remake the island's "exotic settings into high-hat settings where wealth and extravagance became the standard," Flagler set about dolling up Palm Beach as the "Newport of the South." He established the Model Land Company, based in St. Augustine, to oversee his considerable real estate properties on the east coast. And he put Ingraham in charge of developing Palm Beach.

Construction began in spring 1893 on the Royal Poinciana Hotel, a six-story lodging facing westward across the lake, designed in the Georgian style. It opened the following February. Initially 500 rooms, then enlarged and expanded again, it became the world's largest hotel and the largest wooden structure ever erected. Dominating all rooflines on the island, the hotel sprawled along 1,800 feet of waterfront. Eventually there were 1,150 guest rooms and an atmosphere of "eternal spring."

The extension of Flagler's railroad to West Palm Beach was not without ecological headaches. As author Sandra Sammons noted, vines

Guests arriving at the Royal Poinciana Hotel in Palm Beach in 1896, after traveling on the Florida East Coast Railway: (from left) Col. Philip M. Lydig, Miss Helen Morton, Miss Gladys Vanderbilt, Miss Amy Townsend, Capt. A. T. Rose, Mrs. Cornelius Vanderbilt, Miss Edith Bishop, Miss Mabel Gerry, Thomas Cushing, Edward Livingston, Dudley Winthrop, Craig Wadsworth, Miss Gertrude Vanderbilt, Lispenard Stewart, Harry P. Whitney, Miss Sybil Sherman, Cornelius Vanderbilt. STATE ARCHIVES OF FLORIDA, FLORIDA MEMORY.

undisturbed for generations were impervious to a machete. Workers had to avoid highly poisonous manchineel trees and contend with blasting out ironwood trees too hard to chop.

The railroad reached West Palm Beach a month after the Royal Poinciana Hotel opened in Palm Beach. Flagler also built a spur across Lake Worth so that guests could ride in their private railroad cars right up to the hotel's entrance. The rich stayed in the hotel while their servants stayed in the railcar. (Flagler's personal ride was Car 91, built in 1886 and

Jupiter & Lake Worth R.R. (Jackson, William Henry, 1843–1942). LIBRARY OF CONGRESS

nicknamed "Rambler." Today it sits in its own grand salon on the grounds of the mansion he built in Palm Beach.)

When hotel guests wanted to go to the ocean or sightseeing around the island, they rode a wheeled-chair conveyance—Palm Beach's answer to the rickshaw—but instead of being pulled by a bar across the front, it was pushed by a uniformed attendant on a bicycle behind the patrons.

The Royal Poinciana Hotel became so popular with the in-crowd that Flagler built the Palm Beach Inn on the ocean in 1896. It was renamed the Breakers, as guests often asked for a room over by "the breakers." (It was twice destroyed by fire and rebuilt in the Italianate style, continuing a reputation as a top-tier resort famous the world over. While some things changed, hotel ownership did not. Today the Breakers remains in the fold of the Flagler System, along with the stars and diamonds awarded by the arbiters of luxury tourism.)

Flagler built a nine-hole golf course on the island—among the first in the state. Soon the island was a seasonal playground for links-lovers, tennis buffs, anglers, and boating fans. Deciding not to house his workers on the island, Flagler created a town for "have-nots" on the west side of the lake. There, he built his railroad depot.

Within a decade of his purchase of the Jacksonville, St. Augustine & Halifax River Railroad, Flagler renamed the growing system the Florida East Coast (FEC) Railway. The process of getting the hotels built had been a transportation headache, as construction materials were unloaded at his railroad terminal in Fort Pierce, then hauled by boat down the Indian River to Jupiter. There the cargo was loaded aboard the Jupiter & Lake Worth narrow-gauge railroad to Juno, then put aboard vessels bound for the Lake Worth Lagoon. (The "Celestial Railroad," as the Jupiter & Lake Worth short line was called, dated to 1889. Flagler tried to buy it, but was rebuffed. Later, the owners of the line were out of business.)

A cut to open the Lake Worth Lagoon to the Atlantic Ocean had been dug and moved several times during the 1880s (the Palm Beach Inlet currently lies between the north end of Palm Beach Island and Singer Island). Deciding to expand his transportation network, Flagler enlarged the inlet and began to develop a shipping port on the opposite shore; he also stretched a 1,000-foot pier into the ocean.

SCISSORS THE BREAKING POINT

By 1897 Ida Alice Flagler had pushed the envelope of wacky behavior, even attacking a physician with a pair of scissors. She spent time in a mental facility, then came home for spells of relative calm.

Her husband was said to be reluctant to have her committed, until his good friend, Dr. Andrew Anderson, persuaded him that it might be a matter of survival. Apparently, Ida Alice had made some serious threats against Henry, so could be free to run off with "the czar." Then again, perhaps Ida Alice simply railed against her husband's attentions to another woman—someone referred to in certain Palm Beach circles as "a family friend."

In any event, Flagler relied on Anderson to document a telling case for institutional care. Ida Alice was declared legally insane on March 23, 1897, at the age of fifty-one. She would remain in a private sanitarium in New York until her death at age eighty-two. Flagler provided for her care, with a $1 million or so stipend that he regularly increased. In the hands of accountants, the fund grew exponentially by the time she died. (An article in 2005 in the South Florida *Sun-Sentinel* referred to Ida Alice as "the castoff crazy woman," and said her husband's generous trust "kept her descendants in court for decades, squabbling over the remains.")

Despite his wife's condition, insanity was not grounds for divorce in either New York or Florida. A grateful Florida Legislature decided to change the law in August 1901, deeming incurable insanity as legal permission to end the union. (Flagler was the only one who claimed the right, and the state repealed the law in 1905.) Within a matter of weeks, Flagler married Mary Lily Kenan, whom he had met several years earlier. A native of North Carolina, she lived with her family in Kenansville.

Carrying the headline "Divorce From Insane Wife," a 1901 story in the *San Francisco Call* referred to a spate of curious comments coinciding with Flagler's third marriage: "About a week ago, [he] secured a divorce in Florida from his second wife, who had been an inmate of an insane asylum for several years . . . Edward C. Foote, the agent of an office building in New York City, recently sued Henry M. Flagler for $100,000 damages, alleging that by his attentions and liberal presents of money, Flagler has won the affections of Mrs. Foote."

Foote's lawsuit said the previously mentioned $400,000 gift was in the form of shares in Standard Oil, "and it was in consideration of this that she discarded Foote. It appears that Mrs. Foote was merely a footnote," although the lawsuit provided affidavits confirming Flagler had kept her in a comfortable lifestyle from December 1896 to June 1897.

One could speculate that he needed a mistress during those years because he had met Mary Lily in 1891 and was smitten. As her family trained a diligent eye on this older married man paying so much attention to their daughter, Henry was bewitched, betwixt, and between.

Disparate versions describe how they met. One account is that Mary Lily was a summer houseguest at Sherwood, the Newport home of

Pembroke Jones and his wife, and that railroad tycoon Henry Walters made the introductions. The year was 1891, when Henry was sixty-one and Mary Lily was twenty-three. She has been described variously as lovely with a mysterious smile, petite with an hourglass shape, possessing strong features and kind eyes, and "no Gilded-Age hottie."

Eleanor Wright Beane III, who grew up in Wilmington, North Carolina, wrote an anecdotal account of local lore on the third Mrs. Flagler: "The story I was brought up on was that Mary Lily Kenan was a spinster," someone whose family didn't see any promising prospects for their daughter's future, especially as they were the most prominent family around. "So, they took her to Palm Beach and Newport."

The article in the *San Francisco Call* stated that shortly after he completed a Caribbean cruise on a friend's yacht during the summer of 1891, Flagler "dispatched a train with one of his private cars" to North Carolina to bring Mary Lily and her friends to St. Augustine for a ball at the Hotel Ponce de Leon. "Rumors of their affair persisted for years in advance of their marriage."

Another story says Henry and Mary Lily met in St. Augustine, where she was visiting Flagler's niece. (Possibly ironic is that Ida Alice, who knew Flagler's niece, may have arranged the soiree.)

About ten days after his divorce was final, Henry and Mary Lily's wedding took place at Liberty Hall, the Kenan family's summer plantation in Kenansville (built in the late 1700s). As a wedding gift, Flagler is said to have bent his wallet a bit with trophy jewelry from Tiffany's: a 5-foot strand of pearls with a 15-carat diamond clasp. (In another example of shunning Flagler for his ostentatious behavior, his old friend, John D. Rockefeller, did not attend the ceremony.)

Mary Lily wanted them to live in a white marble palace, and they did. The fifty-five-room Beaux Arts mansion Whitehall stood on acreage facing the Palm Beach lakefront, just a short carriage ride from his hotels. Given Flagler's forte at expediting whatever he wanted, the contractor built the Carrère and Hastings design in only eighteen months. Yes, Mary had been aware of her husband's affairs before the marriage, yet her prized Whitehall was a splendid venue for entertaining (and today houses the Henry Morrison Flagler Museum).

Not to imply that Flagler had been too smitten with Mary Lily—or too confounded by Ida Alice's rants—to continue his domination of east Florida. He had learned from Ingraham that his longtime associate and friendly rival, Henry Plant, was planning to build a railroad from Tampa to Miami, vowing to one-up Flagler.

Meanwhile, Flagler had already studied whether to extend his railroad to Miami. It wasn't his priority then, given that area's small population of fewer than 300. There was no "Miami" to speak of—the only port developed on Biscayne Bay was called Lemon City. The area didn't even have a rough wagon road for postal service, receiving the mail only by boat until 1885. Then, the government decided to issue a contract providing for "beach walkers" to carry the mail from Jupiter to Miami.

These men rowed boats to the southern end of Lake Worth, then walked the beach to Delray and spent the night. They then walked the beach to Fort Lauderdale and rowed south on the New River to northern Dade County, walked again to Biscayne Bay, and rowed a boat to Miami. (This service operated from 1885 to 1892. Decades later, literature would give the job the name which today's tourists find familiar—"the Barefoot Mailman.")

A Woman and Her City

The 1880s and '90s were a male-dominated universe, especially in terms of industry and real estate. However, at least two women are responsible for putting Florida cities on the map—primarily by enticing railroad developers to make a commitment to extend their lines.

One of them, Julia DeForest Sturtevant Tuttle, is known as "the mother of Miami" (the previous chapter mentioned that she lobbied Henry Plant to extend his railroad from Tampa, and that he refused). According to Paul George, a history professor at Miami Dade College, Tuttle is the only woman who established a major American city: "She knew early on this place had potential . . . but that it was isolated. She convinced Flagler to [bring] his railroad to Miami."

Tuttle once wrote a friend that, strange as it might seem, "it is the dream of my life to see this wilderness turned into a prosperous country." Known previously as Fort Dallas, a relic of the Seminole Wars, Miami

Portrait of Julia DeForest Sturtevant Tuttle, a widow from Cleveland who made it her mission to transform Miami into a thriving city. Writing to a friend in the 1890s, Tuttle said "it is the dream of my life to see this wilderness turned into a prosperous country." She bought hundreds of acres on the Miami River and converted part of an abandoned fort into her household—adding a wharf, a windmill, a boathouse, and stables. She then persuaded Henry Flagler to extend his railroad to Miami. STATE ARCHIVES OF FLORIDA, FLORIDA MEMORY.

was a colony of a few hundred settlers and the Indians with whom they traded. Tuttle was an exception. She first came to Miami in 1875 to visit her homesteading father and his 40 acres of orange groves.

Author Lynne E. Wright said the Miami that Tuttle first saw had less going for it, transportation-wise, than the Wild West: "[She] rode several railroads, a riverboat, a cattle cart, a schooner and a barge to reach her father's property in what is now Miami Shores."

Widowed since 1886, Julia moved to Miami in 1891, a year after her father died. She sold his orange groves and bought 644 acres of land on the north side of the Miami River. Her friends must have wondered whether she acted out of vision or delusion, considering the hardscrabble conditions.

After converting part of the old fort into her household, she added a wharf, a windmill, a boathouse, and stables. As was the custom among her pioneering neighbors, she learned to trade with the Indians and be grateful for items salvaged from the occasional shipwreck.

Local lore recounts that one of Julia's first acquaintances in Miami was J. W. "Duke of Dade" Ewan, the postmaster and boat captain who showed her the terrain. Hailing from the Carolinas, Ewan is said to have been "smitten" with the forthright widow. (He wasn't the only one; Seminole Chief Matlo brought her gifts of venison and bear.)

A visitor wrote a first impression of the setting: "The scale of living was pretty low. People lived on potatoes and other easily grown vegetables, fish, birds, and once in awhile, someone would have venison . . . It was inordinately difficult to obtain groceries." Travel was arduous and often dangerous, "there being rivers with swift currents, wild animals, snakes and roaming beach tramps with criminal tendencies."

Julia Tuttle's father had been entranced by the aqua allure of Biscayne Bay. She may have been, too, but she saw well beyond the natural beauty and told a friend as much in 1896: "The time will come when the harbor and its approach will be dredged to a depth that will allow the deep sea-going vessels to anchor . . . The South American vessels will finally ply between their home ports and Miami, and Miami will become the great center in all the southland. This may seem far-fetched to you, but as surely as the sun rises and sets, all of this will come true."

Mrs. Tuttle was right.

Having been turned down by Henry Plant, Tuttle made overtures to Henry Flagler, hoping to persuade him to extend his railroad to Miami. The idea held no appeal until a brutal freeze in December 1894 and a frosty encore two months later. Farmers anywhere north of Jupiter lost their citrus groves and vegetable crops.

Mrs. Tuttle, who had met James Ingraham, contacted him and Joseph Parrott to let them know that Miami farmers had been spared. The dual assault of those freezes had left citrus and vegetables in her region untouched. As proof of "life," she sent along some orange blossoms and viable citrus.

In her previous talks with Plant, she'd said she would give half of her land for a town site to whoever built a rail line to Miami. After hearing of the freeze-reprieve, and reminded of Tuttle's offer of land, Flagler put some energy into the idea (also top of mind was the realization that he would qualify for a state land grant of 8,000 acres per mile of laid track).

Days later, Flagler rode the train to West Palm Beach, took a launch to Fort Lauderdale, and finished the journey to Miami in a buggy. As Les Standiford put it, Flagler came prepared to close a deal, having brought along his hotel designers and general manager Joseph Parrott.

Flagler met with Tuttle and countered with his own terms. He would accept her offer of half of her Fort Dallas property on the river, plus he wanted 100 acres to build a hotel. In return, she could retain 17 acres of the river and ocean site for herself. The total of her grant to him would be about 370 acres. In addition, the Brickell family, who owned 640 acres on the south side of the Miami River, donated 320 acres to complement Tuttle's largesse.

Thus, work began and the Florida East Coast Railway reached Flagler's new depot in April 1896—having been built by prisoners leased from the state. With news of the railroad paving the way for new settlement, Miami had a population of 1,500 by the time it arrived.

Flagler had already sent his team to survey and prepare the site for constructing his hotel on Biscayne Bay. With 350 rooms, the five-story Royal Palm Hotel opened in 1897, with two electric elevators, a swimming pool, and an electric generator (as a staunch believer in temperance, Tuttle persuaded Flagler to limit liquor service to the hotel bar).

As was his practice, Flagler put in place the infrastructure that would be needed for his own properties and workforce, as well as an economic base for future settlers. He built schools, churches, and homes for his workers, along with sidewalks, streets, and streetlights, plus an electric company and a water facility. And in 1899, when a yellow fever epidemic hit Miami—sidelining trains and ships—Flagler dumped more money into clinics.

Flagler often demonstrated a sense of social responsibility to help people in need. After one of the winter freezes spelled ruin for many Florida farmers, Flagler wrote to a local minister, asking him to identify "every case of real need where a chance to start again will be appreciated and see that they have that chance." His one caveat was that the person being helped would not know the benefactor's name.

In 1899 Flagler purchased three ships to transport tourists to the Bahamas (where he also had built and bought hotels). This required him to dredge a channel through Biscayne Bay to the ship docks, as the harbor was only 9 feet deep.

Now, with completion of Flagler's railroad to Miami, passengers could enjoy direct, daily rail service to southeast Florida from northeastern cities. In time the umbrella entity of "the Flagler System" would reflect all the subsidiaries of the Model Land Company, the Florida East Coast Railway (1895), the hotels and amenities, and the Florida East Coast Steamship Company (1897).

Henry Plant had died in 1899, after having formed the Peninsular & Occidental Steam Ship Company with the help of his PICO partners. Flagler had been one of them since 1882. In 1910 he merged his steamer line with the Plant System's P & O.

In July 1896 Miami was incorporated as a city—without so much as a stepping stone in the municipal tier. From "don't pass go," having skipped over village, township—not even known as a hamlet—Miami was suddenly legal.

On February 15, 1898, just as the Royal Palm Hotel was delighting winter visitors during its second season, the USS *Maine* blew up in Havana harbor. Fortunately, the Spanish-American War was over by August, but Miami had made some new friends. That's because the government deployed several thousand troops there to protect US interests, thanks to Flagler's rapport with President McKinley; in the process, "Miami" got a bigger spot on the map.

So does one person deserve the credit for birthing Miami, or two?

"Surely, Henry Flagler deserves all the credit he can get for building the railroad to Miami," said Florida Senator R. B. Gautier in 1959. "But he never lived in the jungle that Miami was in the 1890s as Mrs. Tuttle did. He never knew the hardships this lady did."

Tuttle died in 1898, just two years after she accomplished the burning goal of bringing a railroad to Miami. Her coffin was No. 12 in a cemetery she had built. In 1952 US Senator Scott M. Loftin commented on her legacy while dedicating a plaque in Tuttle's honor. He said many astute and farsighted businessmen, including members of the Biscayne Bay Company, had bought property in what would become Miami, "yet [they] failed to realize that they held the site of a future city in their hands. It remained for a wise and remarkable woman to envision its possibilities."

Flagler admired her as a "woman of fire," yet most historians have been confounded by the improbable accomplishments of a Cleveland widow moving heaven and earth to reinvent a desolate swamp. Given their history, Tuttle understood what Flagler was capable of, yet most historians remain amazed at the strata of his achievements, given his humble start and lack of formal education.

Isn't it therefore tempting to make the case that ancestry informed the paths taken by both of these heroic figures?

"WHO WE ARE IS WHO WE WERE"

That quote comes from the script of the 1997 movie *Amistad*, a profound portrayal of the significance of ancestry—and one based on a true episode in history. The speaker is the character of former president John Quincy Adams. Set in 1841, the story involves a group of Mende people kidnapped from their village in Sierra Leone, sold into slavery in Cuba, and chained belowdecks on a Spanish ship bound for the United States.

The Africans overpower their tormentors, only to land in a Connecticut jail charged with murder. Persuaded to consult on the case, then arguing its merits before the US Supreme Court, Adams insists that the defendants cannot be considered slaves, because the ship's log had proof they were born in Africa (since 1808, US policy had banned *international* slavery). The justices concurred, and the Mendes were freed.

A climactic story element addressed ancestry. Adams hears a rumor about the Mende leader, Cinque—a man brave enough to fight off a tiger in Africa—and asks him about the ordeal. Cinque said he was able to summon the courage he needed by calling on his ancestors for backup. Adams asked why he expected that to work. Could Cinque really rely on ghosts?

The gist of Cinque's reply was profound: "They have to help me . . . Without me, they don't exist."

GHOST OF FLAGLER PAST

The concept above stirs images of a young Henry Flagler, making his way at age fourteen, fearless, stoic, and determined. Along the many paths he chose, were his ancestors present—and if so, did he ever call on their counsel or summon their courage?

It has been suggested that Flagler acted boldly at times to impress his old partner, John D. Rockefeller, and/or his beloved Mary Lily. His spirituality was widely acknowledged, so perhaps he was giving a nod to his forebears, because without his deeds, they didn't exist.

Lefèvre's magazine article, mentioned above, was written at a time when the press had exhausted every business angle, financial thread, and cultural nuance on the life and times of Henry Flagler. The writer artfully described the man's physical countenance and demeanor, but came away with a void wherein Flagler's answers left Lefèvre's questions throwing up their hands in exasperation.

Flagler was a tall, vital man who belied his age, with glistening silver hair, clear blue eyes "that gleam but never flame," and a "virile red" complexion. "A handsome old man! . . . But Flagler is not like anyone else and withal is not eccentric. He simply does not 'classify.' You cannot accurately adjectivize him. He does not defy analysis, he baffles it."

Pondering whether the titan had red blood in his veins, Lefèvre asserted that it was not nearly so clear as ice water: "What color is it then? That is the mystery of the soul of Henry M. Flagler."

Lefèvre also described the last session of their interview. The two were standing on the loggia at Whitehall in Palm Beach, gazing westward over the lake at dusk. The writer had plenty of material for publication, but he was impatient to get a living legend to open up about himself: "Doesn't this sky get into your soul? Doesn't that glow light it? Don't you love that water, that line of trees, that sky? Isn't this the real reason why you do things here?"

Always reflective before speaking, the eighty-year-old Flagler paused, put his hand on the younger man's shoulder, and answered: "Sometimes at the close of the day . . . I look at the water and at the trees yonder and at the sunset . . . I often wonder if there is anything in the other world so beautiful as this."

Chapter 11 will address the saga of Flagler's most famous achievement, the building of "the Overseas Railroad" from Miami to Key West. In corporate parlance, it was the Key West Extension, Flagler System.

CHAPTER 10

Outsiders on Board

Reed, Walters, and Warfield

Railroading is a foreign language to many.
—H. A. STIMSON, *DEPOT DAYS*

NO LONGER THE BLUSHING INGÉNUE, FLORIDA HAD REACHED NUBILE territory during the rail-building boom of the 1880s and the heartbreak of failed promises in the 1890s. Many corporations—and entrepreneurs with a giddy attachment—came calling from out of state or offshore.

By then the industry and its powerful lobby had achieved a level of influence that author Gregg Turner called arrogance of "imperial proportions." The frequency of receiverships had prompted Governor Edward Perry to push lawmakers to form a rail commission in 1887. Perry had told the legislature that railroads were "the greatest factor in Florida's progress," but one in need of boundaries. Florida's commission opted to cut-and-paste Georgia's law.

As so many historians have related, the time was ripe for immigration, with newcomers coming to dig for themselves into the outlandish tales of successful farmers and busy merchants. One of the curious was Sir Edward James Reed, a naval architect and member of Parliament who, as noted in Chapter 8, headed a consortium of English and Dutch investors that bought 2 million acres of land in central Florida from Hamilton Disston in 1881 and developed several communities.

The same year, the consortium bought the Atlantic, Gulf, & West India Transit Company, the successor to Yulee's Florida Railroad. The cross-state main line ran 156 miles from Fernandina to Cedar Key. A subsidiary, the Peninsular Florida division, ran from Waldo to Ocala and Silver Springs; another subsidiary, the Tropical Florida Railroad, ran from Ocala to Wildwood. Reed reorganized the trio as the Florida Transit Company; in 1883 he re-reorganized again as the Florida Transit & Peninsular Railroad, with proposed connections to Ocala and Tampa.

A year earlier, Reed had acquired the Jacksonville, Pensacola & Mobile Railroad, which ran from Quincy east to Lake City, with branches to St. Marks and Monticello. (As mentioned already, the railroad's previous owner was the infamous scalawag George Swepson; the J, P & M had built an extension to Chattahoochee sometime before 1873.) Reed also scooped up a subsidiary, the Florida Central Railroad, running from Lake City to Jacksonville. He reorganized both as the Florida Central & Western Railroad.

The Florida Transit & Peninsular merged in 1884 with the Florida Central & Western, the Leesburg & Indian River, and the Fernandina & Jacksonville railroads. The operator built tracks to Tavares via Leesburg, and from Wildwood to Plant City.

A year later, Reed had lease agreements with two smaller lines. He consolidated the lot under one parent firm, the Florida Railway & Navigation Company. Nonetheless, the wolf was never far from the door, and continuing financial snags interrupted its advances. Reed bowed out, and the Navigation entity went into receivership. It continued to operate and built more lines in the vicinity of Jacksonville.

In a reshuffle in 1888, New York financier W. Bayard Cutting and other investors bought the Florida Railway & Navigation Company, then reorganized as the Florida Central & Peninsular Railroad Company. Cutting was a lawyer and legal counsel for a railroad company owned by his grandfather (and his brother, Fulton Cutting, owned a majority of Florida Central stock).

The new company by then owned or controlled tracks from the Atlantic Ocean at Fernandina to the Gulf coast at Cedar Key, with branches to St. Marks and Monticello. It quickly expanded from Plant City south to Tampa, finally getting there in 1890, more than five years after Henry Plant. The Cutting outfit was interested in other areas of central Florida, and studied the investment landscape in Georgia and beyond.

LEASE AND GREASE THE WHEELS

The new South Bound Railroad, completed in 1891, was a 136-mile line between Savannah, Georgia, and Columbia, South Carolina. Three years later, the Florida Central & Peninsular arranged to lease it. The company then built a 138-mile line from Savannah to Jacksonville, to align with routes operating in Florida. By January 1894 rail service was operating from Jacksonville to Columbia, a stretch of 274 miles.

Unfortunately most of the lines Florida Central acquired had been built prior to 1868, and therefore were protected by rules of the Internal Improvement Fund. The holding company defaulted on interest payments on its bonds; the IIF had guaranteed the payments, so those monies accrued to the state agency.

In 1899 a banking consortium bought the Florida Central & Peninsular. The principals were J. William Middendorf Sr. of New York, an investor in the Virginia Railway and Power Company, and a Richmond firm headed by John Langbourne Williams (the latter's son, John Skelton Williams Sr., bought Fulton Cutting's shares).

The Williams-Middendorf banking houses were on the cusp of creating a major new player among Florida railroads, with the Florida Central part of the fold. In 1900 they organized an entity whose origins date to the early 1830s in Virginia's tidewater country.

After a half-century of mergers and shared routes, the Seaboard & Roanoke Railroad was the main line of the Seaboard Air-Line System extending through the Carolinas. The system leased another line into Atlanta in 1892 and Birmingham the following year. Once Seaboard expanded into northeast Florida at Jacksonville, it became one of the state's "Big Three."

Stockholders of the Raleigh & Gaston Railroad met in 1899 to weigh a merger with the South Bound Railroad and a kitchen sink of other lines, including the Florida Central & Peninsular Railroad. (A dizzying trail of ampersands was armchair travel at its most exhausting: the Raleigh &

Augusta Air-Line, the Durham & Northern Railway, the Roanoke & Tar River Railroad, the Seaboard and Roanoke Railroad, the Louisburg Railroad, the Carolina Central Railroad, the Palmetto Railroad, the Chesterfield and Kershaw Railroad, the Georgia, Carolina & Northern Railway, the Seaboard Air Line Belt Railroad, the Georgia & Alabama Railroad, the Georgia and Alabama Terminal Company, the Logansville and Lawrenceville Railroad, the Richmond, Petersburg and Carolina Railroad, and the Pittsboro Railroad.) The result of the merger was the Seaboard Air Line Railway (the South Bound would join the mix in 1901).

The first president of Seaboard Air Line, from 1900 to 1903, was the aforementioned Richmond financier John Skelton Williams Sr. (President Woodrow Wilson would later name him Comptroller of the Currency, and he was instrumental in the organization of the Federal Reserve Board.)

THE BACHELOR, THE WOMAN, THE FAVOR

Baltimore banker S. (Solomon) Davies Warfield had assisted Williams in the formation of Seaboard Air Line. His father was Henry Mactier Warfield, a prominent grain merchant and a director of the Baltimore & Ohio Railroad. During the 1880s S. Davies established the Warfield Manufacturing Company to produce his own inventions of corn cutters and silkers. (Warfield also was president of the Continental Trust Company of Baltimore and was postmaster of Baltimore from 1894 to 1905.)

Within a few years, Warfield became chairman of the executive committee and then president of Seaboard Air Line Railway Company. As a lifelong bachelor, Warfield's motives for extending the railroad past Sarasota may be seen as doing a favor for a lady—but not as the wags would be tempted to frame it.

In 1885 a colony of Scottish immigrants settled in the Sarasota area as part of a promotion by the Florida Mortgage and Investment Company Limited, which had bought about 50,000 acres of land near Sarasota from Hamilton Disston. By the winter of 1910, the bay area had a few small, yawning villages where the descendants of pioneers tried their luck at fishing. The US Census listed the population at 840, and a few forward-thinking tourists from the Midwest maintained winter cottages,

Portrait of Bertha Honoré Palmer of Chicago and Sarasota, where she traveled in a private railroad car with an entourage of family and staff. After touring the bay area for a week, she began buying tens of thousands of acres in what was then Manatee County. She persuaded the head of Seaboard Air Line Railway to commit to extend the company's line to Osprey where she wanted to buy a house.
STATE ARCHIVES OF FLORIDA, FLORIDA MEMORY.

too. The southern terminus for the Plant System's railroad was Tampa, so people and goods traveled by boat down to a wharf on Sarasota Bay.

Arthur Britton Edwards, a "Cracker" cattleman descended from an old Florida family, had come back from serving in the Spanish-American War intent on maximizing the momentum from news that Seaboard Air Line would build an extension from Tampa. Lacking the money to promote the area, he got the bright idea to contact the leading railroads and ask them for a list of people making inquiries about Florida. Everyone on the list got a letter from Edwards.

Meanwhile, Joseph H. Lord had emigrated from Maine in the 1890s to buy phosphate, agricultural land, livestock pastures, and residential property around Sarasota. Lord owned 200 lots and 70,000 acres of vacant land by 1904. Edwards and Lord became partners and opened an office in Chicago, where Lord advertised in the *Chicago Tribune*.

On the morning of January 10, 1910, a mansion on Lake Michigan was shielding the woman inside from freezing winds howling off the water. As she read the newspaper, the words in Lord's ad struck a chord: "Grapefruit and orange groves, beautiful winter homes, fruit and vegetable lands . . . on Sarasota Bay . . . on the Gulf."

Edwards and Lord surely hoped to hook a live one, but neither could have anticipated reeling in Bertha Honoré Palmer—internationally known as an astute businesswoman, arts patron, and socialite on two continents. She also was the widow of multimillionaire Potter Palmer, who in 1870 had declined President Ulysses Grant's offer to become secretary of the interior.

Bertha's sister, Ida Marie Honoré, was married to President Grant's son, Colonel Frederick Dent Grant. Their daughter, Julia Dent Grant, and her Aunt Bertha had traveled in Europe, where Julia met Prince Michael Cantacuzène, Count Speransky of the Romanov family of Russia. The Palmers hosted the couple's wedding in 1899 in Newport, Rhode Island. The setting was Beaulieu, a villa owned by William Waldorf Astor, where the Palmers were spending the summer.

Mrs. Palmer's reputation had a rock-solid foundation. Bertha Mathilde Honoré was a belle born in Louisville, Kentucky, and was well-educated at a convent in Georgetown, Maryland, having graduated with honors in history, geography, the sciences, philosophy, literature, rhetoric and composition, advanced mathematics, and domestic economy. The nuns praised her talents in piano, vocals, and fluent French.

Bertha was the daughter of Henry Hamilton Honoré, who moved the family to Chicago to expand his real estate business. His daughter was about thirteen when she met Henry's associate, a wealthy merchant twenty-three years her senior. She became Mrs. Potter Palmer when she was twenty-one. By then her talks with Potter and her father about their real estate investments had given her a keen appreciation for opportunities and challenges.

Intrigued by the hints of beauty and abundance of land around Sarasota Bay, the widow Palmer visited Florida soon after reading that ad (and only after she had interviewed Joseph Lord to discern his character). Mrs. Palmer made the journey in a private railroad car with her father, her sons—Potter II and Honoré—her brother Adrian Honoré, her general manager, a secretary, and a staff of servants. Having traveled the world over, she offered an informed opinion that Sarasota Bay was "more beautiful than the Bay of Naples."

She scouted the area for a week, and within the year had bought 90,000 acres of what was then Manatee County. And Mrs. Palmer was just getting started.

She had decided to buy a two-story house at Spanish Point, on the bay at Osprey just south of Sarasota. She insisted that Seaboard Air Line commit to extend its railroad to Osprey before she would close on the contract.

So why would S. Davies Warfield acquiesce, and how might she know he would? Perhaps Mrs. Palmer owned a lot of stock in his company (plus her husband's bequest of $8 million). Perhaps she posed a veiled ultimatum—*build my road or watch me build my own railroad.* No matter. In 1911 she extracted a promise and Warfield put in motion a project to extend the tracks 16.5 miles from Fruitville to Bee Ridge to a point south of Roberts Bay. She wanted the terminal named Venice, and she got her way (well, Warfield did have experience as a postmaster).

It isn't certain that she and Warfield knew each other well, but they certainly traveled on the same social plane. The Warfield family had been in America since the Colonial era. They were descended from the Emory family, which had an original land grant from King George III of England.

Mrs. Palmer, with aristocratic ties, was the toast of A-listers in London and Paris. Her late husband had adored lavishing her with luxurious gifts; accordingly, his accountants saw many an invoice from Tiffany and Worth.

She had a friendship with Robert Todd Lincoln, son of the slain president, and the Palmers often hosted American presidents in their home in Chicago. President McKinley appointed her to the US delegation attending the Paris Exposition of 1900—and she was the only woman in the group. Mrs. Palmer was friendly with the Queen Consort of England and golfed with Alexandra's husband, King Edward VII (he was crowned in 1901, the year her husband died).

Warfield, meanwhile, had a niece blessed with the same dusty Baltimore lineage—someone whose name would send the press into a lather years later. She happened to be Wallis Warfield Simpson, *that* Mrs. Simpson, for whom King Edward VIII abdicated the British throne in 1936. (As the Duke and Duchess of Windsor, the couple often visited Palm Beach and other resort towns in Florida.)

An article that year in the *Portsmouth Times* spoke about Wallis Simpson's character as not unlike that of her uncle, S. Davies Warfield, someone who retired as chairman of a conglomerate to plunge into expanding a vintage railroad. The article said many of Warfield's attributes were evident in his niece, Wallis: "He was a man of great nervous energy and drove both himself and his associates. Dominating and self-centered, he was not lacking in social charm."

Meanwhile, Bertha Palmer's velvety Southern purr belied a steel-trap mind, someone whose penchant for ledger-keeping would have had John D. Rockefeller drooling. To deal with her, Warfield would need every ounce of drive and charm. As historian Ernest Poole put it: "She was beautiful, dashing, quick, and smart; and more than that, she was sure of herself."

Sure is right. Warfield began work on the extension within thirty days of their talks. Mrs. Palmer sent for her construction supervisor in Chicago, C. Thompson, who arrived to start work on a dock with rails to transport building materials to Osprey.

SPRUCING UP SARASOTA

The seller of the house Bertha Palmer wanted to buy at Spanish Point was Lawrence Jones, of the John Paul Jones whiskey-folk in Kentucky. Edwards had told her the price for the house and 13 acres was $11,000. She went to Jones thinking she could parlay a lower price, but she didn't really care—she wanted that property, and she bought a few hundred acres around it.

As for Lord and Edwards, they were the sellers of most other properties she bought—covering about 218 square miles. In addition to her initial purchase, Mrs. Palmer bought a 1,300-acre grapefruit grove and a 6,000-acre cattle ranch and 3,000 head of existing livestock in the Myakka River region. Eventually she'd own about 140,000 acres.

Almost overnight the bejeweled socialite became a gentlewoman rancher in boots (with a spur to spare): "The woman who had studied [the fine arts] . . . became an auto-didact in the assimilation of knowledge about crops, cattle ranching, manure, the chemistry of soil and water . . . vegetation as well as wildlife in the area," said University of South Florida scholar Hope L. Black, in a 2007 master's thesis.

Mrs. Palmer already had mastered trees and flowers, as she enjoyed supervising her gardens wherever she lived. According to Black, "She often said that if she had any talent, it was her 'joy in watching things grow.'"

And grow they did. Mrs. Palmer named her house The Oaks at Osprey Point. An architect from Chicago, recently arrived in Sarasota, designed some additions, creating a thirty-one-room house plus outbuildings for her servants and a live-in work crew of several dozen. The 350-acre property had its own water supply, irrigation system, and electric plant.

Janet Matthews describes the transformation in her book, *Venice: Journey from Horse and Chaise:* "She wrapped walkways, formal gardens, reflecting ponds, a tennis court and paths around Indian middens, homestead inns, winter houses, a community cemetery and chapel, boathouses and commercial docks. She beautified those elements around the remodeled Jones house."

To develop the properties, Palmer formed the Sarasota Venice Company. Her brother, Adrian Honoré, was president, and her sons were secretary and treasurer. Her general manager from Chicago, W. A. Sumner, became vice president of the new venture.

Mrs. Palmer's land holdings proved convenient for her growing curiosity about agriculture. She liked the process of attending to her personal gardens, yes, but investing in crops and livestock was a new challenge. She named her ranch Meadowsweet Pastures and fenced lands long open to free-range cattlemen. That was partly because she was building the herd by bringing in Brahma bulls to breed with the wiry, Florida cattle, plus Herefords from Texas and Angus from Georgia. She also built vats for dipping livestock in a chemical solution to eradicate the pesky Texas fever tick.

In 1915 Palmer's ranch shipped 1,000 head of cattle on the Seaboard Air Line Railway, tying up thirty-one cars of rolling stock. In turn, she received shipments of fruit and vegetable plants and seeds from around the country to experiment with new crops that might do well in southwest Florida. She is credited with being the first woman to ship Florida cattle by rail to Texas, of all places. As for her 1,300 acres of citrus groves, they produced and turned a profit quickly enough to impress Mrs. Palmer—whose rail connection was convenient for shipping fruit north by train.

Historians have debated Mrs. Palmer's reasons for replacing silk gowns with cotton shifts—at least until dinnertime. She seldom wore much from her fabled jewelry collection, unless she was promoting one of many community causes at The Oaks or visiting friends in Palm Beach (and this was a woman whose wardrobe trunk held as many diamond stomachers as silk chemises and batiste handkerchiefs).

In 2010 author Catherine O'Sullivan Shorr filmed *A Conversation with Bertha Palmer, The Queen of Sarasota* on the grounds of Bertha's estate, which now is a park. Shorr summarized her contribution to Sarasota: "During a period of eight years, Mrs. Potter Palmer . . . along with her father, her sons, and her brother, masterminded the transformation of a frontier fishing village into a winter haven for the wealthy and a lucrative wellspring of employment for others."

Hope Black's thesis suggests that Mrs. Palmer had a personal-best ambition that outweighed previous accolades: "The advertisement may have ignited a spark of excitement for a new challenge in uncharted territory; a quest for the possibilities of another world. It is conceivable that she sought an opportunity to demonstrate, if only to herself, that she could achieve success in the management of a new enterprise, enriching the family coffers and reinforcing the renown she gained as administrator of the World's Columbian Exposition seventeen years in the past. The wealth she had enjoyed during her lifetime had come from her father and from her husband; this adventure would be hers."

WISE COUNSEL

William Alexander Blount Sr. was born in Alabama, where his father, Alexander Clement Blount, had moved to run a plantation. The elder Blount had been a successful lawyer and state's attorney in North Carolina. Young William's childhood was therefore an agrarian existence, related in family tales as "plowing, gardening, raising poultry, attending to stock, going to the grist mill and the many other things which tend to make a country boy self-reliant."

In the late 1850s Alexander Blount left the plantation in the hands of caretakers and moved the family to Pensacola, where he resumed his law practice. His son William studied law and began practicing in the city as well. His clients included the Pensacola Street Car Company and Daniel F. Sullivan, who bought the Pensacola & Louisville Railroad. On Blount's advice, Sullivan transferred majority control to the Louisville & Nashville Railroad in 1880, which led to the creation of the Pensacola & Atlantic Railroad (as discussed in Chapter 7) in 1881. Blount also was general counsel for many years for the Florida East Coast Railway and was a trustee of the Flagler estate.

William Blount died in 1921, not long after becoming president of the American Bar Association. He had taken ill in Baltimore, and his remains were brought by train to Pensacola. Officials marked the occasion in various ways. The US Supreme Court adjourned for the day; the FEC Railway halted all traffic during part of his funeral; flags in Pensacola were lowered to half-staff. The city's African-American community issued a formal statement: "Though custom forbade us from following the remains of this noble hearted man to his last resting place . . . we as a people loyal to every interest of our community, join with the white citizens in mourning the loss of one of Florida's noblest sons."

A SUIT WITH LEGS

Many examples describe upstanding lawyers steering railroad corporations into wise moves, shysters giving lazy, shoddy advice and a company's general counsel having to mop up messes from the past.

Recall that the Florida Railroad and subsequent outfits were facing bankruptcy in the late 1860s, when David Yulee allowed a Northern investment syndicate to take a controlling interest. A principal, Marshall Roberts, was dismayed to learn the Internal Improvement Fund had no money to pay the interest on his Florida Railroad bonds.

That's when, according to Gregg Turner, the IIF trustees seized the railroad and sold it for a song to Marshall's brother, Isaac Roberts. He requested deeds in the name of Edward N. Dickerson & Associates, which kept the syndicate in control after all. Roberts paid $323,400, less than a third of what it had cost to build the railroad. Turner said bondholders were given a choice to settle up: either take pennies on the dollar, a four-fifths discount on a $1,000 bond, or accept the one-fifth in land the railroad owned.

Enter one Francis Vose of New York, a principal of Vose, Livingston & Company, a firm that imported iron rails and had "sold" a boatload to the Florida Railroad. When its promissory notes and bonds proved worthless, Vose declined to accept either silly offer. Instead, in 1878 he sued the IIF and Governor Harrison Reed in federal court for the full face value of his bonds, "which hamstrung the agency for years until a settlement was made," Turner said.

The Circuit Court of the United States for the Northern District of Florida ruled in favor of Vose and his associate, William H. Wagner of South Carolina. The court issued an injunction to place the IIF into the hands of a receiver, Aristides Doggett.

The IIF was in limbo until 1881, when it was able to settle a lawsuit with such long tentacles. State records for that year show that Doggett itemized the amounts owed to Vose and other creditors, for bonds issued by the Florida Railroad, the Florida, Alabama & Gulf Central, the Pensacola & Georgia, and the Tallahassee Railroad. The total of principal and interest was $979,719 (with the Florida Railroad owing the lion's share of $528,279). Having made payments totaling $171,644, the balance due was $808,075. Of that amount, the fund owed the Vose estate $404,677.

FLORIDA-GEORGIA LINE

Georgia authorities acknowledged a new corporation in 1895, the Georgia Pine Railway Company, to build and operate a road in that state. The company filed a copy of its charter in Florida, received similar rights, and set up an annex to the Bainbridge-based organization. In April 1901 the company took a new name, the Georgia, Florida & Alabama Railway Company.

In 1906 the carrier bought the rights and franchises of another railroad from an out-of-state syndicate. The head of the syndicate was thread manufacturer William Clark, a native of Scotland, and many investors were from New York. The consortium also owned the Georgia & Florida Investment Company, the Gulf Terminal & Navigation Company, and the Scottish Land & Improvement Company.

The Georgia, Florida & Alabama Railway Company acquired the Carrabelle, Tallahassee & Georgia Railroad Company, which dated to 1891. Its previous names were the Thomasville, Tallahassee & Gulf Railroad Company (incorporated in Georgia) and the Augusta, Tallahassee & Gulf Railroad Company (incorporated in Florida).

The Carrabelle company had been incorporated with $1 million in capital stock and a land grant of 206,370 acres. It owned three locomotives and more than four-dozen cars of rolling stock. The route was from Carrabelle on the Big Bend of the Gulf northwest to Tallahassee, then on to the Florida-Georgia border. S. D. Chittenden of Tallahassee was vice president of the railroad.

The Carrabelle line's new owner built a route from Havana, Florida, to Tallahassee, and from Havana to Quincy—which has the distinction of being the first site in America where fuller's earth was discovered. The clay mineral is derived from deposits of ancient volcanic ash, and Quincy remains one of the country's largest mining and processing locations. Florida was producing and shipping 85 percent of US fuller's earth in 1920. Its early uses were to clarify mineral oils (now it's a staple of the cosmetics industry and, well, cat litter).

THE SOUTHERN SYSTEM

Unlike the railroads in Florida and the rest of the South, new construction along the Ohio and Mississippi Rivers continued during the

Reconstruction era after the "First Railroad War." The Richmond and Danville System, for one, expanded but became overextended. Its thirty separate companies operated routes from 6 miles to 552 miles long.

Overextended, the bloated outfit fell on hard times in 1893. As *Railroad World* described the system the following year, it was "much vaunted but intrinsically worthless"—yet valuable to financier J. P. Morgan, perhaps because one of those railroads was the Georgia Southern & Florida.

Morgan reorganized these dozens of companies—whose operations and securities were inescapably linked "in almost hopeless confusion"—into the Southern Railway System. Thus, thirty boards of directors and an equal number of accounting histories "disappeared simultaneously."

In addition to the Richmond outfit, the Memphis & Charleston Railroad and the East Tennessee, Virginia & Georgia Railroad were funneled into the Southern Railway System. Southern Railway owned two-thirds of the routes it operated—about 4,400 miles of track—and had leases, operating agreements, and stock interests in the other one-third. Southern also controlled the Georgia Southern & Florida, which began operations between Macon and Valdosta and extended to Palatka in 1889.

Another line that Southern Railway controlled and operated separately was the Alabama Great Southern. It had been owned by a British holding company whose five railroad entities ran the "Queen & Crescent Route" between Cincinnati and New Orleans.

The first president of Southern Railway was Samuel Spencer, who ran the outfit for a dozen years. On his watch the system acquired more lines and purchased more equipment. Committed to altering the company's focus away from agricultural freight, he looked toward new profit streams. (Either poetic justice or a creepy coincidence, Spencer was killed in a train wreck in 1906.)

By 1916 Southern Railway president Fairfax Harrison was overseeing a thirteen-state system stretching for 8,000 miles. The company also had an interest in the Central of Georgia.

The Royal Palm was a named train of the Southern Railway and one of the earliest named passenger trains to serve the market between Midwest cities and Florida. It ran on its own rails from Cincinnati to Jacksonville; there, passengers proceeding south rode the Florida East Coast

Railway to Miami. Southern Railway was lauded for its service—as even its earliest versions carried sleeper cars of the New York Central. Another of the Southern's named trains, the Kansas City–Florida Special, brought passengers to Florida from the Great Plains. Meanwhile, the Ponce de Leon was the counterpart to the Royal Palm, running between Jacksonville and Cincinnati. The Ponce de Leon collided with the Royal Palm on the day before Christmas Eve 1926 in Rockmart, Georgia, killing 19 and injuring 113. The accident was the subject of a 1927 song released on the Columbia Records label, "The Wreck of the Royal Palm."

It was written and performed by prolific singer-songwriter Vernon Dalhart, known for the genre of railroad ballads. Born Marion Try Slaughter, he chose his professional name from two towns in Texas. Recording as Al Craver, accompanied by violin, guitar, and harmonica, he sang of "one dark and stormy night . . . the Royal Palm was makin' time . . . amid the great crash, the two great engines met . . . an awful sight . . . which no tongue can ever tell."

Not that he targeted the Southern Railway, but true to his genre, Dalhart recorded "The Wreck of the Old 97" in 1924—a classic American train ballad about the derailment of the Southern's Fast Mail train near Danville, Virginia.

WILD CHILD ARCADIA

Arcadia (not to be confused with the city of Arcadia in DeSoto County) was the site of a water-powered sawmill near Milton and Bagdad in the Panhandle. In 1835 the territorial legislature approved a charter for the Pond Creek and Blackwater River Canal Company. Three years later, under a new charter, it was the Arcadia Rail Road Company. Its purpose was to transport lumber over a 3-mile track between Pond Creek and the Blackwater River using mule power.

The first train of the Florida Southern Railway (not to be confused with the Southern Railway mentioned in Chapter 10) arrived in the other Arcadia, DeSoto County, in March 1886 and was the last stop for several months.

As mentioned in a previous chapter, Western artist Frederic Sackrider Remington was a New Yorker who took an interest in Florida cowmen. In 1895 Remington visited Arcadia and later wrote and illustrated an article about the region's men in the saddle, which was published in *Harper's*.

Arcadia and other frontier settlements around the Peace River were said to be as wild as any lawless outpost anywhere. The river originates in south-central Florida and flows toward the Gulf at Port Charlotte. Before rail service, cowboys drove the herds through the river valley to Charlotte Harbor for shipping. The so-called range wars raged in the last decade of the 19th century, and Arcadia once had a reputation as a frontier town as "wild" as any in the American West.

Henry Plant had gained a controlling interest in the Florida Southern Railway and made it part of the Plant System in 1892. Therefore, a few years after Plant's death, the Florida Southern Railway became part of the Atlantic Coast Line Railroad.

In 1914 the Seaboard built the East and West Coast Railroad as a subsidiary to haul lumber and turpentine between Arcadia and Bradenton. Trains began arriving in Arcadia the following spring.

TRAINS, NAMES, AND DEPOTS

A pair of named passenger trains operated daily between Tampa, Sarasota, Fort Myers, and Naples. Names included the Dixie Limited and the Palmetto. Originally known as the Palmetto Limited and put in service in 1909, the latter train was an Atlantic Coast Line through-sleeper operated on a route with the Pennsylvania Railroad, connecting New York City, Washington, DC, and Tampa.

With parlors, lounges, dining cars, and full-Pullman service, the route attracted business travelers as well as the moneyed set. On the freight side, timber, naval stores, citrus, vegetables, and livestock moved to northern markets. Station names included Belspur, Palmersville, Honoré, and Sidell. Adrian Honoré, brother of Bertha Honoré Palmer, was the major landowner along the line.

The Chicago & Eastern Illinois Railroad (C & EI) participated in passenger service on the "Dixie Route" to Florida from the Midwest. Its named trains included the Dixie Limited, the Dixie Flyer, the Dixie Mail, the Dixie Flagler, and the Dixiana.

Trains of the C & EI had dining cars, coaches, a Chicago–Fort Myers Pullman sleeper off the Dixie Limited, and a New York–Naples Pullman sleeper off the Palmetto. The railroad's through-sleepers between Jacksonville and Chicago began service in 1893 to coincide with the World's Columbian Exposition (the one with Mrs. Palmer at the helm). In 1896 permanent service on the C & EI featured the New Orleans and Florida Special, with cars headed for Tampa and Jacksonville.

Many named trains have figured prominently in pop culture, literature, song lyrics—even a lawyer's brief on civil rights and public policy. One often-reflected line dates to 1960, when author Flannery O'Connor said, "Nobody wants his mule and wagon stalled on the same track the 'Dixie Limited' is roaring down." Her railroading metaphor referred to the trepidation Southern writers felt as they struggled in the shadow of William Faulkner.

Author and professor Joseph R. Millichap quotes O'Connor in his 2002 book, *Dixie Limited: Railroads, Culture and the Southern Renaissance.*

BONE VALLEY BLISTERS

As noted in an earlier chapter, William Walters of Baltimore (an original member of the Plant Investment Company) had cobbled together a network of several lines and spurs south of Richmond that would form the core of the Atlantic Coast Line Railroad. His son, Henry Walters, had become chairman of the ACL in 1884 and engineered its takeover of the Plant System's railroads after the death of his friend, Henry Plant.

As soon as Walters settled up with the widow Plant in 1902, the Atlantic Coast Line had twice the reach it had before. Walters would soon outdo himself, however, when the ACL bought a majority interest in the stock of the Louisville & Nashville Railroad, raising the bar on its intense rivalry with S. Davies Warfield's less-dominant Seaboard Air Line.

The tracks of both the SAL and the ACL blistered from the growing freight business out of Bone Valley, which covered about 2,800 square miles across parts of five counties: Polk, Hillsborough, Manatee, DeSoto, and Hardee. As Gregg Turner noted, river phosphate had been found at

Fort Meade in Polk County as early as 1881. Francis LeBaron, a captain with the US Army Corps of Engineers, found it while surveying the lower Peace River environs to see whether there might be a way to join the headwaters of the north-flowing St. Johns River with Charlotte Harbor on the Gulf.

Once the mining industry heard about phosphate deposits, people got busy buying up acreage near the Peace River, and a slew of mining companies formed. Early on, the river pebbles traveled on hopper cars from Arcadia to Punta Gorda, to cross Charlotte Harbor in "lighters" and be loaded onto larger ships in Boca Grande Pass. Joseph Hull, a partner in a Savannah fertilizer company, was among those who established a phosphate mine, and he later consolidated five firms into the Peace River Phosphate Mining Company (the town named for Hull was renamed Fort Ogden).

In 1897 the Florida Legislature granted a charter for the Alafia, Manatee & Gulf Coast Railway, approving a 110-mile route from Plant City to Charlotte Harbor. It was approved for $1 million in capital stock, and the company would receive 6,000 acres of land for each mile of laid track. The principals of the company were from three states: Augustus Shammo, New York; B. F. Myers, Pennsylvania; and F. M. Loomis, G. T. Dickie, and M. B. Harrison, Florida (the railway would be built, but not by them). About the same time, Albert Gilchrist, a civil engineer who would become governor in 1909, recorded a plat to create the town of Boca Grande on Gasparilla Island in Lee County.

Peter B. Bradley of the Bradley Fertilizer Company in New York—and the Boca Grande Land Company—got involved on a scale larger than Joseph Hull when he orchestrated the merger of twenty-two mining outfits into the American Agricultural Chemicals Co. (AACC) in 1899. Thereafter, Bradley acquired increasing numbers of shares in Hull's holding company, finally buying it in 1902.

By this time, many companies sent their phosphate on rail hopper cars bound for Tampa Bay. Bradley, however, anticipated he could lower transportation costs by having a direct rail line from the mines to a phosphate terminal by the deepwater port on Gasparilla Island. As Don Hensley noted in *Taplines*, Bradley needed a charter, and that "paper railroad" chartered in 1897 would suffice. He bought the rights to the Alafia, Manatee & Gulf Coast Railway in 1905, increased the capital stock to $2 million, and changed its name to the Charlotte Harbor & Northern Railroad.

Bradley's agribusiness hired crews of Irish, Italian, and Greek laborers to begin the project by building a wharf, a power plant, and a depot on Gasparilla Island. Turner said "the remarkable rail operation that defied the norm" connected to Atlantic Coast Line and the Seaboard Air Line tracks. One of Bradley's subsidiaries built the "South Dock" terminal at South Boca Grande in 1907. His company also built a 2-mile bridge from the mainland to the island.

Apparently the Charlotte Harbor & Northern is unique in state history regarding its finances. Noting that the company had no public indebtedness and no mortgages—nor were any bonds issued to build and equip the railroad—Hensley said: "The railroad was built entirely with cash from the AACC with them accepting CH&N stock for this cash. As far as I know, this was the only railroad in Florida built entirely with cash!"

A "Rough" Ride to Glory

As noted in Chapter 8, Henry Plant had been swift to act when the Spanish in Cuba tried to impose a tobacco embargo that would have wiped out many of his Tampa amigos. Then, the USS *Maine* blew up in Havana harbor on February 15, 1898. Plant sent his two ships *Mascotte* and *Olivette* back for survivors and refugees. Thus, the Spanish-American War transformed Tampa again, as the vessels became hospital ships.

In the decades following the Civil War, the US Army was still rebuilding its manpower, which prompted Theodore Roosevelt to resign as undersecretary of the navy and organize the 1st United States Volunteer Cavalry Regiment. He and Dr. Leonard Wood, personal physician to President McKinley, recruited cowboys, miners, marshals, and Native Americans, primarily in Western states where the climate would be similar to that of Cuba. These soldiers wore slouch hats and rustic duds, garnering the nickname "Rough Riders."

Members of the regiment boarded a Southern Pacific train in San Antonio and headed east, where they would cross into the Florida

As the United States prepared for action in the Spanish-American War, Florida was ground zero for troop deployment, with Tampa and Miami hosting thousands of troops ready to board ships bound for Cuba. In this photograph, horses are being loaded onto trains in Tampa, where tens of thousands of troops trained before shipping out. Among them, Teddy Roosevelt and the Rough Riders.
STATE ARCHIVES OF FLORIDA, FLORIDA MEMORY.

Panhandle and connect with one of the regional lines operating under the Louisville & Nashville Railroad. Heading south and then west, the troops would arrive in Tampa on Plant's Savannah, Florida & Western Railway.

The Tampa Bay Hotel became headquarters for the military brass, as well as American Red Cross founder Clara Barton and her team. Plant allotted a field near the hotel for a troop camp where the men could drill while awaiting their departure for Cuba. And while he put his hotels and railroads at their disposal for the war effort, he kept an eye on his leisure market.

Roosevelt's "Rough Rider's" [*sic*] arrival at Tampa, Florida, USA c1898. LIBRARY OF CONGRESS.

Word was, Plant had influenced the selection of Tampa as the port of troop embarkation, so Robert Mugge prepared to serve them. The German-born owner of Florida's west coast Budweiser franchise, he anticipated the arrival of 30,000 thirsty customers, courtesy of the US government.

Mugge sent a telegram to the Anheuser-Busch main office in St. Louis to order a trainload of beer. An indignant Adolphus Busch wired back: "There will not be a war and we do not sell beer by the trainload."

But a war there was. Mugge received the shipment, and he sold a trainload of pale lager.

CHAOS ON THE QUAY

Fortunately the conflict was brief. And that train ride from San Antonio to Tampa prompted Teddy Roosevelt to write an essay about it the following year. In "Spanish-American War: The Rough Riders in Tampa," he said the journey took just four days, "and I doubt if anybody who was on the trip will soon forget it."

At every train stop, the locals turned out to cheer, bringing the men flowers, watermelon, sometimes jugs of milk: "Tampa lay in the

9238—Arrival of U. S, Troops, Camp Tampa, Fla., U. S. A.

Arrival of US troops, Camp Tampa, Florida, USA c1898. LIBRARY OF CONGRESS.

pine-covered sand-flats at the end of a one-track railroad, and everything connected with both military and railroad matters was in an almost inextricable tangle . . . The railroad people unloaded us wherever they pleased, or rather wherever the jam of all kinds of trains rendered it possible."

To magnify the confusion, some who had traveled to Tampa would not be chosen to go to Cuba, and disappointment hung thick in the air. One man, Captain Maximilian Luna, commanded Troop F and was from New Mexico. "The Captain's people had been on the banks of the Rio Grande before my forefathers came to the mouth of the Hudson . . . and he made the plea that it was his right to go . . . for he was the only man of pure Spanish blood who bore a commission in the army, and he demanded the privilege of proving that his people were precisely as loyal Americans as any others," Roosevelt wrote.

On the evening of June 7, 1898, orders arrived that the expedition was to start the following dawn from Port Tampa, 9 miles distant by rail. Still more confusion, as the men gathered at the appointed track, but the train was not there. New orders came to march to another track.

Still no train, "but at six o'clock, some coal-cars came by, and these we seized. By various arguments we persuaded the engineer in charge of the train to back us down the nine miles to Port Tampa . . . The railway tracks ran out on the quay, and the transports, which had been anchored in midstream, were gradually being brought up alongside the quay and loaded."

TAMPA GAINS THIRD PLAYER

In addition to the Plant System's rail lines and the onetime Florida Central & Peninsular Railway, Tampa had enough potential for yet another player—the Tampa Northern Railroad. It was organized in 1906 because H. M. Atkinson of Georgia wanted to extend his Atlanta, Birmingham & Atlantic Railroad system. Atkinson aimed to build a line from Tampa northward to connect with his railroad in Thomasville, Georgia. Alas, he was undercapitalized and fell short of his goal.

Atkinson's associate, Preston S. Arkwright, president of the Georgia Railway & Power Company, was vice president of the Tampa Northern. It is he who took up the reins and began building a 49-mile route from Tampa to Brooksville, while buying land for rail yards and a terminal. A short line connected to Fivay Junction—which sat inland from Hudson at the southeast point of an L. (Fivay got its name from a group of men who built a sawmill and were major stockholders in the railroad; their last names began with A. Three were from Atlanta: Atkinson, Arkwright, and Martin F. Amorous. Two were from Boston: Gordon Abbott and Charles F. Ayer.)

The Tampa Northern also operated a 12-mile logging line created by the Aripeka Sawmill Company in 1905. It linked Brooksville with Wiscom and Tooke Lake in one direction and Weeki Wachee and Hudson in the other—with a depot at Sulphur Springs. The railroad also had track rights for the Central Cypress Company into Centralia, which was northwest near the Gulf.

Writing in the *St. Petersburg Times* in 1977, Wilfred T. Neill described the hotbed of activity at George Gamble's commissary in Centralia during the town's brief heyday between 1910 and 1922. The Tampa Northern Railroad hauled "logs in and lumber out" and all manner of goods for Gamble's store, as many as four carloads at a time: "Gamble's commissary sold flour, cornmeal, grits, sugar, salt, coffee, seasonings, medicines, garden produce, clothing, yard goods, household utensils, tools, kerosene—everything needed by the loggers, saw millers and their families."

The merchant imported more than staples—with Greek delicacies such as feta cheese, olive oil, roka, and black kalamata olives arriving on the train. People traveled from larger cities to shop at Gamble's in Centralia.

The town got its name from Centralia, Illinois, the hometown of Edgar A. Roberts. He and his brother owned the Central Cypress Lumber Company, well known throughout Hernando County for its cypress logging operation. Roberts built a rail spur from Centralia to Tooke Lake, about 2.5 miles away, where his friend, Lewis S. Petteway, operated a turpentine still. The lake site had no turnaround, so the trains backed in from Centralia to load the cargo.

Neill said Roberts ran the most efficient sawmill in the county: "Logs were hauled in by train, dumped into a pond and floated to the mill . . . loaded onto a ramp, where heavy chains pulled them into the saws. Double band saws cut the rough timber into finished boards. Power for winching and sawing was provided by four large steam boilers."

One day in 1912, Roberts's sawmill received a gigantic cypress timber said to the largest log ever cut at Centralia. It was such a curiosity that the company displayed the top 20 feet on a rail flatcar for weeks of local entertainment. At the time, the log was said to yield 5,476 board feet of lumber, "enough to build a modern home." A source at the mill said, "The butt cut had to be quartered by blasting before it could be moved."

Centralia went the way of all such towns once the logs ran out. The depot in the ghost town was silent—where once the mill produced 100,000 board feet of lumber a day, on average.

The town of Lutz began as "North Tampa" in the 1880s when a priest, Francis Xavier A. Stemper of Luxembourg, founded a Catholic mission. Just 6 miles away is Odessa, also founded in the 1880s, by previously mentioned Russian émigré Peter Demens, who built a stop for the Orange Belt Railway.

William Lutz, whose father hailed from Denmark, was an engineer for Tampa Northern. His brother, Charles Lutz, ran a sawmill and was an officer of the Tampa & Gulf Coast Railroad. Charles had a rail line built from the sawmill in Odessa to connect with the Tampa Northern tracks; the choppy route that crisscrossed the two railroads became known as the "Pea Vine."

At one time the Tampa Northern Railroad Company owned a one-third interest in Tampa Union Station, which opened on May 15, 1912, with nine tracks, enabling Tampa Northern, the Atlantic Coast Line, and the Seaboard Air Line to consolidate passenger operations in the eastern sector of downtown (all three consigned their waterfront depots to freight operations). Architect Joseph F. Leitner designed the station in the Italian Renaissance Revival style inspired by 16th-century palaces. Corinthian columns on the brick building had cast-stone detailing, featuring the station's monogram of T, U, and S intertwined in bas relief.

Leitner also designed the Plant City Union Depot a few years earlier. The station had a one-story brick passenger depot with a second-story signal tower, and a two-story brick freight terminal. The depot was the heart of Plant City in the late 19th century, as railroad transportation was the lifeline for its main industries of farm produce, lumber, and phosphate mining. The complex housed mail service and contained the telegraph office for "Uncle Wes" (Western Union).

By 1912 the president of Tampa Northern was S. Davies Warfield, and Seaboard Air Line Railway owned all of its capital stock. More maritime facilities were on the drawing board, which involved dredging and filling the southern waterfront near downtown Tampa. The impetus was a terminal for Seaboard on what was then called Grassy Island.

The city had approved a new port complex several years earlier, based on the plans submitted by Seaboard chief engineer W. L. Seddon. Afterward, Grassy Island was renamed Seddon Island, and today is known as Harbour Island. (Chapter 12 will trace the next steps of Seaboard.)

PLEASURE WAS THE ENGINE

As mentioned earlier, the Atlanta & St. Andrews Bay Railway from Dothan, Alabama, to Panama City was completed in 1908. Settlers and homesteaders migrated to the area, and by 1912 the bay region of Washington County had enough population to form its own county. The impetus for the growth was a strong naval stores industry and the location of lumber mills near the railroad.

According to the Florida Memory project, railway mileage in the state increased fourfold during the decade between 1880 and 1890. As noted previously, the Flagler and Plant expansions on the east and west coasts were the spines for a network of railroads linking new population centers, burgeoning industries, agricultural regions, and tropical hideaways for Northern tourists.

Suddenly, Florida was a workable idea.

At least in Flagler's case, his railroad existed for the purpose of transporting primarily wealthy guests to his luxury hotels. In *Billion Dollar Sandbar*, author Polly Redford points out an anomaly: "Flagler's winter palaces civilized what until then had been a real jungle, complete with Indians and crocodiles—one of the first instances where the pleasure industry, rather than farming, mining or lumber, did the pioneering."

STREETWISE

The Palm Beach Railway and Power Company was a Florida railroad incorporated in 1893, although the name is a bit misleading. Its owners were Tampa municipal leaders Edward Manrara, Candide Ybor, and Emilio Pons.

Their aim was to build and operate a line or lines of street railway in Tampa, as long as said street was not part of the route of a competing operation. The Palm Beach line also could extend the railroad from Tampa to any point on Hillsborough Bay that was east of the Hillsborough River. Manrara et al. also got permission to build and operate an electric light plant to illuminate Tampa and the vicinity.

Florida's balmy Gulf coast was becoming a magnet for out-of-state visitors and settlers. Some have said the area suited Midwesterners more than the Atlantic coast because its lakes, rivers, and the Gulf were more familiar in scope than the big blue pond.

In the winter of 1884–85, one of the seasonal visitors to Fort Myers was Thomas Alva Edison, who shipped in a prefab abode and anchored it with the region's first swimming pool. As the inventor of the electric lightbulb and the phonograph, Edison's presence sent a signal to other notables, including automobile inventor Henry Ford and industrialist Harvey Samuel Firestone.

The populations of major settlements from bygone days bear little resemblance to the Florida "hot spots" of today. A map published in 1894 lists "principal towns" and the number of souls residing therein: Key West, 18,080; Jacksonville, 17,201; Pensacola, 11,750; Tampa, 5,582; St. Augustine, 4,742; Palatka, 3,039; and Tallahassee, 2,934. Ocala, Orlando, Fernandina, Gainesville, Apalachicola, Lake City, and Sanford had fewer folks—about 2,000 each. (Notice the list does not mention Miami, Fort Lauderdale, West Palm Beach, or Fort Myers.)

LIMITED OUTLOOK, BLINDERS OPTIONAL

The Seminole Limited was a streamlined passenger train that operated from 1909 to 1969 between Jacksonville and Chicago (the train provided the first year-round service between the two cities). The collaborative line had three operators: the Illinois Central Railroad, the Central of Georgia Railway, and the Atlantic Coast Line Railroad. The Limited was called "the pride of the Illinois Central."

As Peter Gallagher wrote in the *Seminole Tribune* in 2014, it is likely that blues guitarist Tampa Red wrote "Seminole Blues" with the train in mind. The Georgia native was born in 1904, and rode the Limited to find work in the blues hub of Chicago.

The lyrics include the lines, "My baby's gone, she won't be back no more / She left this mornin', she caught that Seminole." Gallagher said the train image is reinforced with the final words to the song: "I'm goin' to find my baby / If I have to ride the blind." (Songwriter Ronny Elliott of Tampa supplied the scoop on what Red meant: "Blinds" are areas of a train between, inside, or under the cars "where a person can sneak a ride and not be seen.")

Another ride on the Seminole Limited gets some ink in *Depot Days*, as writer H. A. "Al" Stimson described a trip from Chicago to Jacksonville. Stimson hailed from De Smet, South Dakota, where his father, Henry Y. Stimson, became the town's depot agent in 1912. His family once lived in the house which author Laura Ingalls Wilder wrote about in *Little Town on the Prairie*.

Once Stimson's "passenger" arrived in Jacksonville, he was in the capable hands of Flagler's FEC Railway down the east coast: "Uncle Henry had a going business and no competition. Train was built for service and delivered the goods."

Stimson described the "Flagler-yellow" depots, coaches, and boxcars as "really just bleached-out orange." The traveler saw grapefruit being loaded in White City south of Fort Pierce, then stayed overnight in West Palm Beach. Proceeding to Delray Beach, he noticed "signs of life, tomato, bean, pepper growers, clearing and plowing." Staying in one hotel, he used the floor rugs to keep warm, as there was "no more provision for cold weather than an African kraal."

The "jug train" from West Palm Beach to Delray Beach carried shoppers. The "hotel train" was a high-class commissary toting groceries to Flagler's hotels. The all-Pullman-car Palm Beach Limited was "the fancy train of the new time-card," as it only stopped at the main resort cities.

As noted in an earlier chapter, the Florida Special was equipped with the first electric lights and the first vestibule sleepers. The train was the setting for a 1936 eponymous movie which sort of bombed at the box office but gave moviegoers a good idea of then-current train travel. The screenplay pits comic pratfalls against a goofy gangster plot—in which five bad guys hijack the Florida Special to steal a fortune in jewels.

The movie poster set the tone: "All aboard for danger . . . excitement . . . romance . . . on the crack train of the Florida run!"

CHAPTER 11

Overseas Marvel

Flagler Tames the Florida Keys

IN 1910 WRITER EDWIN LEFÈVRE WAS IN A CONVERSATION WITH Henry M. Flagler, one of many interviews that were the basis for a magazine article. On that day Flagler made a telling remark: "If ever the Lord made a man who hated traveling, I am that man!"

About two years later, however, Flagler took one for the team when he boarded Car 91 in West Palm Beach and rode his Florida East Coast Railway to Miami to relax for several hours. He had turned eighty-two just three weeks earlier and wanted to be fresh for the final leg of a momentous journey.

At 10:43 a.m. on January 22, 1912, an FEC engine pulling the inaugural train stopped in downtown Key West. Flagler and his wife, Mary Lily, stepped out of his private railcar, nicknamed "Rambler." Thousands cheered and the city launched a three-day celebration. During rounds of speeches, Flagler said: "We have been trying to anchor Key West to the mainland, and anchor it we have done."

Another train, Pullman car in tow, had arrived with dignitaries, politicians, military brass, assorted bigwigs, and other guests invited for a unique hoopla: the completion of the Flagler System's Key West Extension. Assistant US Secretary of War Robert Shaw Oliver was there representing President William Taft. Mexico sent a representative, as did countries in Europe and Central and South America.

Portrait of Jefferson Beale Browne when he was Chief Justice of the Florida Supreme Court. During his career, Browne also was a lighthouse keeper, county surveyor, postmaster, city attorney, president of the Florida Senate, US Customs Collector at the port of Key West, and chairman of the Florida Railroad Commission in 1903. Well before Henry Flagler announced his intention to build the Key West Extension, he told Browne it was a necessity. STATE ARCHIVES OF FLORIDA, FLORIDA MEMORY.

W. R. Hawkins, an employee of the railroad company, wrote in his diary: "Uncle Henry's train ran through to Key West this morning . . . He was the first passenger to cross the bridge."

Had Flagler's career been a picture frame, the fourth corner had just met its miter.

It is tempting to imagine him lost in thought that day as he rode his "own iron" more than 125 miles over dots of islands, vast stretches of teal and aqua water, and brilliant bridges. Surrounded by so much saltwater in the Florida Keys, was there a tiny bit of irony—of being reminded that he lost his shirt in that salt-mining company so long ago? It may be akin to the ghost of an old score to settle—not unlike Clark Gable's character in *Run Silent, Run Deep*.

Jefferson Beale Browne, a native of Key West well acquainted with Flagler, wrote a book in 1912, hinting that, on that point, the two were on the same page: "Hope springs up in me at the expectation of the great prosperity that is to come to Key West with the hundreds of thousands of bushels of salt, that will be made at the new salt works, which will require five hundred vessels a year to transport," Browne wrote in *Key West: The Old and the New*. (During a hopscotch career, Browne was a lighthouse keeper, county surveyor, postmaster, city attorney, president of the Florida Senate, US Customs collector at the port of Key West, chief justice of the Florida Supreme Court, and chairman of the Florida Railroad Commission in 1903.)

As early as the grand opening of Henry Plant's Tampa Bay Hotel in 1891, while other VIPs were taking in the Moorish opulence, Browne and Flagler spoke about the need for a railroad to Key West. In 1894 Flagler told Browne that the logical end of all railroad building in Florida was to reach a deepwater port in proximity to Central and South America.

Building the Overseas Railroad was an official goal, if not yet announced, a year earlier. At a meeting of the FEC board of directors on April 19, 1893, Flagler resolved to extend the railway from Key Biscayne across the Florida Keys to Key West.

That was Flagler's first written intention to build until he ran out of land. According to Keys historian Jerry Wilkinson, that never changed: "The dye was set for the remainder of Florida's east coast, completing each stepping stone per this resolution . . . This is often overlooked, justifying each stepping stone southward as incentives presented themselves."

Concurrent with that corporate communiqué, the Florida Legislature approved an act increasing land grants to boost transportation development. Any company building south of Daytona Beach would get 8,000 acres per mile of built track. As mentioned in Chapter 9, that's when Flagler formed the Jacksonville, St. Augustine & Indian River Railway Company and appointed Joseph Parrott and James Ingraham as directors.

Parrott had assured Flagler the Key West Extension was possible: "Yes, it can be done." However, when the Reverend George M. Ward heard about his friend's commitment to the project, he said, "Flagler, you need a guardian."

Ward said in an interview once that he asked Flagler to explain his purpose in Florida: "What are you trying to do here? Is this investment, or philanthropy, or are you anxious to pose as a state builder?" Ever reflective, Flagler said the Palm Beach pastor's question was pertinent enough: "I believe this state is the easiest place for many men to gain a living. I do not believe anyone else will develop it if I do not."

Flagler ran on fumes of energy and purpose. He was building the Key West Extension with a railroad company, not an engineering company, and the crews would deal with changing water depths, sandy soil, custom-designed bridges, and the vicissitudes in currents of two major bodies of water. In addition, the company needed to house and feed thousands of workers in different locations.

Author Dan Gallagher compared the Extension to the Panama Canal as daunting and stupendous feats of engineering, although the canal took twenty-three years and cost tens of thousands of lives: "Much of this story is about moving earth and rock from one location to another," Gallagher said, estimating 18 million cubic yards of earth, rock, sand, and marl—a limestone mud peppered with the detritus of dead sea life. He cited the Extension as a triumph of logistics, making sure the right materials were at the right location when needed, in a remote environment with many moving parts (and other parts which quite literally didn't stay put).

More about Mooring

In May 1894 state engineer H. S Duval delivered a report to the Florida Trustees of the Internal Improvement Fund, detailing his inspection of the Jacksonville, St. Augustine & Indian River Railway.

At the end of his report, he shared his view of what Flagler might do with intel on the coastal terrain: "No doubt when the great capitalist learns that the Florida Keys are islands enclosed in a harbor made by a natural submerged breakwater called the Florida Reefs, and are therefore not really exposed to the violence of the outer seas and may be connected with ordinary creosoted trestle work as now exists across Escambia Bay, he may rise in a culminating spirit of enterprise and moor Key West to the mainland." (The Keys actually were vulnerable to storm surge, as everyone connected with the Extension would learn.)

By the time the FEC Railway completed its extension to Miami in 1896, Browne was the collector of customs for the Port of Key West. In an article for *National Geographic,* he wrote a shakedown-cruise account of the route the railroad would follow to Key West.

To thrust this project into gear, Flagler built a 12-mile extension southwest from Miami in 1903, to stake out the Cutler Ridge agricultural region for its freight business. The next leg was 16 miles of tracks farther southwest to Homestead—which Les Standiford called, "the last reliably dry land on the continent."

Flagler had a choice to make about which route to Key West would turn an impossible mission into a doable, double-dog dare: No. 1, proceed south from Homestead to the point where land meets water, then build roadbed and tracks on spits of land and dredge, fill, and erect bridges where needed, until his 125-mile Extension reached the southernmost tip of the United States. No. 2, build tracks westward from Homestead to Cape Sable, then build piers and a bridge over 40 miles of Florida Bay to a point in the Lower Keys.

Flagler needed more information, so he directed civil engineer William J. Krome to take a survey party and bring back a report on the feasibility of the alternate route. Krome's take on the situation was a double-wide of no: "There is not enough fill on the face of the earth to build a railroad across the Everglades." (The terrain of voluminous muck, dense palmetto,

Portrait of William J. Krome. At the outset of construction on the Key West Extension, Flagler System, better known as the Florida East Coast Overseas Railway, Krome was assistant engineer. Five years into the project, while Krome was on a leave of absence, chief engineer Joseph C. Meredith died unexpectedly of complications from diabetes. Henry Flagler asked Krome to take over and finish the project. STATE ARCHIVES OF FLORIDA, FLORIDA MEMORY.

and razor-sharp leaves of saw grass was not unfamiliar to James Ingraham. After examining a Tampa-to-Miami route for Henry Plant more than a decade earlier, Ingraham had given the Everglades a colorful if unconventional measuring stick: "You could swing a pint can about on the end of a string and come up with a quart of mosquitoes."

Thus, the die was cast for an east coast extension. And while Key West represented climbing the highest peak, it wasn't the only focal point on Flagler's horizon.

He had visited Cuba several times, and owned shares in several Cuban railroads. Flagler knew railroad magnate Sir William Cornelius Van Horne, who had plans to introduce freight lines for the pineapple, sugar, and tobacco trade in Cuba. A native of Illinois, president and later chairman of the Canadian Pacific Railway, Van Horne had overseen the construction of Canada's first transcontinental railroad.

Van Horne also was a principal of the Whitney syndicate, which created the Cuba Railroad Company to build the country's first transnational line to link Havana with the eastern provinces of Camaguey and Oriente, and the city of Santiago de Cuba, in 1901. (That company was incorporated in Trenton, New Jersey, in 1900 with a capitalization of $8 million.)

With Spain no longer in the picture, commerce between Key West and Havana was open and promising. Flagler could see the potential for Key West being the foremost port on the Atlantic coast. He had only to look at the giant ferries carrying solid trains across the Great Lakes to realize that his ferries could carry his locomotives and cars from Key West to Havana.

Another gold ring dangled on the periphery of Flagler's thoughts, and that was "the big ditch" between the Atlantic and the Pacific Oceans. After decades of political squabbling and engineering setbacks on-site, the US Senate ratified the Hay-Bunau-Varilla Treaty in 1903, confirming the United States would build the Panama Canal and that it would pay Panama sovereignty rights and pay tens of millions to the French to concede their interests.

With plans for the Panama Canal advancing again, Flagler could foresee that it would further elevate the profile and importance of Key West—where a deepwater port would be 300 miles closer to the canal than Port Tampa. It was time to proceed. He wasn't alone in seeing a connection between the two feats. Former secretary of war Elihu Root said, "I regard [the Key West Extension] as second only to the Panama Canal in its political and commercial importance to the United States."

Several historians and authors have cited in exhaustive detail the steps involved in designing and building the Key West Extension. An equal or greater number of writers have delved beyond what Flagler built, more intrigued with the why of it all. Why not enjoy his legion of laurels from a humble upbringing, and the well-earned leisure of advancing age with his wife, Mary Lily? Why keep building?

"That Flagler chose the latter, to go to Key West, says more about the man than anything undertaken in his lifetime," Standiford said in *Last Train to Paradise*.

Lagging behind corporate ways and means, the Florida Legislature authorized the extension in April 1905, granting a 200-foot right-of-way, plus a railhead in Key West and a dozen piers, each 800 feet long and 200 feet wide, for ships. The first estimated completion date was January 1, 1908.

Flagler advertised for construction bids and was nonplussed to receive just one, and an unappealing one at that. The cost-plus proposal would mean reimbursed expenses for the contractor, plus a guaranteed amount of profit. Given Flagler's extensive history with negotiating, a no-risk-plus-profit deal was anathema.

His in-house team could handily build roadbeds and put down tracks, but this project would require the expertise of a master bridge builder (as one of those spans would be 7 miles long). Putting out feelers, Parrott located one Joseph Carroll Meredith.

AN OVER-ARCHING CANDIDATE

A native of Rushville, Indiana, with credentials from Iowa State College and the Stevens Institute of Technology, Joseph C. Meredith was a resourceful, highly respected engineer who had worked the world over and was just wrapping up a harbor pier project in Tampico for the Mexican government.

Parrott and Flagler especially liked the fact that Meredith was an expert in the emerging field of steel-reinforced concrete, as some of the Extension bridges would involve poured columns and arches. (Flagler may have seen himself as having less hubris than those who defied gravity and the elements to build the Roman viaducts.)

Browne waxed at length on this aspect in his 1912 book: "The light that showed [Flagler] the way to Key West dazzled the brightest and appalled the strongest intellects. Who can describe the construction? Why attempt it?" He cited the Roman passages at Segovia, Porta Maggiore, Aqua Claudia, and the Port du Gard as "man's first message in arch building." Browne said the design of Flagler's railroad enlarged, extended, and amplified that message, "and is man's last word on that marvelous style of construction."

While the ancient Romans could live with a string of arches, Flagler needed several dozen. "Where *they* crossed streams, *he* bridged arms of the ocean . . . Obstacles that barred their way they gripped with iron claws, and made them do the work of the master; [Flagler's] obstacles—the bog, the quagmire, the quicksand—evaded, eluded, shifted, swallowed up tons of concrete with their capacious maws and ravenous stomachs."

When the press called the project "Flagler's Folly," the titan gave as good as he got: "It is perfectly simple. All you have to do is build one concrete arch, and then another, and pretty soon you will find yourself in Key West."

Meredith's genius would not go unnoticed, as the national press, and especially the engineering world, took note of this undertaking. An article in *Everybody's Magazine* in 1908 suggested that he mastered every aspect of hurricane and storm weather events in the Keys, and elevated his thinking wholly beyond the stage of experiment: "He made the plans for his mighty viaducts . . . and the foremost engineering authorities in this country looked them over and found them flawless."

The higher-ups in the railroad company called Flagler "the Chief." Now, Meredith was chief engineer, and the not-yet-thirty-year-old William J. Krome became assistant construction engineer. Between 1904 and 1912 they and Parrott employed a workforce of thousands at a time. Exhaustion, heatstroke, and swarms of mosquitoes put in overtime as well.

To combat the insect problem, the men could wear a "head net" fashioned from canvas over the crown of a broad-brimmed hat. Standiford painted a vivid picture of the effective but ungainly gear: Sheets of copper-mesh wire formed netting to drape over the canvas down to the shoulders; with cheesecloth taped to the rim of the mesh, the man tucked the caboodle inside a jacket: "Imagine trudging through 90-degree heat and equal humidity, swinging a 20-pound sledge or manhandling a precarious wheelbarrow full of sloshing marl, with such a getup around one's head."

Equipment for the project was a head-spinning roster as well, with orders for sailing vessels, naphtha launches, and rock-crushing machinery. Among the staples on the list: three tugboats, eight Mississippi River stern-wheelers, two-dozen-plus motor launches, a dozen dredges, eight concrete-mixing machines for barges, two land-based concrete mixers, nine pile-drivers for underwater supports and two more to drive piles for tracks, ten power shovels, a specialized catamaran for building forms for concrete piers, two large steel barges, smaller barges, several locomotive cranes, a floating machine shop, more than a dozen houseboats, and two oceangoing steamships. With work going on six days a week, generators produced electricity for anything afloat.

The distance from the Homestead terminus to Jewfish Creek was 22 miles. There the railroad would cross to Key Largo. FEC officials in St. Augustine called it "a web-footed proposition from start to finish."

In 1925 W. M. Walker wrote a magazine article, "The Greatest Men of Florida," for *Suniland*. In the piece, he talks about the moment when *push* tapped *shove* on the shoulder: "It was here that the road left the mainland and undaunted engineers gazed out across open water that they had promised to bridge for 'The Chief.'"

It's reasonable for a layperson to look at the route and imagine a linear time line from beginning to a terminus 128 miles distant. But Flagler's people did not approach the job as a solitary army proceeding southwest from Homestead—they worked from both ends toward the middle. Based on Krome's surveys, advance teams worked throughout the Keys from the get-go, "taking the beach" as it were, to clear and prepare sites for the phases to come that would require special forces.

By spring 1905 construction crews were dispersed among the islands, starting a functional seaport at Knight's Key, scouting for land for a rail terminal in Key West, and setting up living quarters for laborers and supply lines for provisions.

Under the circumstances, the project was no "field day" for surveyors. The engineers had selected forty-one keys, or islands, for the route. Given the number of gaps between these slivers of sand, they built towers to give them reliable sighting for their instruments. As reported in a magazine in 1908, the distances were so great, "the curvature of the earth hid the rod man on the key from the man with the transit."

The engineers devised a type of shallow-bottom dredge and mounted a steam shovel on the deck. Crews would clear the mangroves and brush to prepare for the dredges, which would send the shovels into limestone muck.

By April 1905 there were ten traveling dredges on duty in Florida City. The pilots of two of them drifted past Cross Key toward Jewfish Creek on the way to the northern end of Key Largo. Working parallel on each side of the soggy surface, the dredges emptied the muck into the middle for the first layer of roadbed. Barges brought in rock for the next layer, and workers laid tracks on the foundation. Where necessary and/or possible, they put in side tracks.

This tedious preparation was to be repeated over and over, until it was time to set up construction of a 100-foot drawbridge over the creek. As modern Floridians and tourists know, all distances in the Keys are indicated by mile marker numbers (local addresses are incidental), with smaller numbers as you go south. For perspective, Florida City is MM 127.5—meaning that many miles north of Key West. The location of that first bridge at Jewfish Creek was MM 107.2. Key Largo, the setting for the first depot of the Extension, was MM 106.

AN UNLIKELY LAKE

In between and veiled by mangroves was a bashful body of water that had escaped the attention of the sharpest surveyors for many decades. Hence, the name Lake Surprise. However, the lady of the lake whispered "fill" instead of "bridge" to the engineers, and that marked a new beginning.

Krome had assigned engineer W. P. Dusenbury to manage the project on Key Largo. He had the materials to put down tracks, but the bridge over Jewfish Creek was still under way when the mystery lake produced a bag of tricks. "Surprise" wasn't certain, and didn't know when she might be, what kind of passage was the best fit.

The lake was about a mile wide and 6 feet deep—"not enough water for swimming and too much for farming." Wilkinson noted the lake's whimsical nature as the menfolk studied how to provide a stable causeway: "When fill was dumped in, it sank and disappeared . . . It took months to construct a satisfactory fill that would support continuous trains across Lake Surprise."

In the process, Meredith weighed his options. Upon drilling, he had discovered the lake bottom was a blanket of indolent peat, way too weak to support conventional pilings. Les Standiford refers to an article by Franklin Wood in *Moody's Magazine*, in which Meredith posed a solution: dredge tons of marl from the nearby sea-bottom and deposit it into the lake, forming an embankment (the fifteen-month process was costly, but it worked).

In late October 1906 the *Florida Times-Union* reported that FEC Engine No. 10 had arrived from St. Augustine and was hauling several box- and flatcars to Homestead, then heading south on the 17 miles of new track to the edge of Jewfish Creek. The rolling stock was loaded onto barges and taken to Key Largo, where 27 miles of track had been completed. About three months later, the newspaper's update was cause to cheer over completion of the bridge over the creek and tracks over Lake Surprise: "The first train crossed from the mainland to Key Largo . . . with Henry Flagler and a party of friends aboard."

Word was getting around, according to a *Key West Citizen* report in May 1907: "When the F.E.C. Railway was first completed to Homestead and later to Jewfish Creek, an occasional passenger train was sent down to accommodate sightseers. Later, it was found necessary to inaugurate a daily passenger train to accommodate the hundreds of settlers arriving in that district."

Month by month, key to key, the chain of roadbed and tracks resembled a 13-foot-wide zipper up and down the terrain. For staging the work, Flagler had bought and leased as much heavy marine equipment as the Atlantic Seaboard could spare. The rest had to be built. As for land, there was the acreage from land grants; he bought and leased the rest (and manufactured the turf he needed in Key West).

In fall 1905 the *Miami Metropolis* informed readers that the steamer *Biscayne* had towed two recently completed double-decked houseboats to the Keys. They were to be living quarters at work camps at Planter on Key Largo and on Matecumbe Key. Crews had built a sizable work camp and equipment staging area on Long Key almost from the beginning, as it would involve a major bridge. The setting on Long Key was so congenial that Flagler built some screened frame cottages for management (while ovens at the bakery popped out 1,000 loaves of bread a day).

Writer Joy Williams set the scene for the ephemeral aspect of that vista and so many others throughout the Keys: "Water loves light. The light changes. Dawn and sunset break. Thunderclouds mass. The water is black, emerald, azure, sheer, and the vault of sky becomes the vault of water."

While the endgame of all that eye candy was Key West, the deepwater dock built off of Knight's Key was a pivotal point, involving a 4,000-foot wooden trestle, warehouses, and space for two tracks. Through 1911, it was the southern terminus of the Extension.

Vintage postcard of the Knight's Key Pier construction. LIBRARY OF CONGRESS

BOOZE ON THE LOOSE

Those double-decker barges doubled as portable work bases and living quarters for the crews. Field kitchens served good food, fresh water and pure ice but, per Flagler's edict, "no liquor in or near the camps." The usual sources for booze in Key West balked at the risk of breaking that rule (and perhaps taking a bullet for delivering sneaky-pete hooch).

But what about a short boat ride away from camp? Where there was a will to make extra money, there was a way for certain settlers in the Keys to smuggle liquor to bored and weary workers. Standiford wrote about an enterprising boatman who enlisted some cohorts to retool an old freighter for their new sideline. Thus converted, the vessel was "a floating saloon-cum-bordello to which a desperate man might catch a ride via skiff for an evening's entertainment."

Managers of the camps had strict orders from Parrott et al. in St. Augustine to dissuade their men from slipping off the quarters boats for such excursions, but some looked the other way because desertion among the ranks was a routine worry. Meredith got a note from one of his supervisors noting the "great difficulty in the prevention of the liquor traffic." The worst case to date owed to "the unfaithfulness of our own steward in the matter."

In a letter to Parrott, the teetotaler Flagler seemed more intrigued with how the men drank than the fact that they broke company rules: "There was this noticeable difference . . . the Negroes were regular, but moderate drinkers while the whites who drank would get on a spree of several days before returning to work."

Reliable labor for the project was an ongoing headache. Management recruited a melting pot of workers: black and white Americans, Swedes and Norwegians, Cayman Islanders, Italian steelworkers, and deepwater divers from Greece to work on the foundations. The pool broadened by 1907, when laborers from Cuba signed on in considerable numbers. The men received wages of $1.25 a day plus food, lodging, and medical care. Despite the cultural potpourri, or perhaps because of it, the men worked together pretty well, because a united front was stronger against weather, injury, and isolation.

Freshwater and plenty of it was a priority, with more than four million gallons consumed each month. The only existing source was rainwater in cisterns. Flagler's solution was to pump freshwater from the Everglades, store it in holding tanks near Homestead, and send it south every day in cypress water tanks aboard trains.

Trained medical staff monitored working conditions. If someone got sick, they traveled on a ship for care in Miami or Key West, Standiford said: "Most problems were dehydration, flu, snake bites, fractures or lacerations," plus boredom from the intense isolation. To address the latter, Flagler built accommodations for visitors—a kind of boarding camp for workers' families.

Nonetheless, the press embroidered criticisms that characterized Flagler as a heartless master of slave labor. In New York, the government sued the FEC in 1908, alleging slave-labor practices. Flagler offered forthright answers to the complaints: "I gave orders . . . that no pains or expense should be spared to house and feed the men in the best possible manner," including field hospitals with medical personnel. He referred critics to the opinions of an associate, Major General J. R. Brooke, who said he had never seen any American troop installations "where the men were as well quartered and fed."

A Chicago newspaper reported in November 1908 that the government's labor case had been quashed. Five days later, Flagler said in a note to Elihu Root that he would resume work on the Extension.

From the outset, crews were scrambling to put down as much track as possible. That enabled Parrott to send the railroad's rolling stock to expedite construction. Construction locomotives would leave Homestead pulling cars loaded with material and deliver them to a designated site (one of eighty camps operating at any given time).

In areas without tracks, and where the water was too shallow for ships, supplies came ashore on scores of barges. Hence the need for the Knight's Key Dock in a channel about 25 feet deep. Wilkinson called construction of the dock one of the largest supplementary parts of a larger project ever built (meaning it was critical up to a point and then dispensable). Between 1906 and 1908 it was a relay station to deliver rock and other material from deep-draught ships to shallow-draught barges to construction sites on land. Afterward, until the winter of 1912, it served as a transfer point between the FEC Railway and ocean liners.

Chief Engineer Meredith worked from a base at Knight's Key, moving from point to point by water, Edwin Lefèvre said: "In and out of the construction camps he flitted in his launch, his binoculars to his eyes, like a general observing the movements of his troops on the battlefield."

BRIDGING AN OCEAN

The Overseas Railroad would involve three extraordinary bridges: the Long Key Viaduct (MM 64), the Seven-Mile Bridge below Knight's Key (MM 47), and the Bahia Honda Bridge (MM 37). Construction on those could not proceed until the company could assemble some outsize floating concrete mixers. With about 16 miles of track already in place on Grassy Key below Long Key, the first mega-mixer left Miami on the steamer *Columbia* in June 1906, a sign that bridge work was imminent.

Initial work got under way on the Long Key Viaduct—the second-longest bridge of the Extension. It would be a structure of solid-concrete

Artwork shows a Florida East Coast Railway express train crossing the iconic Long Key Viaduct. Located at Mile Marker 64 in the Florida Keys, the chain of solid concrete Roman arches stretches for 2.7 miles. STATE ARCHIVES OF FLORIDA, FLORIDA MEMORY.

Roman arches stretching for 2.7 miles. In water depths varying from 10 to 30 feet, crews would erect 180 arches (50-foot spans) and 42 arches (35-foot spans). About 800 workers participated in building the Extension's signature feature.

In the era of no communication system in the Keys, and therefore no way to send weather alerts, forecasting was rather unsophisticated. In every engineer's pocket was a small tube of water with weeds in the bottom. If the weeds wiggled upward, it meant that air pressure was dropping and a storm was on the way.

The weather asserted the upper hand while the Long Key Viaduct was under construction. In October 1906 a hurricane hit Barbados, then Central America, and finally Long Key. The killer storm claimed 240 lives, including 135 laborers working for the FEC, and wiped out the bridge construction at Long Key. Meredith braced himself and his team to handle the losses: "No man has any business connected with this work who can't stand grief."

Of the workers lost, 104 of them were on Houseboat No. 4, like the vessels mentioned in the *Metropolis* article. A steamer rescued dozens of workers; the ocean swept away the others in a toss of barges and flatboats. W. M. Walker described Flagler's reaction to the loss of life among men doing his bidding: "Orders went out to spare no expense in rescuing the men, and money was cabled all over the world in order that workmen picked up by passing ships might return to this country."

Krome, who was in Key West at the time, wrote his father about the tragedy at the Long Key plant. He said the men had been housed in these big Mississippi River tie barges "with houses on top of them. The barges themselves rode about 12 feet out of the water and the hulls were used as kitchens and dining-rooms."

Houseboat No. 3 also broke away from its mooring, but it washed ashore. No. 4 floated toward the Gulf Stream. The engineer Dusenbury took a battering but was not seriously injured. He told Krome the barge drifted southeasterly across Hawk's Channel to the outer reef: "The dragging anchors caught for a moment or two but soon gave way, letting the boat drift out into the ocean. She soon began to go to pieces."

An article in the *Miami Herald* reported the account of a survivor, William H. Sanders, chief engineer of a tugboat who lived aboard the No. 4 quarters boat. When he was rescued, he said a lot of the men had raided the first-aid kit, consumed all the laudanum, and "lay down to die."

When work resumed on the Long Key Viaduct after the 1906 hurricane, Parrott had chartered every steamship available. A flotilla of barges and workhorse boats were involved, according to details of the work compiled by FEC division engineer William Mayo Venable for *Engineering Record*.

Only Designer Cement Would Do

To create the arches for the viaduct, the engineers chose Portland cement from England and Germany for all the underwater concrete work. By the numbers, the bean-counters' ledgers showed 286,000 barrels of cement, 177,000 cubic yards of crushed rock, 106,000 cubic yards of sand, 612,000 feet of pilings, 5,000 tons of steel rods, and 2.5 million feet of timbers.

Imagine rectangular wooden cofferdams (forms), pilings, and coral rock formations; cement, sand, and gravel; low tide, high tide, shifting currents, and heavy machinery dancing on a swaying barge. Then imagine needing 33 forms for each of the 180 arches.

Venable described the stages: drive the pilings through sand and muck into bedrock; set a wooden cofferdam on the sea bottom and place submerged sandbags to hold the base in place, leaving the top out of the water; pour a layer of underwater cement into the bottom of the form to surround the pilings and form a watertight seal up to 5 feet thick; allow the concrete to set for a few days, then place another form within a form to hold a lattice of reinforced steel woven around the pilings; fill the whole with concrete to form a pedestal above the water, with the rods waiting for the next level; and let the concrete harden for a week. Then, in the final step, a barge would deliver another form in the shape of an arch and it would be topped with layers of concrete. Standiford said the result was one gracefully curved 55-foot link "in what would eventually become a breathtaking chain of arches across the sea."

Meredith employed a conservative strategy to avoid placing stress on the bookend piers which might occur when drying concrete spans contracted. Workers would leapfrog their way, connecting two piers and leaving an opening. Once all the concrete was cured, the crews filled in the gaps.

When Meredith consulted with "the Chief" about the engineering challenges of the design, he told Lefèvre that Flagler opted for a viaduct because he abhors anything makeshift: "Permanence appeals to him more strongly than to any other man I ever met. He has often told me that he does not wish to keep on spending money for maintenance [of what is] . . . but to build for all time. [Others] make improvements gradually, as the profit comes in. But that is not Mr. Flagler's way."

The ordeal of the 1906 hurricane had caused a year's delay while the railroad replaced machinery, repaired equipment that wasn't on the bottom of the ocean, and rebuilt 17 miles of washed-out tracks on Key Largo. The FEC also gave up houseboat facilities and built the workers barracks on land up and down the Keys. Quarters boats were limited to bridge construction crews and evacuated for hurricanes.

Walker's article reinforces the stress level among the crews who might have felt stranded between Flagler's resolve and their own physical limitations: "Indian Key was reached at last and the work proceeded steadily, the pressure of anxiety growing stronger daily as the project was farther and farther away from its beginning. It was too late to turn back now."

In addition to the commotion at Long Key and the lower end of Upper Matecumbe Key, trains were running to Tavernier and Snake Creek, and Lower Matecumbe was a central supply depot. Workers had built a half-mile trestle at Tavernier Creek to reach Plantation Key (MM 90). The job involved clearing 5 miles of mangroves and palmetto scrub, dynamiting in the shallows to bring up limestone, grading the roadbed, putting down rails and ties, and filling in with riprap.

NAVY AIMS A SQUIRT GUN

While the legislature had approved a railhead in Key West, the location hadn't been determined at the outset. Flagler had bought a few parcels there, mere smidgeons, but there was nothing suitable for a rail and shipping terminal with adequate space for docks.

Early on, Parrott had gone to Key West to scout for terminal sites in an already overbuilt city surrounded by water. A thriving port since the 1820s, and a reliable haven for pirates since the 17th century, Key West for the FEC's purposes was starting to resemble a soggy cul-de-sac.

Parrott's exchange with "the Chief" was pithy:

Parrott: "There is no more dry land in Key West."

Flagler: "Then make some."

Parrott hired Howard Trumbo of Trumbo American Dredging Company to enlarge the footprint of Key West by 174 acres. The engineer created a breakwater and foundation, extending the bulkhead in a broad arc above the northwest corner of the island. He dredged thousands of cubic yards of marl from the flats to fill in the parcel, and prepared the site for a 1,700-foot-long pier that would be 134 feet wide. This would allow trains to stop alongside a ship at "Trumbo Point."

However, in midsummer 1907, the US Navy threw up a roadblock with sticky consequences for the Extension. The FEC received instructions from the War Department to shut down dredging for the rail terminal at Key West. The government's stated rationale was the area's strategic military presence.

The FEC put a halt to construction in Key West in fall 1907 and scaled back the project's workforce. During 1908 work in the Lower Keys was quiet. Crews who had worked there transferred north to expedite completion of the Knight's Key Dock. The company shut down its offices and put its floating construction equipment into a mothball fleet on the Miami River. Cagey, effective, and guaranteed to frustrate the navy's stalemate.

Parrott was equal to the standoff, and asserted a droll comment which appears in Standiford's chapter on the topic: "If the time ever came when the Navy needed its mud," the government had Parrott's word, "it would be returned from whence it came."

Once the navy and the politicians got their skivvies out of a twist, it was time to resume construction at Key West and other phases.

A newspaper reported in January 1908 that the first engine and cars passed over the Long Key Viaduct and proceeded to within a short distance of Knight's Key, the terminal of the railroad at that time. Train service between Miami and Knight's Key began on February 4, 1908, with two trains leaving Miami in the morning and returning from Knight's Key the next day. That meant the FEC was now complete for 477 miles south of Jacksonville.

Rewind to completion of the Long Key Viaduct, which became the FEC's alter ego. Marketing minions used photos of the striking arches to milk public interest in the Extension. (Eventually a train on the bridge became the corporate logo.)

TESTED TO THE UTMOST

Catastrophe, however, was about to inject a major test of will. Any honcho can say no one on the team is indispensable, but the Overseas Railroad had relied for at least five years on the critical expertise and judgment of master bridge-builder J. C. Meredith. By spring 1909, he was losing a struggle with diabetes. He went into a coma and died on April 20 at age fifty-three, five years into the Extension project.

On the day of Meredith's funeral, the FEC shut down operations, "silencing every wheel" between 2 and 3:05 p.m., and suspended work for the rest of the afternoon.

Meredith's obituary in the *Miami Times-Union* referred to his scientific deductions as proof of his professional greatness. The engineer had been tasked with solving "knotty" engineering problems that were unique in the history of his field. The article cited the Long Key Viaduct as his entree to immortality: "Mr. Meredith was the first civil engineer ever called to measure the force of the tides and waves and construct a roadbed over miles of ocean waters . . . [His work] is a marvel to the thinking classes of this age."

Meredith had been a retiring, quiet sort with few intimate friends but well-admired and respected, and someone who had refused—just a year before his death—the offer to take a much-deserved vacation.

Standiford's insight into this deliberate man's character doubles as a timeless eulogy: "Meredith's devotion to his job and loyalty to Flagler were as steadfast as any military officer's. For him, and for most of the engineers and supervisors, the successful completion of this singular project meant everything, their sense of duty inextricable from their sense of self."

When Meredith had taken Lefèvre on a tour of the construction site at Knight's Key, he told him, "There isn't one of us who wouldn't give a year of his life to have Mr. Flagler see the work completed."

Haunting words from the man who, when he outlined his plans for the bridges and incomparable route, received no questions about what they would cost. Meredith said that Flagler issued just one caveat: "I want to see it done before I die. That is all he said." That the Extension itself became a bridge too far for Meredith is more than poignant.

At age seventy-nine, "the Chief" had a decision to make. Observers at the time wondered whether the loss of his chief engineer would be the death knell for the project—given that the greatest bridge challenge was still ahead. Assistant engineer Krome could take over, but would he?

At the time Meredith died, Krome was taking a break to tend to his groves near Homestead. Surrender was not in Flagler's vocabulary, and perhaps it didn't sit well with Krome either. When asked to take charge, he agreed. At the time, Krome was only thirty-two.

Another hurricane hit the Keys in October 1909, and a dozen railroad workers died with the sinking of the tugboat *Sybil*. The storm pitched a 19-ton steel girder span into the ocean, washed out 40 miles of track, and tossed boulders the size of a tin lizzie. Walker's purple prose aptly set the scene: "Nature, sensing man's victory imminent, gathered its forces for one last assault upon the encroachments of the conquistador . . . A terrific hurricane broke from the leaden clouds, whipping the waves into a frenzy, and driving the seabirds in mad flight headlong into the girders of the pitiful little strip of steel, wood and concrete that Man had dared to place in the roaring majesty of the sea."

Rail service had begun in the Upper Keys and Middle Keys in the winter of 1908. At the time of the 1909 hurricane, a train that left Miami stopped at Quarry Station on Windley Key to wait out the worst of the storm. The engineer, crew, and passengers were stranded there for three days due to washed-out tracks and roadbed between the stations at Jewfish Creek and Everglade. Fatigue was the worst of it for them, as the engine was hauling a Pullman car with plenty of provisions.

WAITING TO EXHALE

The combined losses of Meredith that spring and the workers in the fall storm gave Flagler more pause than anyone on the project except Parrott and Krome would ever realize. The project had reached Knight's Key and faced the most daunting challenge of all—the Flagler Viaduct. Days went by while the crews at construction camps between Homestead and Knight's Key dusted off and took stock of the damage.

Lots of machinery was on the bottom of the ocean, and segments of railroad track were in a tangled heap or washed aside. Most of the dredges, pile drivers, concrete mixers, and other gear were either dented or taking on water.

Flagler called Parrott to his office and told him to collect all the remaining equipment and "sell to the highest bidder." Gambling that "the Chief" might be having an off day, Parrott did something he'd never considered before—disobey his boss. He kept the directive to himself and ignored the order to collect and sell equipment strewn along the right-of-way. Work on the Extension proceeded.

Arrival of first train at Key West, Florida, over sea, Florida East Coast R. R., January 22, 1912. LIBRARY OF CONGRESS

According to W. M. Walker's account of 1925, Flagler called Parrott several days later, asking him to itemize the rolling stock, vessels, and machinery he had put up for sale. "Parrott told him the truth. Flagler received the news quietly, wavered a moment in what must have been horrible suspense for Parrott, and then smiled grimly. It was all right, the work would continue." Flagler's rationale was simple: "If we quit now we'd admit defeat and have no harbor. We'll go on."

Another hurricane hit in 1910, with no casualties among the railroad crew. The material loss was 17 miles of roadbed washed away. By now Flagler and Krome had become experts in the world according to the Florida Keys—especially railroad design, given the frequency of this organic, on-the-job crash course.

Hurricanes had taught them that topography created natural outlets for storm surges between the keys, and that placing filled embankments for roadbeds only served to bottle up that ferocious energy. In addition, Krome determined that most of their washouts occurred from receding tides. Standiford said that's why Flagler decided to build more bridges instead of less: "If something were to be suddenly dropped in the path of these surges, obviously, there would be hell to pay."

Once Krome explained that the rock and gravel got washed away, but not the bottom layer of limestone marl, Flagler suggested they reverse the process of roadbed building. The bottom layer would be rock; next, a topping of "slimy" marl from the sea bottom, which dried in the heat and hardened like a natural concrete seal. The sun-cured marl was "far more likely to resist stormy waves than the usual riprap thrown on top of the grade," Standiford wrote.

Flagler told Krome why he was willing to take more time and spend more money to finish the line: "What we need is permanent construction . . . I would rather be two years completing the line to Key West and have it be permanent, than to have a repetition of the disaster [the hurricane on October 11, 1909]."

Of course, storm surge wasn't the only hazard in a hurricane, as a foreman learned the hard way. Stranded on a remote key which others had evacuated, he climbed a tree and used his belt to fasten himself facing the trunk. Suddenly, his hands were burning, then his face and lips; within moments, his eyes were swollen shut. The foreman had the misfortune to not realize the tree he climbed was a highly poisonous manchineel (the word adapts from *manzanilla*, which is Spanish for "small apple," as the lovely, innocent-looking tree bears small round fruit. The Spanish word for the tree is *arbol de la muerte* (tree of death), hence the proverb: "He who sleeps under a manchineel sleeps forever."

Luckily, the foreman was rescued and spent several months recovering in a hospital.

Another lesson from hurricanes surfaced when Krome let Flagler know what he planned to do next time around: sink all the floating equipment, then raise it after the storm and repair it.

"SEVEN MILES OF HELL"

That is the catchy title of a chapter in Standiford's *Last Train to Paradise*, one which that fortunate foreman who strapped himself to the manchineel might appreciate if it had been written at the time he recovered.

The town of Marathon (so-named after workers began saying the Extension was "turning into a marathon") had become general headquarters and had rail service, as it was located at the beginning of the remaining construction to Key West. For the purpose of this chapter, the bridge from MM 47 south of Marathon to MM 40 will be called by its historic name, the Flagler Viaduct. In modern times, it became known as the Seven-Mile Bridge (the original was actually closer to 9 miles when counting the approaches). Nothing even remotely like this aspect of the Extension had ever been attempted. At the time it was completed, the bridge was the longest in the world.

Originally called the Flagler Viaduct and renamed the Seven-Mile Bridge, it seems intent on forcing the horizon to hold steady. The bridge stretches south from Marathon at Mile Marker 47 and was close to nine miles long when counting the approaches. Nothing like this aspect of the Key West Extension had ever been attempted. When completed, it was the longest bridge in the world. STATE ARCHIVES OF FLORIDA, FLORIDA MEMORY.

"The Flagler" was actually built in four sections south of Marathon. It would be almost four times as long as the daunting Long Key Viaduct. The four named spans were the Knight's Key, Pigeon Key, Moser Channel, and Pacet Channel bridges. At a total length of 35,815 feet, it consisted of 335 steel girder spans, 80 feet each; 9,000 feet of concrete-arch viaduct; and a 253-foot swing-truss span. Pigeon Key, a 5-acre patch, became a base camp, or "railroad village," for about 400 workers between 1908 and 1912. The outpost had a post office and a commissary.

The first task at hand was for surveyors to identify where the piers and arch supports would be placed—no easy task away from dry land. The surveyors couldn't properly use their transits and sighting instruments on a swaying vessel dodging waves, so management built platforms at 500-foot intervals across 7 miles of ocean, anchoring each one in bedrock. Those platforms could not impede other work, so they were a few hundred feet south and east of the route's actual line. A surveyor in an observation tower on Pigeon Key checked the alignments.

Standiford spelled out the high science of their communications: "When the surveyors had completed their calculations and triangulated

A Florida East Coast Railway train moves across the "Flagler Viaduct" in the Florida Keys. The bridge was later named the Seven-Mile Bridge, beginning south of Marathon as part of the Key West Extension, Flagler System. STATE ARCHIVES OF FLORIDA, FLORIDA MEMORY.

the necessary positions, they used flag and hand signals to direct workers in the precise placement of the initial piling for each of the 756 bridge supports."

After preliminary site preparation and staging, construction on "the bridge" began in early 1909—before the death of Meredith and before the 1909 hurricane. It is said that each concrete pier gargled and swallowed enough sand, gravel, cement, lumber, and steel to fill one five-masted schooner. As noted previously, the cement wasn't garden-variety (the type used underwater came from Alsace-Lorraine).

Dredges worked in places too shallow for barges, forming man-made islands from the deposits of sand and marl. Pilings pierced the limestone cap on coral reefs, although some had to reach through caves 50 feet down. Divers then set the outer cofferdams, poured the cement seals, pumped out waste, and placed wooden molds and anchored them to the base. Other workers descended into the molds to place the reinforcement rods. Bucket by bucket, derricks on barges transferred concrete, leaving the final stage of each pier above the water line. Concurrently work proceeded on the spandrel section at the south end, involving molds for arches and prefabricated forms on top of the piers, followed by steel support spans between the piers.

The roadbed for the Moser Channel Bridge was almost 30 feet above the ocean. Each girder weighed 19 tons and arrived on a barge pulled by a tug. On another barge, a 70-foot boom lifted the girder into place.

In the days before diesel, electrical, and hydraulic tools and equipment, the workers were all but shackled to steam-powered gear. As Standiford pointed out, they were massive, noisy, and notoriously undependable: "Imagine having to work on a yawing, heaving, pile-driving barge from dawn till dusk, never more than a few feet away from one of those roaring, foul-smelling behemoths."

The Knight's Key Trestle would reach Pigeon Key a mile offshore. The shorter second section, Pigeon Key Trestle, traversed shallow water to the west to connect with the main section, the Moser Channel Bridge and the swing-truss section for tall vessels. The final 2-mile section, the Pacet Channel Viaduct, went to Little Duck Key. The first three segments involved 546 concrete support piers capped with steel deck girders. The fourth bridge had 210 spandrel arches similar in style to the Long Key Viaduct. The route deliberately strayed a bit to avoid some of the deeper water between Knight's Key and Little Duck (a point spelled out in Browne's essay of 1894).

A fire in March 1910 was blamed on flying cinders from FEC Engine No. 11. An article in the *Key West Citizen* reported the location as Key Largo: "Everything being dry, the flames spread quickly and are now out of control. Practically all of the fruit trees and crops between Jewfish Creek and Newport are either burned or in danger of being destroyed." The article referred to a Captain Watkins of the schooner *New Venice,* who said the flames were moving north and south. Subsequently all locomotives in the Keys switched their fuel from coal to oil.

In June 1910 engines No. 10 and No. 12 rode by barge to Stock Island (MM 5) for construction use. In September they steamed across company tracks into Key West.

Work continued in various stages, and Flagler was pleased at the smoothness of train service at the Knight's Key Dock. Passengers on trains from New York and points south connected with one of his steamships headed for Havana—demonstrating the success of his vision in advance of the done deal. "Already the time between New York and the Cuban capital is reduced by half a day by the new route," *Cement and Engineering News* reported at the time, "a fact which has its readily apparent political and economic bearings."

Concurrently construction proceeded on the large terminal at Key West, with track and bridgework under way across Stock Island and northward, for the next difficult phase.

CLOSE BUT NO CIGAR

Although a 1-mile stretch sounds simple, the Bahia Honda Channel Bridge (MM 37) would be complicated and challenging. The Spanish had named it "Deep Bay" for a reason, with water depths from 20 to 35 feet.

Just as Krome had stepped in after the death of Meredith, Clarence Stanley Coe stepped into the shoes of assistant engineer responsible for overseeing bridge and trestle work. (Coe, a native of Indiana, had been the first city manager of Miami.) He and Krome followed a simple formula: 1 foot above water for every foot below water, so that the tracks would be above any storm surge.

The Bahia Honda project was the only camelback-style bridge on the Extension. It consisted of twenty-seven through-truss spans and nine deck plate girder spans, thirteen spans at 128 feet each, thirteen spans at 186 feet each, and one span 247 feet long.

Yet another hurricane hit in October 1910, making landfall in Cuba but lashing south Florida as well. It claimed two lives among the workers, and wracked the project with substantial damage. High winds lasted for thirty hours and struck the Lower Keys. The center span of the Bahia Honda Bridge took the biggest hit, causing the foundation to wobble.

That called for boatloads of material to rebuild it.

In addition to storms and occasional wildfires, the crews encountered another hazard, as some Keys settlers were disturbed by the railroad's presence. Standiford referred to one character, Montenegrin Nicholas Mackovtich, who may have been "disturbed" to begin with. He was a recluse who set booby-trapped spring guns all over his property.

Bahia Honda Bridge, c. May 27, 1926.
LIBRARY OF CONGRESS

When railroad workers weren't tiptoeing around the likes of Mackovtich, they might encounter eccentric or dangerous drifters, gunrunners recovering a shipment, or mercenaries aiming to join *la revolución de día* in Cuba.

In early 1911 Krome told the company that a year hence, in time for Flagler's eighty-second birthday on January 2, 1912, the Extension would be complete—that is, without any more hurricanes or major, unforeseen delays. The last span in the Knight's Key trestle settled in on January 21, just nineteen days late.

In terms of blood, sweat, tragedy, and treasure, the project had taken eight years. But Flagler's determination to see it through had shackled his thoughts for two decades. And that fact fascinated everyone else. Why, when he had achieved so much already, was he looking longingly at the Keys, those seagirt islets which Lefèvre draped in such artful angst in 1908: "Worthless, chaotic fragments of coral reef, limestone and mangrove swamp . . . aptly called the sweepings and debris the Creator hurled out to sea after He finished shaping Florida"?

Flagler was not the first dreamer or visionary to see the potential of an overseas rail line. The editor of the *Key West Gazette* suggested linking the city to the mainland by rail as early as 1831. While US Senator

Stephen Mallory of Key West was in Washington in the 1850s, he had promoted the advantages of a Key West railroad. In 1866 J. C. Bailey created a survey route that could be used to run a telegraph line to Key West for his client, the International Ocean Telegraph Company.

In 1880 the state of Georgia granted a charter to the Great Southern Railway Company to build a railroad to Key West, with plans for steamship service to Central and South America. In 1883 former Confederate general John B. Gordon began building from the Georgia side; before reaching Florida, Gordon changed his mind.

HENRY'S "IRON," HENRY'S MONEY

Henry Flagler has been quoted many times as saying that he would have been "quite a rich man" were it not for Florida. His railroad company bankrolled the vast majority of the Overseas Railroad until the project was about 45 miles short of completion. That point was the leg from Knight's Key to Key West.

In 1909 the *New York Times* published an account of Flagler's dealings with investment banker J. P. Morgan. Per their agreement, the FEC Railway issued $12 million in mortgage bonds, with Flagler taking $2 million of the total. Morgan's syndicate sold half of the rest, $5 million in mortgage bonds, to major players in the life insurance sector: New York Life, Equitable, Prudential, and Mutual Life. The trade-off was a first lien on all of FEC's existing and future rail lines.

Not that Flagler was broke . . . His stock dividends from Standard Oil were robust and regular—$150,000 a month during certain years. His concern, however, was that he wouldn't live long enough to finance the object of his obsession.

The words of George Perkins, a partner at Morgan, typified adulation in the financial world over Flagler's dedication to finishing what he started: "That any man could have the genius to see of what this wilderness of [fresh] waterless sand and underbrush was capable," Perkins wrote, "and then have the nerve to build a railroad here, is more marvelous than similar development anywhere else in the world."

POWER OF THE PRESS

While preoccupied with the Overseas Railroad, Flagler expanded his involvement in newspapers—through events stemming from the failed Fort Dallas National Bank. As someone who held a sizable note on the bank, Flagler was on the to-do list of Illinois lawyer Frank B. Shutts (federal authorities had sent him to Miami in 1909 to close out the bankruptcy case). According to Nixon Smiley in his book The *Miami Herald Front Pages,* Flagler was so impressed with Shutts that he persuaded the lawyer to move south and become counsel for the Flagler System.

The *Miami Morning News-Record* had suffered from a recession in 1907 and was deeply in debt—with Flagler the major creditor and Shutts the receiver. According to Smiley, Shutts tried to persuade Flagler to buy the publication so that he would have a voice to defend regular attacks in the afternoon *Metropolis.* "The wealthy man's control of Miami was deeply resented by the residents, and [the paper's] caustic criticism of the sometimes callous and uncompromising Flagler System proved much to their liking," Smiley said.

Shutts had used the wrong argument, as Flagler was impervious to criticism. He did, however, warm up to Shutts's suggestion: "If you want to publish the newspaper yourself, I might consider acquiring it."

Thus, the Flagler System took over the *News-Record* in 1910 and renamed it the *Miami Herald.*

WHY KEY WEST?

Stephen Mallory of Key West called it "America's Gibraltar," a strategic outpost with established industries in fishing, cigar-making, shipbuilding, salvage, and sponge-diving. In the 1890s Key West was the largest city in Florida, with a population of 17,000. It also was an important military installation, as a fueling station for US Navy vessels. Flagler's rail extension could do more than benefit Key West, and his own empire—it could grow the US economy as well.

The day after that engineer threw the switch to open the Flagler Viaduct, connecting the project's last segments, "Rambler" brought Mr. and Mrs. Flagler to the Key West celebration, along with Joseph Parrott and other FEC officials. Thus a vision voiced in 1892 had come full circle.

Surveyors on the Key West Extension had to deal with a lot of moving parts and some tough challenges. In addition to using precise instruments for their calculations, hand signals and flags were essential for communications. STATE ARCHIVES OF FLORIDA, FLORIDA MEMORY.

In August of that year, a newspaper in Havana published details about express train service from New York to Key West—using the Pennsylvania Railroad, the Atlantic Coast Line, and the Key West Extension, Flagler System—connecting with Flagler's Peninsular & Occidental Steamships to Cuba. The trip featured only two nights en route to Havana: "This train carries the latest design all-steel Pullman drawing room and Standard sleeping cars, is electrically lighted and equipped with electric fans throughout. There is no change of cars between Key West and the Pennsylvania Station in the very heart of New York City."

Reportedly Mr. Flagler told an associate that he believed his fortune was given to him to help his fellow men to help themselves, and that "he wanted to see if a plain American could succeed there where the Spanish, French and English had not."

Despite his disapproval of Flagler's choices for companionship after Mary died—and the attendant publicity over his extravagant gestures with wife No. 2 and wife No. 3—John D. Rockefeller continued to credit Flagler with his financial status. In 1902 Rockefeller wrote to his longtime associate: "You and I have been associated in business upwards of thirty-five years, and while there have been times when we have not agreed on questions of policy, I do not know that one unkind word has ever passed or unkind thought existed between us . . . I feel my pecuniary success is due to my association with you, if I have contributed anything to yours I am thankful."

Edwin Lefèvre had a precise grasp of Flagler's mental prowess as he approached his eightieth year: "It is characteristic of men who see clearly and think in straight lines that they have no illusions about their capabilities or those of others . . . What we call knowledge is not merely the collection but the proper classification of facts." He called Flagler a genius for detail, with a broad grasp of essentials, a vivid imagination, and a very highly developed creative impulse. Flagler spoke more plainly: "I never wanted to leave a thing unfinished."

W. M. Walker's account of the time referred to Flagler's longtime confidant, the Palm Beach pastor George Ward: "I confess I was worried when the Extension finally reached Key West . . . I wanted him to see his undertaking completed, but I dreaded the withdrawal of this spur to living. He loved to overcome obstacles but once they were overcome they lost their charm." Walker gave Ward's sentiments a spiritual context: "The Extension proved Flagler's final mammoth task, for men cannot go on forever growing greater and greater. Immortality would be no gift."

Many writers have guessed at what Flagler invested in the Extension, as well as all of his developments in Florida. The total is in the neighborhood of $50 million, or one-third of the state's valuation at that time. Of the total he spent, about two-fifths of it "anchored" Key West to the mainland. Flagler had told Henry Walters he expected the project to cost $7.5 million, which would be true if he had quadrupled that estimate. One guess is that it would cost him $625 million in 2006 dollars to build the Extension. Spoiler alert for younger generations who played hooky from history class: *The Railroad That Died at Sea* is not fiction. The Overseas Railroad existed from 1912 until the deadly 1935 Labor Day Hurricane, when portions of the FEC tracks were washed away. See the following chapter for that phase of the story and the fate of Flagler's vision.

CHAPTER 12

Plus and Minus

Loss, Gain, 1920s Boom, 1930s Fallout

SLIGHTLY MORE THAN A YEAR AFTER KEY WEST HAD SALUTED HENRY Flagler's triumphant arrival, riding his own iron into the city—after he said, "Now, I can die happy"—he fell down some stairs at Whitehall in Palm Beach. Flagler languished for a few months and died from complications of a hip fracture on May 20, 1913, when he was eighty-three. His wife, Mary Lily, was at his side.

His only surviving child, son Harry Harkness Flagler, had visited his father while he was in a coma. It has been said that Harry had not met Mary Lily before, and that she didn't notify Harry until Henry was unconscious. Harry had been estranged from his father since Flagler's ill-fated marriage to Ida Alice. Harry also had no interest in the family business, preferring the music circles in New York (though he did spend two years running aspects of his father's companies, and he was a director of the Jacksonville, St. Augustine & Indian River Railway).

According to Palm Beach historian James Augustine Ponce Jr., a native of St. Augustine whose father owned the funeral home that prepared Flagler's remains for the final resting place, the rift between Harry and Henry went on for decades: "I don't think father and son ever spoke during the last twenty years of his father's life."

A Florida East Coast Railway train carried Flagler's body to St. Augustine for interment in the mausoleum beside his first wife, Mary;

his daughters, Jennie Louise and Carrie; and his infant granddaughter Margery.

In a stately eulogy below a banner headline, the *St. Augustine Record* reported that the railroad company had ordered all trains halted at the hour of his funeral: "Mr. Flagler, who was a true practical philanthropist, believed it to be his duty in the management of the great fortune that he made to use it for the greatest benefit to his fellow man—to help men to help themselves." (John D. Rockefeller did not attend the funeral or a later memorial service at the Royal Poinciana Chapel in Palm Beach.)

Flagler's fortune, which his forty-six-year-old widow inherited, was about $100 million. Despite the estranged relationship with Harry, his father had provided for him all along. The will specified that Harry would receive another 5,000 shares of stock in the Standard Oil Company, and that each of Harry's three daughters would get 8,000 shares.

Mary Lily became a director of Standard Oil, and looked to her brother, William Rand Kenan Jr., and her cousin, Owen Kenan, for advice on the Flagler System's vast holdings. In an odd bit of irony, her future would collide with tragedy, myth, lore, memoirs of another family's secrets, stories about a "love child," one or two suicides involving railroad tracks—even suppositions of murder.

Back in 1891, when she met Henry Flagler, the socially prominent Miss Mary Lily Kenan had been keeping company with Robert Worth Bingham, whom she met while he was in college at the University of Virginia. Robert came from a family of educators, and while he wasn't on her same social plane, he hoped that her family connections would be the ticket to a prosperous future in law and politics. Their relationship had been "what you might call an affair," Mary Lily later said in a North Carolina newspaper, the *New Bernian.*

Apparently Mary Lily and Henry were infatuated from the outset, perhaps equally. She broke off her youthful dalliance with Robert and began a long-term romance with the still-married Henry (literature at the Henry M. Flagler Museum in Palm Beach refers to her as "a family friend").

Around 1896 the talk around Wilmington, North Carolina, was about a new baby in the Kenan family, as Mary Lily's married sister, Mrs.

J. K. Wise, had just had a daughter named Louise. Around the same time, Henry gave Mary Lily $1 million in Standard Oil stock and reassured her parents that he was dedicated to her. It is said that her parents objected more to the press attention over their "friendship" than what might have occurred behind closed doors.

Convincingly rebuffed, Robert Bingham abandoned North Carolina and moved to Louisville, Kentucky, where he married Eleanor Miller the same year Louise Wise was born. Eleanor came from a comfortable family, which fit his profile for his professional ambitions, and they had three children. Robert practiced law and became a circuit judge. And because Eleanor's mother was a widow (her husband had killed himself on a railroad track while Eleanor and Robert were engaged), he became his mother-in-law's lawyer, trustee, and confidant.

Author Sallie Bingham, the judge's granddaughter, wrote about the relationship in one of her books. Perhaps because everyone in Louisville knew Robert had entertained "a lingering interest" in Mary Lily, or because Eleanor was otherwise an unhappy woman, Bingham speculates that her grandmother chose to follow her father's path.

Eleanor died on April 29, 1913, shortly after an accident at a railroad crossing. She was a passenger in a car full of family members who had taken her husband Robert to the train station for a business trip to Cincinnati. Her youngest son, Barry (Sallie's father), was on his mother's lap, Bingham wrote: "Perhaps the emotional amnesia which crippled my father began that rainy day when the 7-year-old boy felt his mother push him off her lap before she sprang out of the car door."

Reports varied. The driver was Eleanor's brother, Dennis Miller, who spoke of a trolley "bearing down" with no way to avoid it. But the trolley didn't ride on the railroad tracks, and the family was in a big touring roadster. If a train had hit the car, there would be more injuries. No one else was really injured, yet Eleanor Bingham had a crushed skull.

About three weeks later, Henry Flagler died in Palm Beach; not in the mansion, but at "Nautilus," his private cottage on the ocean north of The Breakers. It was there that doctors had been keeping him comfortable and often sedated, and where Mary Lily's cousin, Owen Kenan, supervised the nursing staff.

The judge's outward expressions of grief over Eleanor's death did not keep her mother from worrying about all the sensitive information her son-in-law possessed. Henrietta Miller replaced him with another lawyer and trustee, and Bingham's finances began to deteriorate. When the judge was about $1 million in debt, with creditors pressuring him, a story circulated around the city, Sallie Bingham said: "The creditors suggested he go and visit a certain well-known widow in Florida."

Not that it would be the first time. Since Mary Lily's marriage to Flagler, Robert had made a few winter excursions to see for himself the kind of lifestyle they enjoyed—one that he coveted as much or more than he wanted his former lover.

Hence, the newly widowed pair, Robert and Mary Lily, became reacquainted. They married in New York in November 1916 in the home of Mr. and Mrs. Pembroke Jones, the very couple who had hosted Henry Walters when he introduced Mary Lily to Flagler. In this case, Mary Lily was four years older than Robert versus thirty-seven years younger than Henry.

Of course, her family and company advisors insisted on a prenuptial understanding to protect her large fortune. Just days before the wedding, Mrs. Flagler announced that her "niece," Louise Wise, then age twenty, would be her heir. She also set up a trust fund to protect her Florida properties: the Florida East Coast Railroad, the Flagler System hotel company, the Model Land Company, a utility in Miami, and the Peninsular & Occidental Steamship Company.

KISS OF DEATH
When Mrs. Bingham gave her new husband a certified check for $50,000, he gave her a kiss. Later rumors would suggest he had already given her something not talked about on the verandas where refined families took tea and sipped mint juleps.

Suddenly, this relatively young and vibrant woman was in failing health, complaining of chest pains. It was whispered that during the years of her soirees in Palm Beach, she had developed a taste for alcohol, which Mr. Flagler had not.

An article in the *Los Angeles Times* in 1987 reported her husband's actions: "Within weeks [of their marriage], however, something clearly was wrong. Mary was shuttled off to a Louisville hotel and placed in the care of one of Judge Bingham's friends, a dermatologist. It was during this period that she secretly revised her will to include a bequest to her new husband." In the codicil of June 1917, she wrote: "I give and bequeath to my husband, R. W. Bingham, $5 million to be absolutely his . . ."

The dermatologist's treatment consisted of regular shots of morphine. In July 1917, after she was found unconscious in her bathtub, the doctor gave her more morphine. During an episode of convulsions, Mary Lily Kenan Flagler Bingham died, only eight months after their wedding.

The death certificate referred to brain edema and a heart condition. But the Kenan family found that suspicious, found fault with giving the judge that $5 million, and contested Mary Lily's will. If she were resting in peace in September of that year, it would have been disturbed when her brothers and a team of doctors exhumed her body to perform a secret autopsy.

Doctors from Chicago, New York, and Baltimore traveled in a private railcar to Wilmington, then rode in curtained limousines to the cemetery after midnight (this appeared in the *Los Angeles Times* according to coverage of a lawsuit that the judge brought against author David Chandler). After the "hasty" pathology exam, tissue samples went by train to New York for a more complete examination. Her body reportedly contained "enormous amounts" of morphine and heavy metal poisons, possibly arsenic and mercury. According to Chandler, the Kenans dropped their lawsuit and locked away some troubling details of the autopsy results.

The true cause of Mrs. Bingham's death became an unresolved cold case with less and less official action and lots and lots of tabloid attention—speculating murder, reckless medical treatment, and, gasp, tertiary syphilis. The latter was much discussed in Chandler's book, *The Binghams of Louisville*. While Chandler posed a menu of scenarios—one was that the judge "caused her to be addicted to morphine" and she died suddenly because she didn't receive proper treatment—more sensational was his theory that America's richest woman "died of the ultimate complications of tertiary syphilis." The author found that angle the most probable: "Tracing it back, the likelihood was that she received it from Robert Worth Bingham during their youthful affair"—as he might have contracted the disease during some "bawdy house" encounter. Chandler agreed it was strictly speculation, but said it "answers the question why [Mary] was in the care of a dermatologist rather than a heart specialist. In those days dermatologists treated syphilis. It also explains the curious settlement of the Kenan family, obviously not wanting a scandal of that sort."

The judge used his $5 million inheritance to buy the *Louisville Courier-Journal* newspaper and other businesses—and likely felt less jealous of Flagler with every profitable investment. He bought a large house in the city and furnished it in a style which Sallie Bingham said was similar to that of Whitehall. In 1932 President Franklin D. Roosevelt appointed him ambassador to the Court of St. James. As to Robert's fate, granddaughter Sallie's memoir alluded to health problems, "possibly syphilis." Bingham died in 1937.

When all was said, done, and speculated about, nothing got in the way of Henry Flagler's accomplishments. Not the possibility that Robert Bingham had schemed heartlessly to get that $5 million; not the notion that he was so preoccupied with ambition that sloppy medical care would suffice. He got his $5 million, and Mary Lily's family got control of the other $95 million.

One of the trustees of the H. M. Flagler Trust was William Beardsley, who was president of the FEC through the early 1920s. Mary Lily's brother, William Rand Kenan Jr., also was a longtime trustee and succeeded Beardsley as president. That meant the Kenan family retained control of Henry's personal fortune as well as the Flagler System assets. Mary Lily left portions of her estate to her sisters, Jessie and Sarah. Louise Wise got a large bequest, along with Mary Lily's houses.

William Kenan and his sisters remained owners of the FEC Railway until 1931, when the bankrupt line went into receivership (a bruising bit of news which would have vastly disturbed the eternal rest of Henry Flagler).

WARTIME WORRIES

Several months after the United States entered World War I, President Woodrow Wilson took action. In December 1917 he decreed that all American railroads were under federal control. This decision placed more than 690 firms nationwide under the aegis of the US Rail Administration.

As author Frederick Lewis Allen pointed out in *Only Yesterday: An Informal History of the 1920s,* "One bought one's tickets at United States Railroad Administration Consolidated Ticket Offices." Secretary of the Treasury William McAdoo became director general of the railroads, and Henry Walters of the Atlantic Coast Line was part of McAdoo's inner circle.

In his book, *A Journey through Florida Railroad History,* Gregg M. Turner notes that many firms had tried to organize themselves to help the war effort by forming a Railroad War Board. Its purpose was to maximize the national fleet by discontinuing needless passenger routes, and to transport matériel to military sites. Some firms balked, so the Interstate Commerce Commission directed facilities to be run by the government.

The feds commandeered 100,000 railcars and 1,930 steam locomotives. After the war, such equipment was returned to owners, who had received a so-called rental fee (standard return) based on an earnings average from 1915 to 1917. Many owners were unhappy over the seemingly arbitrary stipends, and most were exasperated when the feds relinquished control—as they returned locomotives and rolling stock in a sorry state.

Seaboard chairman S. Davies Warfield was among the unhappy ones who objected to an arrangement in which revenues suffered, while cars and engines came back damaged or well-worn. In 1917 he spoke in Baltimore to members of the National Association of Owners of Railroad Securities. About 500 people attended, some from Tampa and other Florida cities, and those in the room represented more than $3 billion in railroad securities. As the program noted, the railroad capital of the country at the time was about $17 billion, "far in excess of the total annual receipts of the United States Government."

Warfield said that stabilizing railroad securities therefore must be integral to successfully financing the nations at war, because railroads were performing valuable services to coordinate the government's efforts to safely and successfully transport troops, matériel, food, and other essentials: "All interests are pulling together. We have telegrams and letters from [1,000] owners, amongst them many women, offering their cooperation in the purposes of this conference."

Wartime was also a hardship for some businesses owned, operated, or purchased by people of German heritage. In the settlement of Millville on Watson Bay near Panama City, a group of men had organized the St. Andrews Lumber Company right before the turn of the century. Henry Bovis ran the operation until 1910, when he sold it to foreign investors. Members of European royalty were among the founders of the German-American Lumber Company in Pensacola.

They built a new lumberyard, a logging railroad, and a shipyard near Millville. During World War I, however, the federal government confiscated the property and assets of German-American Lumber after receiving a lead—and finding pro-German literature and weapons in a secret tunnel. In 1919, when the government offered the assets for sale, W. C. Sherman bought them and rebuilt the operation as the St. Andrews Bay Lumber Company.

For many others, the war was a true stimulus to Florida's economic growth, even boosting revenues for the railroads, as there was greater demand for the state's goods nationwide. Also, its climate was appealing for year-round training of military personnel—for the navy at several ports and at bases for the army air corps and the marines.

Railroads got extra business when federal officials built an 8-mile spur at Arcadia to Carlstrom Field, an aviation training facility, plus lines to other military sites. Arcadia began calling itself "Aviation City" during that time, with Carlstrom and Dorr Fields.

The navy had acquired Trumbo Point in Key West from the Flagler System and began building Trumbo Naval Air Station there in 1917. During World War I the base was the deployment point for the navy's dirigibles such as the big C-1 blimp. Seaplanes taking off from Trumbo were a vital element in submarine patrol throughout the Caribbean.

The sprouting of such facilities, as well as new cities and roads to assist the war effort, created a natural springboard for economic expansion.

War would always disrupt Florida's orange blossom–induced reverie, but before long, people were back on track to explore parts of a state newly open to all kinds of traffic. The time was right to be on the move, given the boffo doings by the Wright Brothers and Ford Motor Company. The "plane, train, and automobile" era was bursting at the seams with new fans.

ALL RAILROADS LEAD TO FLORIDA

In fall 1925 an unprecedented land boom gripped Florida, with fistfuls of silly dollars changing hands along the east coast. Early action took place from West Palm Beach to Miami, then Jacksonville. At the height of the craze, people were exposed to what Frederick Lewis Allen called "the most delirious fever of real-estate speculation which had attacked the United States in ninety years."

The author spelled out what mapmakers were scrambling to convey: "The whole strip of coast line from Palm Beach southward was being developed into an American Riviera . . . The fever had spread to Tampa, Sarasota, St. Petersburg, and other cities and towns on the West Coast. People were scrambling for lots along Lake Okeechobee . . . Sanford . . . all through the state."

As noted in the *Gainesville Sun*, train travel increased dramatically during the era of Coolidge prosperity: "More money was available to more people who wanted to mirror the bluebloods," even if the pretense had to be packed away with their vacation duds. "Coming down as a guest on a private yacht may have been out of the question, but a ticket on the Seaboard or the Atlantic Coast Line was not."

This turned Florida into a very busy fishbowl, one which caught railroad operators off-guard. During wartime conditions already described, owners had to neglect basic maintenance, never mind upgrades, so they were abjectly unprepared for the whirlwind of demand.

The boom had been gaining a head of steam for several years, and it popped the lid in 1924. Allen credits the newfangled automobile with a big role in the appeal of real estate that seemed inaccessible in the past— "by bringing within easy range of the suburban railroad station, and thus of the big city, great stretches of woodland and field."

Addison Mizner had gotten bored after dressing up Palm Beach in Mediterranean Revival–style mansions, so he turned his attention to what would become Boca Raton, 25 miles south on the coast. He built a railway depot, a grand hotel (The Cloisters), and golf and yachting amenities, and promoted a Venetian-style canal. In the words of brother Wilson Mizner, Boca Raton would be "a platinum sucker trap."

Carl G. Fisher was busy creating lagoons and islands in Miami Beach (thanks to the foresight of Julia Tuttle). D. P. Davis bought two small isles in Tampa Bay which were little more than mangrove stands. There he dredged, filled, and created Davis Islands. "Still the public bought . . . blindly, trustingly . . . [making] out their checks for lots in what they were told was to be 'another Coral Gables' or just next to the right of way of the new railroad," Allen said.

The "Big Three" railroads at that time were the Atlantic Coast Line, the Seaboard Air Line, and the Florida East Coast Railway. Per Turner's research, they controlled 80 percent of the tracks statewide, "and they conveyed more passengers and freight than any other mode of transportation."

Henry Walters of the Atlantic Coast Line put the crush of boom traffic into perspective: "No one . . . could have foreseen the phenomenal growth and development that has taken place [in Florida] in less than a year's time, thrusting suddenly upon the railroads such a volume of business that they were unable to give normal service and resulting in a congestion of traffic which could only be overcome by drastic measures."

All the major players were vying for plum extensions, and many acquisitions occurred during the boom. According to Turner's analysis of the 1920 report of the Railroad Commission, twenty-nine carriers had a presence in the state, in addition to the "Big Three." Three of the twenty-nine had lines covering more than 100 miles: the Louisville & Nashville (246), the Georgia, Southern & Florida (162), and the Charlotte Harbor & Northern (112). By the end of the 1930s, because of so much merger madness, the industry in Florida would rely on a much leaner twenty-two railroad companies.

Rainin' Trains

The summer of 1925 should have spelled off-season traffic for the railroads, but waves of real estate speculators made it a scorcher. Florida had a torrent of train schedules, to the point of traffic gridlock. This prompted experts to call for a freight embargo on nonperishables in October 1925. It was an unprecedented move which lasted until May 1926.

From an article in *RailwayAge* in November 1927, one can sense the crisis that arose from orders arriving in Florida without a manifest, orders for merchandise going nowhere: "Enormous orders placed by merchants, the heavy movement of building and highway materials, coupled with one of the largest crops in the history of Florida, together placed an enormous burden upon the Big Three which became increasingly difficult to carry."

As one example of the embargo's effect, a contractor expecting building materials for a project in West Palm Beach got only one category: "So only the bathtubs arrived" for what was to be a trophy property in the South.

Developer Joseph W. Young, engrossed in his vision for Hollywood-by-the-Sea, was irate when the rail embargo sidelined his building materials. His solution was to buy his own fleet of vessels. "The railroads had been forced to place an embargo . . . to avert the danger of famine; building materials were now being imported by water, and the harbor bristled with shipping," Allen said.

The Atlantic Coast Line and the Seaboard Air Line were major freight carriers in Florida and had decent passenger traffic. To meet market demand, the ACL founded the Atlantic Coast Dispatch, with refrigerated cars to carry citrus.

The Flagler System's Florida East Coast Railway, however, had an edge over competitors because of the properties in its subsidiary, the Florida East Coast Hotel Company: the Hotel Ponce de Leon, the Alcazar, and the Cordova in St. Augustine; Ormond-on-the-Halifax in Ormond Beach; the Royal Poinciana and The Breakers in Palm Beach; the Royal Palm in Miami; the Long Key Fishing Camp on Long Key; and Casa Marina in Key West (begun in 1914). Up and down the east coast, the FEC hotel company was checking in tens of thousands of guests a season (on the high end, rooms at The Breakers were costing people $40 a night).

As noted in the previous chapter about the Overseas Railroad, Flagler had built a work camp and construction staging area on Long Key during work on the signature viaduct. When those facilities were no longer needed, he built a village, the Long Key Fishing Camp. The property had a seventy-five-room hotel, fourteen cottages, a two-story clubhouse, a general store, a post office, and a fleet of a dozen fishing boats with guides on standby.

Quite the destination, it drew the likes of dentist-cowboy-writer Zane Grey. He spent the winter of 1911 there, fishing and writing *The Light of the Western Stars*. And before novelist and artist John Dos Passos had cut off his friendship with Ernest Hemingway, he told him about making "a dream journey" over the Long Key Viaduct for a visit to the tropical hideaway.

That coincides with the tone of W. M. Walker's magazine article, noting the reams written of that colossal arched wonder "in treatment both technical and non-technical. There it stands. One must ride over it in a comfortable Pullman to appreciate its magnificence."

MILEAGE COUNTS

With corporate headquarters in St. Augustine and its east coast domination (a main line of more than 500 miles between Jacksonville and Key West), the FEC was in the catbird seat as geyser-like demand bubbled up. According to Turner, company revenues in 1920 were $13.7 million, net operating income was $1.8 million. Besides the main line, the railroad had eight branch lines operating over another 233 miles.

The FEC began to advertise in advance that the travel time between New York and Havana would be two nights. However, the railroad reached Key West a year before the terminal there was ready to dock the freight vessels. In 1915 the company was able to introduce those ferries carrying trains from Key West to Cuba. The first one was named the *Henry M. Flagler*.

There were two channel bridges in the Upper Keys due for upgrades, as the company replaced wooden trestles with concrete spans. Trains ran daily, however, and the Key West Extension was pronounced completely "done" in 1916. Mail, telegraph, and telephone services completed the train-connection equation.

The East and West Coast Railway was a petite line from Bradenton on the west coast running southeast to Arcadia in the Peace River valley by way of Myakka City. It began in 1915 as a freight carrier hauling mail, lumber, grain, naval stores, and sometimes phosphate. The E & W had tracks but no rolling stock of its own, and leased engines and cars from Seaboard. (As noted in an earlier chapter, the forerunner of Seaboard Air Line was the Florida Railway and Navigation Company, which dated to the mid-1880s. Nicknamed "the Key Line," it reflected the shrewd maneuverings of Sir Edward Reed.)

At Arcadia, the E & W line intersected with two other carriers: the Charlotte Harbor & Northern Railway and the Atlantic Coast Line, which had a route from Lakeland to Fort Myers. Seaboard leased all of

Florida Railway and Navigation Engine No. 28, near Baldwin, circa 1887.
COURTESY OF DONALD R. HENSLEY JR.

the E & W line in 1925, and purchased the Charlotte Harbor & Northern a year later. Gradually the East and West Coast was less useful and Seaboard removed the line in 1934.

Well before the 1920s land boom, John Dunn and his associates in Dunnellon built a shipping basin near the mouth of the Withlacoochee River. They named the depot Port Inglis after John L. Inglis, a North Florida investor in Dunn's phosphate mining firm.

Albertus Vogt, the next man to run the Dunnellon Phosphate Company, organized the Standard & Hernando Railroad to link phosphate mines around Hernando with a port on the Gulf of Mexico. According to the Interstate Commerce Commission reports for 1903, the railroad's charter was to build a line from Standard, Florida, to Hernando with a branch to Port Inglis—as its dock on the river connected with Seaboard's tracks at Dunnellon.

The first ship loaded with phosphate, a Dutch steamer bound for Hamburg, Germany, cleared the port in 1902. Soon, with increasing demand for the mineral essential to making fertilizer, ships full of phosphate were headed to buyers in England, France, Sweden, Denmark, and other countries. By 1907 Port Inglis led the world in phosphate shipments.

In 1916 Seaboard created the Florida Central & Gulf Railroad so as to acquire the Standard & Hernando's property and franchises. Under an agreement finalized in 1919 between Seaboard and the Port Inglis

Terminal Company, the Florida Gulf & Central "bought" the Standard & Hernando's assets.

Before the boom years, S. Davies Warfield, chairman of Seaboard Air Line Railway and its affiliated Baltimore Steam Packet Company, was busy with expansions and other acquisitions. The company also upgraded the routes with heavier rails and rock ballast.

Seaboard had purchased the construction bonds of the United States & West Indies Railroad and Steamship Company, and made a traffic agreement with the company in 1903. Reorganized as the Florida West Shore Railway, the Seaboard subsidiary completed a line from Durant to Bradenton in spring 1903—and built an extension to Sarasota and westward to Fruitville in 1905. Four years later Seaboard absorbed the Florida West Shore Railway and extended it to Venice in 1911.

Seaboard acquired the Warnell Lumber and Veneer Company line in 1905 and the Tampa & Gulf Coast Railroad in 1912. In the boom years, Seaboard absorbed the Tampa Northern Railroad in 1925, the Tavares and Gulf Railroad in 1926, and the Jacksonville, Gainesville & Gulf Railway in 1927. In 1928 Seaboard leased the Georgia, Florida & Alabama Railroad.

After buying the Tampa & Gulf Coast, Seaboard extended the rails past Gulf Pine to Tarpon Springs, a town that began as a winter vacation spot and became famous for sponge diving. Then the T & G absorbed a line from Tarpon Springs to Port Richey.

Seaboard also built a 47-mile branch from Sulphur Springs to Clearwater and St. Petersburg. A line on the Pinellas Peninsula in 1915 went to Indian Rocks Beach. This so-called Orange Belt Route also ran to Gulf Coast Junction, where Seaboard switched the trains onto its Tampa Northern Railroad into Tampa.

In 1926 Seaboard built a 43-mile extension from the Charlotte Harbor & Northern connection at Fort Ogden south to Fort Myers on the Caloosahatchee River. Another 30-mile branch went to Naples, and a 9-mile spur reached Punta Rassa. Yet another 30-mile branch ran eastward to LaBelle, an old cattle town named for the daughters of cattleman Francis Hendry.

As Don Hensley wrote in *Taplines*, a personnel appointment led to altered connections for the Charlotte Harbor railroad. In 1916 T. W.

Parson resigned as superintendent of Seaboard's South Florida Division to run the CH & N. Previously the railroad's preferred connections for passenger and merchandise trains were aligned with the Atlantic Coast Line's schedule. That all changed once the former Seaboard exec took charge. From then on, CH & N trains were attuned to Seaboard's schedule.

By the end of 1925, Peter B. Bradley (of American Agricultural Chemicals) agreed to sell the stock of CH & N and lease the railroad's property to Seaboard. It took the ICC three years to approve the sale and lease deal, with Seaboard merging the CH & N in 1928.

In the Panhandle, Seaboard had built a line west from Jacksonville to River Junction near Chattahoochee, where it connected with the Louisville & Nashville Railroad and went westward to Pensacola and points north. Warfield's most ambitious expansion was a 300-mile route from Coleman Junction south of Wildwood over to West Palm Beach, Miami, and then Homestead. Another was a branch from Tampa to Fort Myers and Naples on the west coast.

Seaboard organized the Florida, Western & Northern Railroad to handle the extension from Coleman to West Palm Beach, including stops in West Lake Wales, Avon Park, Sebring, Okeechobee, and Indiantown. Seaboard called the route the Orange Blossom Special. The Florida Western was in service in 1925, when its name was changed to the Seaboard All-Florida Railway.

Warfield visited Indiantown in central Martin County in 1925 and was enamored with the former Seminole trading post. Anticipating it would become a popular stop on the line, he organized a street layout, built a sizable passenger depot, and put up the Seminole Inn as a hunting lodge for friends (the latter is now on the National Register of Historic Places).

By 1927 the Seaboard All-Florida had gone farther, past Fort Lauderdale and Hollywood to Miami. With another 30-mile extension, it had reached Homestead. With each advance of major carriers, remote outposts had a raison d'être—as a new town with a rail depot (Boca Raton and Hollywood were just two of them). Seaboard Air Line Railway Company absorbed its own creation, the All-Florida line, making SAL the only carrier with a presence on the southeast and southwest coasts.

The Seaboard system had been extravagant, however, and its finances were weaker than some of its competitors. Government records indicate that in 1903 the company had issued $5.9 million in thirty-year first-mortgage gold bonds and $7.9 million in twenty-year second-mortgage gold bonds. Author and historian Richard E. Prince noted the dilemma in a book he wrote in 1969: "Unfortunately, the Seaboard . . . was wedged between the wealthy Atlantic Coast Line and the rich Southern Railway System."

Warfield traveled to Arcadia in January 1927 for the inaugural run of the Orange Blossom Special into southwest and southeast Florida. He had been confident Seaboard could grow and erase its indebtedness, based on the potential of Florida. But that was during the boom; he misjudged the part about him not being present to turn things around. As author Eliot Kleinberg wrote, "Warfield died suddenly in late 1927, and his dream for Indiantown died with him."

Afterward, Legh R. Powell became president, presiding over Seaboard headquarters in Norfolk, Virginia, and 4,500 miles of railroad tracks. The company was in receivership by 1930 (and would be a ward of the federal district court in Virginia for almost fifteen years). Seaboard would be the first railroad casualty of the Great Depression.

By 1933 Seaboard had abandoned service to Fort Myers, Naples, and the Manatee-Arcadia branch—given that the Atlantic Coast Line had parallel service. However, SAL's Cross-Florida extension into West Palm Beach, Miami, and Homestead became a profitable investment for the company. (Of course, Seaboard's east coast presence was viewed with disdain in the Flagler System boardroom, where FEC executives considered the competitor a trespasser.)

Despite the financial pressure, Prince said that bond-holders who survived the crisis became stockholders in the reorganized Seaboard Air Line Railroad Company which emerged in 1932.

From its entry into Florida in the early 1900s, Seaboard had gained a foothold running tracks through Ocala and Plant City and westward toward Tampa. Branch lines went to St. Petersburg, Bradenton, Sarasota, and Venice (thanks to Warfield's association with Bertha Honoré Palmer). By then the system originating in Richmond had forty-one railroads with routes covering 2,600 miles.

Five predecessor lines were based in Virginia and the Carolinas. As noted earlier, one of its acquisitions in 1900 was the Florida Central & Peninsular Railroad, which had seven predecessors—one in Georgia and the rest in Florida.

By 1924 southwest Florida had four regular routes: the Florida Southern Railway route toward Fort Myers; the Florida West Shore Railway route toward Venice; the Charlotte Harbor & Northern Railway route toward Boca Grande; and the Tampa Southern Railroad route toward Sarasota.

With its passenger trains running from Richmond to Tampa, Seaboard also had year-round freight service on the Seaboard Fast Mail and passenger service on the Seaboard Florida Limited. The latter used dynamo-power to provide electricity. And its marketing slogan taunted the snowbound, as if one had only to wave a wand to go "From Zero to 80 [degrees] in 24 Hours."

COASTING IN HIGH GEAR

The Seaboard had competed all along with the Atlantic Coast Line Railroad, which had acquired the Plant System's railroads after the death of Henry Plant (and similar to the FEC's sentiments, the Coast Line found Seaboard's expansions irksome). Both operators had absorbed numerous short lines and spurs until they had the Tampa Bay area cross-stitched and crocheted.

The ACL's main line in Florida ran from Jacksonville to Tampa via Orlando, Lakeland, and Plant City. But its west coast headquarters was Tampa—where the ACL built maintenance shops, rail yards, switching tracks, and shipping facilities.

As mentioned in an earlier chapter, the Atlantic Coast Line Railroad's passenger trains from New York City were popular with tourists: the Atlantic Coast Line Express, the Havana Special, the Palmetto Limited, and the Florida Special. When the latter train arrived in Jacksonville, it continued south to Miami and Key West on the Florida East Coast Railway tracks. Passengers heading westward proceeded on ACL tracks.

During the winter season of 1920–21, the ACL expanded its schedule to meet demand with the Everglades Limited and the all-Pullman

The "Havana Special" passenger train idles beside the dock in Key West, where passengers and cargo transferred to the "Governor Cobb," a vessel owned by the Peninsular & Occidental Steamship Company. It formed in 1900 with the merger of the Plant System's People's Line and Henry Flagler's Florida East Coast Line of steamships. STATE ARCHIVES OF FLORIDA, FLORIDA MEMORY.

Everglades. Still keeping up with passenger business, the ACL added the Florida West Coast Limited and the Florida East Coast Limited. And as Turner noted, the ACL revived the West Indian Limited.

In 1902 the Atlantic Coast Line Railroad had gained a majority of stock in the Louisville & Nashville Railroad, which continued to operate as a separate company for several decades. The L & N had bought, leased, or otherwise acquired twenty-nine railroads. Four lines had "Pensacola" in the name, but most originated out of state.

By the peak of the 1920s boom, the ACL had nine Pullman trains running between New York City and Jacksonville; five were year-round and four accommodated the winter crush. The system comprised the parent firm, Atlantic Coast Line Railroad of Virginia, its ten railroads, and a dozen other lines.

In 1920 the ACL had 4,900 miles of track in the South—of which almost 1,800 miles were in Florida. Reported assets were $318 million. Its main line ran from Richmond, and the southern terminus was Jacksonville. Driven by the real estate frenzy, the ACL put down new steel rails; built a larger freight yard at Lakeland; upgraded its shop complexes in Sanford and High Springs; and built new depots in Avon Park, Lake Wales, Frostproof, and Richland.

Turner describes one major improvement the ACL began before the boom, the 167-mile Haines City Branch, which went through the central Florida ridge country's regions of agriculture, lumber, and mining. It added service to Sebring in 1912, then went on to Immokalee and Deep Lake.

In addition, the ACL built a 15-mile spur from Harrisburg to Moore Haven at the western tip of Lake O in 1918, where sugarcane growing was asserting its dominance. That branch would later proceed another 25 miles via Clewiston to reach Lake Harbor.

Another major expansion was the Tampa Southern Railroad, which was chartered in 1917 to build a route from Manatee County's agriculture region and link Tampa to Sarasota and later Bradenton. The Tampa Southern also built a branch to Southfort (Fort Ogden), as directed by the ACL, which owned its stock.

Even more significant to the ACL was the Perry Cut-Off built between Perry and Monticello in the Panhandle, and from Thonotosassa to Richland. This project positioned the ACL to have an important connection between Tampa and major cities in the Midwest—via Thomasville, Georgia—avoiding a lot of time-consuming east and west travel.

The Southland was part of the ACL's Perry Cut-Off service. As advertised in the *Sarasota Herald* in 1929, it ran from Sarasota to Thomasville and arrived two stops later in Atlanta. Passengers later boarded in Cincinnati, Columbus, and Cleveland, Ohio, and Grand Rapids and Detroit, Michigan, with the northern terminal in Chicago.

As noted earlier, the ACL had other famous named trains. One of them, the Pinellas Special, ran between Jacksonville and St. Petersburg, with a spur to the Hotel Belleview-Biltmore built by Henry Plant. Some of its streamliners, such as the Florida Special and Havana Special, operated jointly with the Florida East Coast Railway to Key West.

During the mid-1930s the ACL reduced the route of the Palmetto Limited so that it terminated at Savannah. The Depression era also brought competition from cars, airplanes, and the growing trucking industry—putting a dent in Florida's railroad business. The Florida Special, however, was still in demand.

Early in 1939 the company's first streamliner to Florida made its debut and got raves on service. William C. Vantuono, editor of *Railway-Age*, wrote about the striking Art Deco–style paint schemes which two railroad companies favored that year, when they premiered new streamliner passenger trains and recently introduced diesel-electric locomotives. The Florida East Coast Railway's first diesel escorted the Jacksonville-to-Miami train Henry M. Flagler, and like all new FEC units, it strutted its stuff in a bright red, yellow, and silver palette.

The Atlantic Coast Line's first new locomotives were assigned to the Champion, giving every passerby from New York to Miami a flash of its purple and silver livery and vivid yellow striping. Competing with the Champion was the Seaboard Air Line's Silver Star and Silver Meteor. Each unit pulled identical consists of seven cars.

The Florida Southern had merged in 1902 with the Savannah, Florida & Western Railroad, which ran its trains in downtown Tampa to stop at various hotels. The Florida Southern's 310-mile route merged with the ACL in 1903.

When the Florida land boom collapsed, the state's railroad footprint reflected the extent of so much corporate participation. The map showed 5,700 miles of railroads, a record not likely to be seen again.

As noted in an earlier chapter, J. P. Morgan had organized the Southern Railway System around the turn of the century. Morgan and Atlantic Coast Line chairman Henry Walters had become friends and congenial competitors—close enough for the press to call the ACL a "Morgan" railroad.

When Walters died in 1931, his nephew became the new chairman. Lyman Delano was the son of Walters's sister Jennie and Warren Delano III (who died when his startled horse hit a train). Lyman Delano, first cousin of Franklin Delano Roosevelt, joined the Atlantic Coast Line team in 1910. He held posts as general manager and vice president, and was the railroad's federal manager during the World War I period of nationalization.

The ACL was able to punt its way through the Great Depression because management promptly put in place substantial cost-cutting measures. Freight business dwindled by half, and passenger traffic dropped off by more than 60 percent. However, the Coast Line credited its subsidiary, the Louisville & Nashville, with helping to stave off receivership and bankruptcy.

POSTWAR PROPS

After World War I, William Beardsley had invested in major upgrades for the Florida East Coast Railway. Its capacity had been limited by having a single track, so the company built a new second main line between Jacksonville and Miami in 1926.

The FEC upgraded its equipment during the 1920s to service all the plus-business, ordering modern oil-burning "Mountain-class" locomotives. The company also built a new double-track drawbridge over the St. Johns River to handle boom-time commerce.

The company's Florida East Coast Limited traveled over Pennsylvania Railroad tracks between New York and Washington, then traveled on the Richmond Fredericksburg & Potomac Railroad to Richmond. From there, FEC trains traveled on ACL tracks to Jacksonville. Then, Turner wrote, "the FEC advanced the crack train to Miami."

Alas, the FEC failed to generate the sustaining revenue streams that Flagler had envisioned. After the collapse of the Florida land boom and the national crisis of the stock market crash, the FEC went into receivership in 1931. William Rand Kenan Jr. ran the Flagler System from the time of Flagler's death in 1913, through the boom-time prosperity and the financial crisis. Unlike other operators, the Kenan family opted not to sell the FEC to Atlantic Coast Line.

As for the Overseas Railroad, it was a big hit with passengers who overlooked the fact that the schedule was a bit loose. As Les Standiford put it, "on time" was a relative term for trains heading south from Miami. When a bridge tender raised a span to let a ship through, passengers could fish from the rail platform.

And ice became "a small miracle" enabled by the railroad. The author described a family living on Big Torch Key whose order for large blocks of ice arrived at a depot. They bought a Model T Ford to transport the cool stuff to a dock and then floated it over to their cottage.

BUSTED AND BROKE

Decades of dreaming, planning, and executing had put Florida on the map, and railroad developers had driven much of the enthusiasm, literally becoming an economic "engine." Of course, the piper would expect a handsome reward for all this effusiveness. And debates about supply and demand merited as much sympathy as "the dog ate my homework."

From Allen's splendid account in *Only Yesterday:* "Exactly as the developers of the tropical wonderlands of Florida had learned that there were more land-speculators able and willing to gamble on houses intended for the polo-playing class than there were members of this class, so also those who carved out playgrounds for the rich . . . elsewhere . . . learned to their ultimate sorrow that the rich could not play everywhere at once."

Well before the Crash of '29 gripped the national economy, Florida was feeling the crush of defeat upon the collapse of the real estate boom in 1926. As the Department of State described conditions, it was a time "when money and credit ran out, and banks and investors abruptly stopped trusting the 'paper' millionaires."

Two more hurricanes, in 1926 and 1928, put huge dents in the economy as well. The following year, the citrus industry suffered from an invasion of the Mediterranean fruit fly. That prompted a quarantine, with a ban on any exports or imports of citrus, plus grove production dropped by 60 percent.

Between 1928 and 1933, revenues for the rail industry were off by half, nationwide and in Florida. In an article in the *Gainesville Sun* in 2005, historian Chris Monaco said that 1932 was "the beginning of the end" for the original Florida Railroad route, one which had been acquired by Seaboard. "The tracks were torn up between Fernandina and Cedar Key. Once that happened, the whole concept of linking the east coast as a sort of cross-state barge canal ended."

Despite the economic realities of the real estate bust and the Depression, Florida grew. People settled in towns that the railroads had created, and the lack of a state income tax held a lot of appeal. According to the 1930 Census, the state's population increased by 50 percent in that decade.

COLLABORATIVE COMPETITION

Inasmuch as Jacksonville was the major railroad gateway into Florida, Henry Flagler had insisted that the city have a proper train depot. About 1890 he began a clandestine scheme to buy land west of the city for a union station. Historian John Cowart says Flagler whipped other railroad owners into line and obtained a public bond issue.

Along with the Florida East Coast Railway, co-owners of the Jacksonville Terminal Company were the Atlantic Coast Line Railroad, the Seaboard Air Line Railroad, Southern Railway, and the Georgia Southern & Florida Railway.

In 1916 it was time to expand the Jacksonville Terminal, so the company acquired more land to build a station that would make a statement. The owners hired architect Kenneth Murchison, who designed a Beaux Arts structure not unlike the aesthetic of Pennsylvania Station in New York. Once it opened in 1919, the terminal received more than a hundred trains a day. By the late 1920s, the station was Jacksonville's second-largest employer.

SIEGE FROM THE SEA

The hurricane "blew that coast to ragged tatters, destroying last chances, scattering hopes. It sucked the last turquoise from the inshore waters, shrouded the mangrove in caked sandy marl, transformed blue sea and blue sky to a dead gray. It blew the color right out of the world."

That immortal imagery is courtesy of the late Peter Matthiessen, author of *Killing Mister Watson*. And while it refers to another storm entirely, one which occurred decades before the 1935 Labor Day Hurricane, it provides a telling description of its "dead" and bleak effects.

The holiday hurricane of 1935 was the strongest and most intense hurricane to make landfall in the United States in recorded history. It also was the first of three hurricanes to hit the US during the 1900s that were Category 5 strength at landfall. This monstrous killer hid its intensions until it was too late to rescue people living and working in the Keys. Hundreds of people were killed, either battered to death, blown into the sea, or drowned on land in the storm surge.

A lot of the tracks of the fabled Key West Extension were destroyed. FEC Engine 153, a 1922 Pacific-type passenger locomotive, hauled the last train out of the Keys and reached Miami before the tracks were washed away. Those marvelous bridges, however, were intact—a testament to Flagler's passion for permanence.

Catastrophe loomed in late August, when a minor tropical disturbance formed near the Bahamas. As it moved westward toward the Gulf Stream, weather forecasters acknowledged its potential as a tropical storm. Early on September 1, near Andros Island in the Bahamas, it was strong enough to be called a Category 1 hurricane. Barreling above the warm waters of the Gulf Stream later that day, it gained strength with nothing to impede its intensity.

Having turned toward Islamorada in the Upper Keys, the hurricane hurled its peak intensity of 185-miles-per-hour winds and 20-foot waves at Craig Key. Landfall was between 8:30 and 9:30 p.m. on September 2. In addition to Craig, the hardest hit areas were Long Key and both of the Matecumbes. The hurricane braked somewhat as it proceeded parallel to the west coast and made a second landfall near Cedar Key two days later.

At the time about 1,000 people occupied the devastated areas, a few hundred settlers living in frame shacks, and more than 600 veterans of World War I housed in tent camps on Matecumbe Key (the word is a variation of the Spanish phrase *mata hombre*, or "kill man"). The veterans had been sent to Islamorada to work on a New Deal highway, bridge, and tunnel project financed by President Roosevelt's Works Progress Administration (the section would link Grassy Key and Lower Matecumbe to eliminate a ferry trip for motorists). For all of these souls, the FEC Railway was the only means of evacuation, so they awaited rescue.

Elsewhere in the Keys, people were beginning to take notice of the weather forecast. One was author Ernest Hemingway, who had a home in Key West and a dock for his fishing boat, the *Pilar*. According to Les

Standiford, Hemingway was wrapping up an afternoon of writing *To Have and Have Not* at his home on Whitehead Street late on Saturday afternoon of Labor Day weekend. Had he not sat down to read the newspaper just then, he would have been on his way to Sloppy Joe's on Duval Street, and later Captain Tony's.

But a troubling headline about an approaching storm altered his routine. Hemingway left the house to attend to securing the *Pilar*. After waiting out the hurricane, the author took a boat to Matecumbe to help with rescue efforts. Officials had been hindered until the day after because of persistent gale-force winds and high seas.

According to FEC records, the office in Miami began receiving distress calls from the Keys early Monday. About 2 p.m. an administrator with the Florida Emergency Relief Administration requested a special train to evacuate the veterans. Because of the holiday weekend, the FEC scrambled to round up a crew to assemble a consist.

Engineer J. J. Haycraft left Miami about 4:25 p.m. in "Old 447," pulling six passenger cars, two baggage cars, and three boxcars. There was a fifteen-minute delay at the Miami River, as the turntable bridge "yawned open" for holiday pleasure-boaters oblivious to the emergency.

Another delay occurred in Homestead, where Haycraft stopped at the rail yard to move the engine to the rear of the train—a logical step which would allow him to quickly head north from the Keys. More precious time evaporated when a snapped cable slapped itself around Old 447. The engine stalled and it took an hour to find the tools that could cut it loose.

Dealing with obstructions blown onto the tracks and poor visibility, Haycraft guided the train into the Islamorada station on Upper Matecumbe Key about 8:20 p.m. Just then, there was an abrupt shift in the direction of the brutal winds. This northeast-to-southeast whipsaw pushed a 17-foot tidal wave over the islands.

Haycraft and his crew survived, but the hurricane swept eleven cars off the tracks. The only upright equipment was the 106-ton Schenectady "Old 447" and a tender. The eye of the storm meant a forty-minute calm at Lower Matecumbe, followed by storm surge and winds at the veteran camp there. Another calm lasted almost an hour at Long Key. Shortly before that tidal wave, winds were close to 200 mph at Snake Creek south of Islamorada. Once the surge waters receded, the Middle Keys had new topography and some new channels between Florida Bay and the Atlantic.

Officials documented 577 bodies, of which 288 were veterans. Headlines in the *New York Times* and local newspapers offered up the horrific fate of those in "shredded" camps.

An article in *USA Today* in 2005 recounted the events for one particular family, in an interview with Bernard Russell. He was seventeen during the 1935 hurricane; of sixty-one in the Russell clan on Matecumbe Key, fifty died that night, including his mother and three sisters: "[Russell] felt his sister's grip on his hand pull away in the darkness as the 200 mph wind whipped his body and waves crashed over him for what seemed like an eternity" as a tidal wave crossed over the island. "There were so many dead people and no place to take them . . . They stacked them up and burned them."

The article referred to a letter Hemingway wrote to his editor, Max Perkins, describing a search effort that turned up sixty-nine bodies: "Indian Key was absolutely swept clean, not a blade of grass . . . We made five trips with provisions for survivors to different places but nothing but dead men to eat the grub."

Some victims were swept into the Gulf or the Atlantic, and some "were literally sandblasted to death." Dr. Lassiter Alexander, attending at one of the veterans' camps, said that while the surge waters were still rising, "we made our way to the railroad track" and hung on to it. No truly accurate death toll was possible, given the transient nature of Keys dwellers and visitors.

One such hail fellow had lived on a houseboat on the Miami River for many years, probably not far from Julia Tuttle's original homestead. Charles Van Vechten and his wife, Jesse, decided to set sail for the Keys one day with their German shepherd and pet canary. Of course, carefree Charles never checked the weather forecast. His nephew, Jay Van Vechten II, recalled the story of their adventure: "A hurricane swept them up off of Tavernier . . . carried them and their boat inland a few blocks, then plunked them down in some woods. And that is where they lived out their remaining days."

Charles Van Vechten's account of the hurricane's aftermath was vivid: "You can't imagine how sudden—and how awful—it was . . . There was a big wall of water . . . it swept over those shacks and messed them up like they were match boxes." (While Charles was living a tropical version of bohemian joie de vivre in the Keys, his brother, Jay Henry Van Vechten Sr., was moving comfortably in New York business and cultural circles. His wife, the former Isabel Henderson, was a protégé of Jerome Kern and starred in six of his musicals. She also opened daytime shows at Radio City Music Hall.) No small bit of irony, too, is the presence of Jay's Uncle Charles in the vicinity of Henry Flagler's ruined masterpiece. Isabel Henderson Van Vechten was the niece of Ida Alice Shourds (the second Mrs. Flagler, who had died in 1930), which means that Henry Flagler was Jay's late great-uncle by marriage.

Charles Van Vechten's reference to "sudden" is a vivid reminder of how unpredictable hurricanes can be. As Standiford wrote in *Last Train to Paradise,* "The intertwined skein of design and fate that brought [Hemingway, Russell, Haycraft, those 600 veterans, and scores of others] together on that ill-fated Labor Day night is complex indeed . . . but impossible to have been foreseen."

The damage to the Overseas Railroad cannot be measured in any terms that correlate to what it took to create it: not the years of planning and back-wrenching construction; not the aforementioned blood, sweat, tragedy, and tears; and certainly not the vision and grit of the man who moored Key West to the mainland. The FEC says that 42 miles of filled roadbed was washed out and countless miles of railroad ties were torn and twisted (one remnant is visible today in the waters off Summerland Key). The company built a temporary track to rescue "Old 447," since it was worth $60,000.

Already bankrupt from the effects of the Great Depression, the FEC opted not to rebuild the Overseas Railroad. In one respect, it can be suggested the Extension was not the victim of a hurricane, but that it succumbed to death by bean counters who chose to short-sell the assets rather than rebuild what Flagler had devoted so many years and dollars to create. He had invested $27 million to build it, and it could have been repaired for about $1.5 million (talk about salt on a certain psychic wound).

It was business. Those insurance companies, the principals at the Morgan syndicate, could have seen the merits of investing more to rebuild the roadbed and tracks because the difficult parts—the bridges—were intact. Such a project would have created jobs at a time when sorely needed, and given the country an "8.2 Wonder of the World."

But Flagler was long dead, and no one at the FEC had his passion for the Extension. Adhering to the cold calculations of their accountants, the company's directors sacrificed the remains of the railroad. On the flip side of that decision, the much-touted freight business had not materialized, but the tourist business was robust.

So the FEC accepted $640,000 from the state for the miles of surviving roadbed, the bridges, and 156 miles of right-of-way. Unlike old soldiers, however, the original Flagler bridges have not faded away. The signature Long Key Viaduct, the Seven-Mile Bridge, and the Bahia Honda Bridge are highly visible listings on the National Register of Historic Places.

A year after the hurricane, this imposing trio became the platform for the Florida Overseas Highway, the first continuous overseas highway, which was completed in 1938—and operates to this day. At Bahia Honda Bridge, the new highway was welded to the top of the camelback spans. The rails were recycled as guard railings on the bridges and are still visible. These structures have withstood many hurricanes since 1935 (near the Long Key Viaduct, there is a railroad museum on Pigeon Key).

Regarding the dearly departed Key West Extension, author Pat Parks said the FEC phenomenon lived "a brief romantic life and a spectacular death . . . which gave it a highly individual personality." In addition to the deaths from the killer hurricane, hundreds of laborers had died during its construction, and it had "shortened the life span of a few engineers."

That masterpiece survived for twenty-three years, "through disasters of finance, wind and flood . . . Half a million passengers had enjoyed the marvel of riding across 29 islands, fording the waterways over bridges and embankments." Author Dan Gallagher cited folklore about the hurricane which "destroyed the railroad and Henry Flagler's dream, and those who had once derided the roadway as 'Flagler's Folly' probably said, 'I told you so.'"

Francis McKindall, in a review of Gallagher's book, enlivened the topic in a way that might have tickled Flagler pink: "The tragedy? That you and I never got to ride the [156] miles in a fine old coach pulled by a coal-fired engine, hauling it across the thirty-eight great bridges and viaducts between Homestead and Key West. What a trip that would have been, eh? The velvet curtains swaying, the sea air blowing in through the coaches, the plume of smoke from old #447 blowing away in the wind, the engineer up there ahead in the engine, whistling to let the people know—on Indian Key, Key Largo, Key Vaca, Pigeon Key, Torch Ramrod, Sugarloaf, Saddle Bunch, Islamorada, and Bahia Honda—that we were on our way. In style."

Florida Woos, Characters Fall Hard

If there is one common denominator in Florida history, it is that few—rich or poor—are immune to the mind-set that overtakes reason in this climate, whether they are industrialists, entrepreneurs, settlers looking to prosper, immigrants with and without a pedigree, or just plain "characters."

Chapter 10 described the Chicago socialite Bertha Honoré Palmer, who transformed Sarasota and persuaded S. Davies Warfield to extend the Seaboard Air Line and name the depot Venice. After her death, her sons, Honoré and Potter Palmer II, further developed her extensive land holdings.

Bertha's niece, Julia Dent Grant (Ulysses S. Grant's granddaughter), lived for many years in Europe with her husband, Prince Michael Cantacuzène, Count Speransky. The prince had been a general in service to Tsar Nicholas II, and the fallout from the Russian revolution prompted the family to leave Europe. They made their way to Sarasota, where Cantacuzène went into business with his wife's relatives. The prince, along with Honoré and Potter Palmer, formed the Palmer National Bank and Trust Company in July 1929, after taking over the First Bank and Trust Company building. The Palmer Bank survived the Great Depression and became one of the strongest banks in Sarasota.

In another instance, topography was quite a character, too, with a role in shaping events.

Deep Lake, on the western end of the Big Cypress Preserve, is called a unique feature, which gives one pause because it's impossible to know

256

whether something like it exists elsewhere on the planet. At 90 feet deep, it is one of the deepest lakes in Florida and the deepest one south of Lake Okeechobee. Studies show that its top half is freshwater, and the bottom half is saltwater (maybe that contributes to its "unique" label).

The freshwater aspect was a draw for settlers and a positive influence on agriculture. Historically Deep Lake was a Seminole settlement where fertile lands with good elevation were conducive to citrus and other crops. Enter a pivotal pair: Walter Galloway Langford of Live Oak, a second-generation cattle rancher, banker, and real estate investor, and John M. Roach, president of the Chicago Traction Company, who had purchased Useppa Island off the coast of Fort Myers as his first land holding in Florida.

Shortly after 1900 Langford and Roach acquired about 300 acres around Deep Lake to develop grapefruit groves. After clearing the pinelands, they planted seedless grapefruit trees. That part of southwest Florida then had scant infrastructure, so there were snags to overcome. It was difficult for the two partners to get their supplies and specimen trees from Fort Myers, and equally tough to ship their grapefruit to market via oxcart.

This was a part of Florida without passable roads, canals, or railroads, so they built a 13-mile tram-style railway system in 1913 to go from Deep Lake south to Everglades City on the west coast, on the cusp of the Ten Thousand Islands. The men fashioned a gas-powered railroad car out of a Ford Motor Company engine and mounted it on a four-wheel railcar. The flanged wheels ran on the rail with small flatbed cars, likewise on flanged wheels. A cockeyed mishmash perhaps, but the tram's components did the job of getting crops to market.

By 1915 Langford and Roach were shipping 17,000 boxes of their grapefruit. Sometimes the fruit arrived in a soggy state: The Deep Lake roadbed and track had been laid without being graded, so occasional flooding was a concern.

Because of their citrus venture and the allure of Useppa Island, Barron Gift Collier Sr. took an interest in Florida. As it happened, Roach was friends with Collier (who had persuaded him to sell Useppa Island in 1911 for $100,000). Collier, a native of Memphis, saw southwest Florida's potential as a winter retreat, yes, but its business potential intrigued him as well. As a high school dropout, Collier had worked on the Illinois Central Railroad and began his own business at age twenty. Six years later, with the success of his Consolidated Street Railway Advertising Company in New York, he was a millionaire.

In 1922 Collier purchased the Deep Lake lands, the grapefruit grove, and the Deep Lake Railroad. Gradually he bought up land in the area to grow a business he would call the Deep Lake Grove & Cannery. He turned Everglades City around by 1923, after buying most of the land in and around the town. About five years later, it had roads, a railroad, a bank, a telephone, sawmills, docks, workers' barracks, and its own streetcar.

Collier wanted more substantial rail service, so he and some Fort Myers business leaders formed a joint venture with the Atlantic Coast Line. The Fort Myers Southern Railroad built an extension from Fort Myers to Bonita Springs and Naples. The company extended the line to Marco Island on the Gulf coast south of Naples in June 1927.

Seaboard Air Line had its own track into Fort Myers and a line to Naples by the end of 1926. Historically the Florida Southern Railroad had been building in this area since the 1880s, with a line from Arcadia to Punta Gorda. The Atlantic Coast Line had built an extension from Punta Gorda to Fort Myers (by the early 1900s, the ACL had bought the Florida Southern Railroad). Collier, meanwhile, sold the Deep Lake Grove Railway to the ACL. In 1929 the ACL rebuilt the tracks and extended it to Everglades City, which would become the company's southern terminus.

While the association between Roach and Collier was significant, it is noteworthy that Langford was instrumental in getting the attention of the Atlantic Coast Line Railroad, and those northern visitors who decided to buy winter homes in southwest Florida. No small irony, given that Langford's wife was the former Carrie Watson, daughter of Edgar J. Watson, who was immortalized when Peter Matthiessen wrote his trilogy set in the Ten Thousand Islands.

Yes, Edgar was *that* "Mister Watson," a firebrand of a planter at Chokoloskee, south of Everglades City, who was murdered in 1910 by a band of angry neighbors. His travels by rail, boat, and horseback were the stuff of 19th-century legends, with enough nuggets of probable truth to keep the Florida wags busy and the townsfolk for miles around very nervous.

Did Watson really ambush Belle Starr in Oklahoma in 1889? Perhaps "the Shadow knows," but no one else could prove it.

Myra Maybelle Shirley Reed Starr had grown up with the James and Younger boys in Missouri and was twice widowed (Jim Reed and a Cherokee man, Sam Starr). At the time of her death, she was married to Sam's younger relative, Jim July Starr. Suspects with a motive included her husband, her children, and Edgar J. Watson, a sometime sharecropper on her land.

Watson's sinister intent would have stemmed from suspicion that she would turn him in, as he was wanted for murder in Florida. Lore in Oklahoma indicates that Watson was tried for Belle's murder and acquitted— which doesn't mean he didn't do it, nor does it mean there wasn't probable cause to stifle his violent bent elsewhere. What got Watson killed in Florida was the growing body count in the Ten Thousand Islands (which Matthiessen so lyrically related).

As for other characters in Florida, outlaw John Hopkins Ashley was often compared to train robber Jesse James due to his daring escapades. Born in Fort Myers in 1888, he was the son of Joe Ashley, a trapper, alligator hunter, and onetime sheriff. John had learned the ways of a trapper, but he formed a gang with his brother Bob and their nephew, Hanford Mobley. This came about in 1911 after John was accused of murdering Seminole trapper Desoto Tiger.

Known variously as "King of the Everglades" and "Swamp Bandit," John and the Ashley Gang robbed trains and banks, smuggled rum from the Bahamas during Prohibition, and helped themselves to the loot of others. They also taunted every badge in south Florida, which fueled the headlines.

Joe Ashley and his older sons had worked on the Florida East Coast Railway when Flagler was building tracks near Fort Lauderdale. So the company might have been a bit miffed when John, Bob, and Chicago bad boy Kid Lowe robbed an FEC passenger train in 1915.

For the next nine years, the gang acted out at will, until someone tipped off a sheriff and lawmen set up a sting in 1924. The snare tightened on the St. Sebastian Bridge near Fort Pierce, where John Ashley pulled a gun. He and several others died in the shootout. He was thirty-six.

CHAPTER 13

War and Peace

Hostile Takeover, Rational Mergers

The US government chose not to repeat that costly experiment in "nationalizing" railroads during World War II, given the Great War's cost to the industry of more than $1 billion.

From the time of the Japanese attack at Pearl Harbor, while American troops waged war in the Pacific and battled in Europe and North Africa, Florida was in the throes of a riveting campaign to assist the national cause. Oodles of vacant land and warm weather for year-round training purposes made Florida a magnet for military base construction. Between 1941 and 1945, more than 200 installations were built or expanded, covering more than 1 million acres of land and ringing up a tab of more than $300 million.

Gordon D. Gaster, a native of Avon Park who was seven years old at the beginning of the war, lived in a town where aviation training was big business: "Florida had so many military bases and training facilities all over the state, it was being seen as a big bull's eye for our enemies. Thus, we had air raid warnings and 'air raid wardens' who rode around on bicycles and horses to give folks the 'all clear' signal."

World War II created an enormous rush of business for the railroads. As Gregg Turner noted, the offshore menace of enemy submarines shifted the way that maritime cargo could be moved securely; therefore, railroads took up the slack, making their lines another target for sabotage.

Military personnel and stewardesses wait by a train in 1941. With so much vacant land and weather conducive to year-round training, Florida was a magnet for military base construction. More than 250,000 Floridians served in the military, which involved more than a few train tickets to boot camps. Trainloads of personnel also arrived from out-of-state to report to hundreds of military installations. STATE ARCHIVES OF FLORIDA, FLORIDA MEMORY.

Reflecting the "real and present danger" in February 1942, enemy submarines attacked four merchant ships off the east coast near Cape Canaveral. German spies came ashore near Jacksonville, intent on blowing up railroad lines and therefore halting the shipment of war supplies. Fortunately they were captured before doing any damage, but the breach put US intelligence forces on a sharper alert.

While agriculture was still the leading industry, shipbuilding grew into Florida's primary manufacturing endeavor during the war. Defense contracts boosted the economy of a lot of cities, prompting some to say "Steel State" instead of "Sunshine State." Coastal shipyards on the Gulf coast were big employers, with 15,000 working in Panama City—building more than 100 vessels—and about 9,000 producing hulls in the Tampa area. Railroads assisted with transporting vessels built inland in Orlando, where workers assembled thousands of assault watercraft used in amphibious landings like the Normandy invasion.

Prices for crops and commodities saw increases, too. Florida citrus production reached eighty million boxes during 1943, while the price of cotton doubled.

More than 250,000 Floridians either enlisted or were drafted into the military, which involved more than a few train tickets to boot camps. Meanwhile, trainloads of personnel arrived at stations all over Florida to report to those military bases. In addition to the main branches of the service, the state passed an act to create the Florida Defense Force—which would replace the National Guard if its members had to go on active duty. In 1943 the "force be with you" became known as the Florida State Guard.

The US Army Air Corps established a bombing range on more than 210,000 acres of vacant swampland east of Avon Park. Pilots learning to fly B-17s and B-29s added a lot of thunder to the skies as they went through their paces. After World War I, two airfields near Arcadia had become inactive. The Embry-Riddle Aeronautical Corporation reactivated both Carlstrom and Dorr Fields as primary training schools before World War II in "Aviation City."

Some municipal airports also doubled as a campus environment for cadets and civilian employees. Trainees flew PT-17 Stearman aircraft provided by Albert Lodwick, a Lakeland aeronautical entrepreneur acquainted with reclusive billionaire Howard Hughes. Lodwick had established a school in Lakeland, and enrollees there included cadets in Great Britain's Royal Air Force.

The Jacksonville Naval Air Station and the Camp Blanding army base near Starke were two of the state's large wartime complexes. Jacksonville was already a major commercial hub, and Camp Blanding became Florida's fourth-largest city, housing 55,000 soldiers on an installation covering 180,000 acres.

The US Navy beefed up its presence at Key West and the Pensacola Naval Air Station. The army air corps expanded at MacDill Field and Drew Field in Tampa, and at Eglin Field near Fort Walton Beach. Smaller camps were set up at the Sopchoppy Bombing Range and Immokalee Army Air Field. By the mid-1940s about forty airfields in Florida were training pilots.

The economy in Key West had been dormant after the Depression, but wartime activities caused a rebound. Seaplanes at Trumbo Naval Air Station played a vital role in submarine patrol throughout the Caribbean. Such seaplanes escorted Allied convoys and helped to win the war.

Eventually three major air bases were located in southeast Florida, all with substantial rail connections: Homestead, Morrison Field in West Palm Beach, and the Boca Raton Army Airfield. The latter developed from an existing municipal airport. The government appropriated $11 million to convert it into the army air corps' only radar training station during the war. The base grew to 800 buildings and garrisoned more than 16,000.

Despite the number of installations, many facilities began to get overcrowded during the war. Several luxury hotels that had been built by railroad magnates were allocated for "satin-sheet barracks," while others doubled as temporary clinics for injured troops.

With so many men participating in the armed forces, civilian jobs needed to be filled, and wages improved for women and minorities who filled those positions. This rush to serve became a springboard to a post-war economic boom which almost reminded Floridians of the early 1920s. The state's population increased by more than 46 percent in the 1940s, and even more so during the '50s (compared to the national increase of 15 percent).

In Boca Raton, for instance, Florida Atlantic University today stands on lands once used for that army air corps radar base. Like many other cities, Boca began to grow after the war when the men and women who trained and served there returned to settle.

MOMENTUM LED TO MERGERS
As noted, the ACL and other railroads provided a safer alternative to coastal shipping and served the fast-emerging military industry in the Southeast.

For the remaining years that it was known as the Atlantic Coast Line Railroad, the company raised the flag's image by upgrading its equipment. Starting in 1942, when Champion McDowell Davis became president of the ACL, the company completely switched its fleet of locomotives to diesel power. Concurrently, Davis attended to infrastructure, rebuilding several hundred miles of track, upgrading rail yards and shops, and installing modern signaling systems. During the period through 1955, the railroad spent more than $268 million to retool its physical plant.

Freight business blistered the rails up and down the coast and across the state, a traffic increase for the ACL of 150 percent. Wartime passenger traffic was closer to 200 percent higher, as the ACL expanded to meet demand for regal streamliners such as the Champion (named after Davis). That dolled-up rolling hotel had been introduced in 1939 and, as noted, it rode from Pennsylvania Station to Jacksonville. From there the Champion traveled south on a Florida East Coast Railway track—and raced to Miami with the FEC's new streamliner, the Henry Morrison Flagler, on a second track. Both were still competing with Seaboard's streamliner, the Silver Meteor, also introduced in 1939 and the first diesel-powered streamliner between New York and Florida. These lightweight streamliners ran faster on diesel than steam, which made a Florida getaway seem like more vacation for the price of a train ticket.

As noted, the ACL collaborated with the Penn and the FEC on segments of service. The railroad also ferried other companies' prestigious passenger trains to and from Florida: the Everglades (New York to Jacksonville); the Florida Special (New York, Miami, and St. Petersburg); the Gulf Coast Special (New York, Tampa, Fort Myers, and St. Petersburg); the Havana Special (New York to Key West until 1935); the Miamian (Washington to Miami); the Palmetto (New York, Savannah, Augusta, and Wilmington, North Carolina); and the Vacationer (New York to Miami).

Between 1940 and 1971 other streamliners ran between Lake Michigan in Chicago and Biscayne Bay in Miami: the City of Miami, Dixie Flagler, and South Wind. The routes of these three trains landed in the wheelhouse of a consortium. As the passenger coaches and sleeping cars traveled on the tracks of different companies, the relevant operator would simply switch locomotives and move on. This consortium included the Illinois Central Railroad, the Central of Georgia, the Atlantic Coast Line, the Seaboard Air Line, and the Florida East Coast Railway. The City of Miami consist was the only one of the streamliners on that Midwest-to-Florida route to operate with Pullman Standard cars, and the only one to run on all-diesel power from terminal to terminal.

With its strategic routing all across Florida, plus corporate attentiveness and heavy investment, the ACL's passenger revenue stood at more than $28 million in 1946. That would drop to about $14 million by 1959, given the growing industry competition from automobiles, trucks, and airplanes.

THE SPHERE WAS IN BALL'S COURT

As pointed out in the previous chapter, financial misery had visited the Florida East Coast Railway in the early years of the Great Depression. Unable to pay the interest on bonds issued during the land boom, the company went into receivership in 1931. It had the court's protection until the beginning of World War II, when the FEC was forced to declare bankruptcy. Before that point, however, one could say the ghost of Alfred Irénée duPont had a message for the ghost of Henry Flagler.

But idle that engine and back up that flatcar a few years to 1903 and the origins of the Apalachicola Northern Railroad. By 1907 the pioneering outfit had built a line from Apalachicola to Chattahoochee, which was a Louisville & Nashville hub. The primary industries of interest to the railroad were fisheries and lumber. In 1910 the St. Joe Lumber & Export Company built an extension from Apalachicola to Port St. Joe, using special trains. The impetus was the anticipated shipping trade through the Panama Canal, whenever it might be completed. When the Depression hit, business dropped off and the Apalachicola Northern was financially strapped.

Around 1916 Alfred I. duPont resigned from E. I. duPont de Nemours and Company after years of bitter disputes over control of the family gunpowder-manufacturing empire. Five years later he and his wife, Jessie Dew Ball duPont, were living in Jacksonville, where he began to make some investments. In the mid-1920s duPont acquired a major interest

Crowds greet passengers on the Apalachicola Northern Railroad in Port St. Joe in the 1920s. Alfred I. duPont bought the company in the 1930s when he went on a buying spree in the Panhandle. STATE ARCHIVES OF FLORIDA, FLORIDA MEMORY.

in the city's Florida National Bank. He gained a controlling interest by the outset of the Depression, and kept the bank solvent by depositing as much as $15 million of his personal fortune to discourage bank runs. By the early 1930s, the bank had six branches around the state.

Jessie's younger brother, Virginia native Edward Gresham Ball, had accompanied them to Florida. The brothers-in-law had become close friends, and duPont eventually put Ball in charge of his business dealings. DuPont had begun by buying up Panhandle property and owned almost 100,000 acres, mostly stripped forests where new growth was coming along. He organized the Gulf Coast Highway Association to build roads and develop the transportation infrastructure in northwest Florida.

Accepting Ball's advice and structuring of the deal, duPont acquired another 240,000 acres of land in 1933. The plum assets were in four counties and included the Apalachicola Northern Railroad, a settlement on St. Joseph Bay, a sawmill, the St. Joseph Telephone & Telegraph Company, the Port St. Joe Dock & Terminal Company, and several other entities.

An Atlantic Coast Line Railroad streamliner is shown at the depot in Fort Pierce, where it rode on tracks owned by the Florida East Coast Railway. STATE ARCHIVES OF FLORIDA, FLORIDA MEMORY.

In 1935, just as work was proceeding to build the St. Joe Paper Company, duPont died at age seventy-one. He had established the Alfred I. duPont Testamentary Trust, and his $56 million estate was valued at $27 million after taxes. Mrs. duPont was the principal trustee, but she accepted her brother's advice on assets of the trust—including the banks and the vast Florida land holdings.

St. Joe Paper at that time was a weak link in terms of revenue, but Ball followed duPont's expectations for launching the paper-making operation. The 100-mile railroad was hardly a contender, and the company's telephone company had a mere 167 lines—most allocated to the railroad. Ball incorporated the St. Joe Paper Company in 1936 and entered into an operational joint venture with the Mead Corporation of Ohio two years later. Mead ran the St. Joe mill until 1940, when Ball was able to exercise the duPont Trust's option to buy out Mead's interest. Ball then became president of St. Joe Paper.

After the Depression, there was new demand for packaging, especially the new corrugated cardboard, which was becoming a popular shipping alternative to wooden crates. Business increased significantly during World War II, and St. Joe Paper was able to expand. Ball, meanwhile, had long coveted the Florida East Coast Railway, despite its ailing finances. Over a period of two decades, he had played tough with Champion Davis of the Atlantic Coast Line, who also looked to buy the FEC.

With a bit of experience running St. Joe Paper's puny railroad, Ball believed that the time would come when he could eventually gain control of the FEC. In 1941 he began to buy and hold the Florida East Coast's defaulted bonds—a move the industry viewed as a bad investment.

Once the duPont Trust owned 51 percent of the outstanding bonds, Ball expected to take over. However, Davis sued Ball in federal court to block the maneuver. Their feud lasted seventeen years, at an estimated cost of $5 million each. Historians are fond of the term "hostile takeover" when they refer to the actions that enabled Ball and the duPont estate to take control of the FEC—but there are nuances to being seized.

In 1959, when William Rand Kenan Jr. retired as president of the FEC Railway, the court remained unwilling to turn over the railroad to the testamentary trust. So Ball asked for the court's permission to be president of the company. Ball got what he wanted and a salary of $12 a year. Gradually he asserted control over the FEC, first by putting in place accounting procedures that gave him daily snapshots of company finances. Then he modernized the systems for maintenance, mechanized other practices, and realigned job functions.

Finally, in 1961, St. Joe Paper Company received legal permission to take over the FEC. Then Ball really went to work, cutting the workforce of 3,300 by one-third. In 1963 unions objected to the rapid pace of cutbacks and called for a work stoppage. Ball's response was to eliminate the railroad's money-losing passenger service. By the mid-1960s, no longer bleeding red ink, the FEC was operating as a profitable intermodal/freight line.

In 1964 the FEC employed fewer than 1,000 employees. A long ordeal ensued, complete with sabotage of the tracks and equipment, and overall disruptions. Union resistance lasted in some form, including threats, shootings, and vandalism, into 1975. Unable to reach an accord with the union, the FEC replaced striking employees with other workers. Eventually federal intervention reduced most of the violence, and the US Supreme Court upheld the railroad's right to use replacement workers during the strike.

Rick Brautigan is a lifelong railroad buff who once owned the historic Delray Beach train station and housed his practice, Rick Brautigan Architecture, there. He commented on the infamous standoff: "This strike against the FEC became the longest strike in labor union history. It also changed the face of railroad labor as we know it today. No more cabooses, and two-man crews instead of five."

Not that Ball ignored the St. Joe Paper's railroad during this time. With both outfits, he reinvested earnings, such as they were, into operations. Eventually both railroads were on solid footing. According to company history, by 1980 the FEC had become a more consistently profitable enterprise than its parent, St. Joe Paper.

Author Gregg Turner described Ed Ball as a non-politician who was a powerbroker, someone who exerted immense influence in Florida businesses and controlled assets and fortunes which he never owned. Because of vast land holdings, and the banking group, Ball was the largest taxpayer in a dozen counties or more.

In 1999 the *Florida Times-Union* published an article by Raymond Mason, who was Ed Ball's confidant. Mason said managing duPont's wealth probably made Ball "the largest landowner in the state, the largest banker, the largest railroader and the largest political force." Mason described an insightful incident that occurred during the protracted labor strike against the FEC, when "the unions were demanding pay increases and were routinely blowing up tracks."

Even though Ball had eliminated passenger service, he was aware that the state could intervene and a court could order him to resume it. Ball asked Mason to arrange a meeting with Governor Farris Bryant. Mason was invited to come along, and they took the train to Tallahassee the night before. That's when Ball showed Mason a copy of duPont's will, which confirmed that he had no interest in the estate and was paid only $1 a year by the railroad.

The point was to impress upon Mason that he had no financial stake in the effect of the strike, and that his views on the strike and passenger service were a strict matter of principle: "[Ball] told me to keep my mouth shut during lunch with the governor at his farm . . . After lunch, he told me to ask the governor for a ride downtown. He wanted me to explain to the governor that Ball had no financial interest in the situation. My whole duty was that conversation with Gov. Bryant."

Ball was indeed a man who controlled wealth and wielded influence, but had little personal interest in material things. Edgar M. Turner, a third-generation banker in Pensacola and now retired, has fond memories of his dealings with the man who built the Florida National Bank building in Jacksonville in the 1970s: "He reserved the top floor for his own offices and decorated it as if it were during the 1930s. Art Mullin, a respected interior designer from Pensacola, visited Mr. Ball along with my dad [Frank Malone Turner Jr.] and told him that his was the first office he had ever been in that was fifty years old the day you moved in!"

Turner's grandfather was Edgar Robert Malone, who owned American National Bank, one of the banks that Ball purchased to form the Florida National Bank group. As a result, Ed Turner became a large stockholder in Florida National Bank: "I visited Mr. Ball and mentioned that he needed to raise the dividend on Florida National Bank stock. He responded, 'I'm doing you a favor by saving you taxes' by keeping the dividend low [to lower the bank's taxes, Ball would donate excess earnings to charity, thus avoiding corporate taxes]. I replied that if he did not raise the dividend, I would have to sell my stock. His reply, with a wide grin on his face was, 'And if you do, you will then have to pay taxes!' I have to say, I loved the guy."

Ed Turner said Ball was a very clever businessman, with cunning ways to avoid unnecessary expenses. While purchasing vast tracts of land in northwest Florida for duPont to develop into subdivisions, Ball would donate portions of the property to the state. That way, "the state would build access roads that Ball would otherwise have had to pay for himself."

Florida East Coast Industries (FECI) was incorporated in 1983 and became the holding company for the FEC Railway and the real estate holdings managed by Flagler Development Company (a separate company which today focuses on commercial real estate). In 2000 FECI began to operate independently of the St. Joe Company, and in 2007 the company was purchased with private equity funds managed by Fortress Investment Group (the next chapter will describe its current plans for the next generation of railroad service in Florida). Today the FEC operates from its headquarters in Jacksonville, and its route closely parallels the one Henry Flagler developed in the 1890s.

As for duPont's first little rail line, the Apalachicola Northern Railroad continued to operate through various reorganizations until 2002, when the Rail Management Corporation leased the line, its locomotives, rolling stock, and equipment. The Apalachicola Northern still has a route almost 100 miles long from the Gulf coast north to the Georgia line. Today the old Port St. Joe route, called the AN Railway, is owned by the Genesee & Wyoming, which bought Rail Management in 2005. The line hauls chemicals and lumber and intersects with CSX.

SEABOARD—THE LONG AND THE SHORT OF IT

In receivership by 1930, the Seaboard Air Line Rail*way* reemerged stronger after World War II as the Seaboard Air Line Rail*road* Company.

In 1949, in a venture with the Louisville & Nashville, Seaboard opened a line from Jacksonville to New Orleans. The Gulf Wind streamlined passenger train replaced the heavier New Orleans–Florida Limited, with regular stops in Tallahassee, Chattahoochee, Pensacola, Flomaton, Mobile, and Biloxi. In Chattahoochee, L & N locomotives replaced those belonging to Seaboard. And like the Atlantic Coast Line, Seaboard had been absorbing several short lines until the tracks of these two companies intertwined throughout central Florida.

Seaboard's route to New Orleans, involving a company controlled by the ACL, is one example of events that created opportunities for a conversation about a possible merger as early as 1958. And despite decades of intense rivalry and one-upmanship, people in both camps were putting a lot of time into smoothing the path toward uniting them. (Some have compared their squabbles to the Pennsylvania Railroad and New York Central, who were working out differences in the same era.)

In the mid-1920s, Seaboard Air Line Railway decided to expand with a 300-mile route from Coleman Junction south of Wildwood over to West Palm Beach, Miami, and then Homestead. Another phase was a branch from Tampa to Fort Myers and Naples on the west coast. Seaboard called the route the "Orange Blossom Special" with stops in West Lake Wales, Avon Park, Sebring, Okeechobee, and Indiantown. STATE ARCHIVES OF FLORIDA, FLORIDA MEMORY.

While proposed in 1958, the merger became official on July 1, 1967, when W. T. Rice of the Atlantic Coast Line and John W. Smith of Seaboard Air Line formed the Seaboard *Coast* Line Railroad. The new entity enjoyed thirteen years of profitable operations before it once again became fashionable to consolidate. Seaboard *Coast* Line merged with the L & N and other systems to become the Seaboard System Railroad Company. The South Florida Railroad—which was part of Atlantic Coast Line from 1902 to 1967—was part of Seaboard Coast Line from then until 1980.

Meanwhile, the Chessie System Inc., a Virginia-based parent company, had incorporated in 1973. The same year, Chessie acquired the Chesapeake & Ohio Railway, which controlled the Baltimore & Ohio Railroad, the Western Maryland Railway, and some smaller outfits. In fall 1980 Chessie System merged with Seaboard Coast Line Industries to form the CSX Corporation. Its successor, CSX Transportation, was founded in 1987.

CSX Locomotive 617 pulls a train by the Railside House Museum in Hawthorne, a small town in Alachua County east of Gainesville. Hawthorne is the location of the Marjorie Kinnan Rawlings Historic State Park—forever famous as the location of the author's home near Cross Creek between Lochloosa and Orange Lakes. STATE ARCHIVES OF FLORIDA, FLORIDA MEMORY.

Company literature indicates the acronym was part logic and part serendipity. During merger talks, the two chairmen said it was important not to use the names "Chessie" or "Seaboard" because it was going to be a partnership. Employees made suggestions and most included the initials C and S. Meanwhile, the companies needed a temporary nickname during discussions with the Interstate Commerce Commission. The lawyers decided to use CSX, and it took on a life of its own.

So what does the *X* stand for? "CSX is singularly appropriate. C can stand for Chessie, S for Seaboard, and X, which actually has no meaning." But the company conceded that *X* could be slang for Express, thus giving the X a job to do.

Today CSX operates and maintains more than 2,800 miles of track in Florida and employs more than 5,000 people. Its reports for 2014 show an investment of $247.6 million in its Florida network.

The Tallahassee Railroad Company, formed in 1834, gets points for longevity as well. It began operations in 1837 with a route from Tallahassee to St. Marks. As noted, the single-track roadbed went for 22 miles and began with mule power.

In 1839 the company acquired a steam engine and extended the line to Port Leon. With a seaport terminal and surrounded by abundant agricultural lands, the railroad had plenty of business transporting cotton during the antebellum era. In the early 1980s the line was absorbed by the Seaboard Coast Line Railroad (now CSX), which still operates freight trains over much of the original route today.

The Seminole Gulf is a short line railroad headquartered in Fort Myers that operates two former CSX freight lines in southwest Florida (it is part of a commonly owned affiliate, the Bay Colony Railroad Corporation, based in Massachusetts). The route follows the old Charlotte Harbor & Northern tracks from Arcadia to Fort Ogden, then continues on the former Florida Southern Railway tracks to Punta Gorda, Fort Myers, and Naples.

Seminole Gulf operates with CSX to transport lumber, newsprint, propane, stone, steel, scrap metal, and other commodities. Just for fun, and a little extra cash, it rides around Fort Myers as the "Murder Mystery Dinner Train," offering passengers a meal and entertainment. The cast puts on comedy, satire, and all manner of whodunits, with passengers playing "super sleuth."

"PLEASE PASS THE RATTLESNAKE"

According to the Florida Memory history project, George Kenneth End of Arcadia became fascinated with rattlesnakes in the 1930s. On a whim, he cooked one after skinning it and decided to market it as a delicacy. He formed the Floridian Products Corporation, Rattlesnake Division, and took orders for skins, charms, skulls, liniment, venom, and, of course, rattles. One very popular item was "Diamondback Rattlesnake with Supreme Sauce" (reptile meat cooked in a meat stock with mushrooms and heavy cream).

Business was so good that End moved the operation to larger quarters in Tampa and called it the Rattlesnake Cannery and Emporium. He and his sons put on traveling shows for tourists, milking the snakes for their medically valuable venom. When war loomed, and many of his snake-hunters were enlisting in the military, he vowed to continue the business, "in spite of hell, Hitler and high water."

In another ironic twist, just as Southern Railway president Samuel Spencer died in a train wreck, George End died from a snakebite in 1944. Despite many years of handling snakes, it was his first and last experience with the fangs. End got a taste of immortality for a while, having established the US Post Office in Rattlesnake, Florida.

Amtrak Arrives

Before the merger with Atlantic Coast Line, Seaboard trains continued to stop at the Indiantown depot through the 1960s, but eliminated passenger service in 1971. The depot was demolished several years later, and the Seminole Inn is the only extant building with significant ties to the 1920s boom era. S. Davies Warfield's contributions to Indiantown remain, however, as the main road through town is Warfield Boulevard. But the loss of train service there is a microcosm of what befell the passenger rail industry.

Trains had been carrying people across parts of Florida since the mid-19th century, but none of the geniuses who developed railroads had figured out how to make the service profitable. Adding in the competition from autos, trucks, and airplanes, passenger service took on the life of a permanent thorn. Perhaps some operators envied Ed Ball's ability to persuade the courts to uphold the decisions he made to reduce FEC's expenses.

With no end to the money drain in sight, Congress passed legislation in the fall of 1970 to split freight and passenger travel. President Richard Nixon signed it into law, forming the National Railroad Passenger Corporation (nickname Amtrak, from morphemes suggesting "American" and "track"). Railroad companies that became "members" of the corporation could then pay for the privilege of abandoning passenger service. This was before the SAL-ACL merger, before the dawn of CSX, and Seaboard Air Line was in front of the line to join the national corporation. Thus, it became No. 1 on Amtrak's roster of railroads that could provide passenger service in Florida. (Perhaps Warfield would appreciate the fact that passengers on Amtrak trains travel from central Florida to south Florida on the route he built.)

Amtrak's Silver Service trains—the Silver Meteor and the Silver Star—bring passengers from New York, Washington, DC, Charleston, and Savannah. Stops in Florida include Jacksonville, Palatka, DeLand, Orlando, Winter Park, Kissimmee, Lakeland, Winter Haven, Sebring, Okeechobee, West Palm Beach, Delray Beach, Deerfield Beach, Fort Lauderdale, Hollywood, and Miami. For the route from Chicago to Florida, Amtrak dropped the City of Miami streamliner and reinstated the South Wind.

In the 1980s Amtrak also resurrected a service popular among people who spend the winter season in Florida. Previously handled by Auto Train Corporation, the route takes snowbirds and their vehicles between Sanford, Florida, and Lorton, Virginia.

TRI-RAIL FOR COMMUTERS

Tri-Rail is a railroad for commuter passengers in South Florida traveling between West Palm Beach and Miami. It has eighteen stations: six in Palm Beach County, seven in Broward County, and five in Miami-Dade County. Many of its stations connect with Amtrak.

The current system was formed by the Florida Department of Transportation and began service in 1989. The aim was to provide temporary service while construction crews widened I-95 and the other primary north–south artery, the Ronald Reagan Turnpike. The South Florida Regional Transportation Authority manages Tri-Rail, along with a division of CSX Transportation.

The line on which Tri-Rail operates was built in the 1920s by the Seaboard–All Florida Railway. DOT officials had hoped to use the Florida East Coast Railway line, but the FEC declined to adjust its priority on freight service.

Due to ridership demand, Tri-Rail outlived its initial objective as a temporary stopgap to alleviate auto traffic congestion. Line extensions now bring passengers to South Florida's three international airports. In 2007 the state completed a double-track upgrade from the Mangonia Park station in West Palm Beach to Miami; the project included a high-level fixed bridge over the New River near Fort Lauderdale.

In the old-school realm, Tri-Rail also plans to modify some train cars to accommodate passengers' bicycles. There will be bike racks to park your ride until you reach your train stop.

The Legacy Factor

Harry Harkness Flagler died in 1952. One of his daughters, Jean Flagler Mathews, acquired and restored Whitehall as a memorial to her grandfather. The Henry Morrison Flagler Museum opened in 1960. Several decades later, the museum added the Flagler Kenan Pavilion on the south side of the mansion on the lake. The venue is popular for black-tie dinner dances and other charity galas—as a portion of the ballroom is devoted to an alcove for "Rambler," Flagler's restored private railroad car.

Numerous museums in Florida are devoted to its railroad history, and in many cases these institutions are housed in historic depots. And even though frequent rail travel took a lengthy pause in the 1960s, railroads continue to be revered for their role in state history. In addition to museums, trains became a running theme in many Florida theme parks and tourist attractions.

The displays and props range from vintage and romantic to rustic and/or rusted relics; at other times the treatment is contemporary, futuristic, and sci-fi. Just as there was a time before railroads in Florida, there will come a time to rethink role, route, design, and optimum gear—the way old boys and girls managed to do.

Right and Left, a Step on the Rail

Flounder's Chowder House on Pensacola Beach is popular with visitors who like to sit outdoors overlooking Santa Rosa Sound. In addition to table seating—to savor the restaurant's famous shrimp and spinach gratinée, perhaps—there is a horseshoe-shaped bar. The footrests are vintage iron rails from old tracks on the mainland.

And in Tallahassee, an old train depot houses the All Saints Cinema, where a brick wall of the former passenger station features a wall-size logo. An old-fashioned reel of "film" curls above the stylized locomotive. The cinema, which is operated by the Tallahassee Film Society, is inside the current Amtrak station.

CHAPTER 14

Private Places

Love-and-Less for All Aboard Florida

THANKS TO THE VISIONARIES, SCHEMERS, CONSTRUCTION ENGINEERS, and overworked-underpaid laborers, Florida has a rich history of railroad development. As offered in the previous chapters, those primitive-pioneering-modernized iron horses transported people and goods around the state and to points north, south, and west for more than a century.

Rail passengers went up, down, cross-state, out of state, and out of the country. Florida fish and shellfish, cattle, citrus, vegetables, sugarcane, molasses, cotton, indigo, lumber, naval stores, and phosphate rode the rails to shipping ports and connection hubs with other rail systems.

Versions of the original main lines run today carrying commuter passengers on Tri-Rail and over long-distance routes on Amtrak, and hauling freight as they did all along. There are alternatives to rail travel, yet Florida's size and shape still get in the way of efficient auto trips and affordable interstate air travel.

Orlando is four hours by car from Miami; Pensacola is eleven and Jacksonville about six. Airfare within the state costs as much or more in money and time than a flight to New York or Chicago. Yet thousands of people get on the road or in the air every day, to conduct business, visit a relative, or tour an attraction. And they do that primarily because existing passenger rail service is inadequate.

Enter a relatively new and somewhat controversial enterprise, All Aboard Florida (AAF), a private company preparing to offer express passenger service over a 235-mile route from Miami to Orlando. The $2.5 billion endeavor is being financed with debt and equity. When operational, it will become the first passenger rail line in the United States to be privately owned, operated, and maintained. As the company weighs its initial performance, it may extend All Aboard Florida to Tampa and Jacksonville (which would make Pensacola the "redheaded stepchild" in that equation).

AAF expects to be operating thirty-two passenger trains a day over the 70-mile route between Miami and West Palm Beach by early 2017. The component northward to Cocoa Beach and west to Orlando International Airport would follow by the end of that year.

Sources following the debate say the swan song of passenger rail service came at a time when Americans fell in love with their sedans and ragtops. Now, Florida lacks enough highways and other infrastructure to grow into its potential as an international tourist destination and a major player in the logistics of global intermodal cargo transportation (from ships to railcars to trucks). In an article in the *Palm Beach Post,* Robert Poole, the regional director of the Reason Foundation, said that AAF "appears to have identified a market niche" in which passenger trains are faster than cars and less aggravating than planes.

All Aboard Florida is a wholly owned subsidiary of Florida East Coast Industries LLC, which has historic ties to Henry M. Flagler (featured in chapters 9 and 11). In fact, the AAF trains will run on existing Florida East Coast Railway tracks—a tangible tie to the Flagler legacy—and a new 40-mile segment to be constructed between Cocoa and Orlando. FECI is in the process of placing a second track along the FEC freight corridor between Miami and West Palm Beach—because cargo consists snail along compared to the express passenger trains.

As noted in the previous chapter, FECI was purchased with private equity funds managed by Fortress Investment Group LLC in 2007. According to Bloomberg Business, Fortress paid $2.65 billion for FECI. At the time Fortress assumed control, the official statement said the firm made a co-investment commitment of $275 million in connection with its acquisition of "various Fortress-managed funds of Florida East Coast Industries."

Wesley R. Edens and Randal A. Nardone were two of the cofounders of Fortress in 1998, with about $400 million in assets under management. When the company issued its initial public offering in 2007, assets under management were about $30 billion. At the time, *Institutional Investor* called it the first publicly traded alternative-investment firm (private-equity and hedge-fund manager) in the United States.

Fortress had $72 billion in assets under management, Bloomberg Business reported in July 2015. All of which makes All Aboard Florida not even a trickle into the coffers, nor a miniscule drain—just another investment that hasn't dimmed the financiers' commitment despite some opposition to the project.

The non-independent directors at Fortress include Peter Lionel Briger Jr., Edens and Nardone, and Michael E. Novogratz. Independent directors include David B. Barry, Douglas L. Jacobs, and George W. Wellde Jr. At the helm of All Aboard Florida are seasoned professionals who joined the company in the past few years. Co-presidents Michael Reininger, chief development officer, and Donald Robinson, chief operating officer, are alums of the Walt Disney Company, where they were at the helm of high-profile national and international projects.

Chief financial officer Jason Bewley has spent his career in passenger transportation, travel, and tourism. Bewley was formerly with World Fuel Services, and AirTran Airways (later acquired by Southwest Airlines).

Until 2014 All Aboard Florida expected to borrow $1.6 billion from the Federal Railroad Administration to finance the project. Rather than experience the delays associated with awaiting approval for a government loan, the company opted to seek $1.75 billion in tax-exempt, private-activity bonds. In August of that year, AAF applied to the US Department of Transportation for approval of the private-activity bonds, as a government entity would issue them. (Despite a low interest rate on these debt instruments, investors like them because they don't pay taxes on the profits.)

At the time, Reininger said the bonds would expedite the start of construction on the second phase of the line between West Palm Beach and Orlando.

Geography Driving Opposition

As writer Kimberly Miller cited in the *Palm Beach Post* at the time, the move by All Aboard Florida to drop the Federal Railroad Administration loan application was "an abrupt departure . . . and a jolt to people working to derail the project."

Critics are primarily located in the counties of the Treasure Coast—Martin, Indian River, and St. Lucie—areas that are considerably less populated, with far less traffic congestion, than the Gold Coast's tri-county region of Miami-Dade, Broward, and Palm Beach Counties. Opponents cite lifestyle concerns such as noise, increased traffic congestion, and delays for boaters when drawbridges must be lowered more often.

Florida Trend magazine editor Mark Howard addressed the Treasure Coast's angst in an article in December 2014: "Three counties that won't get stations initially . . . have worked against the train. It's unclear whether they're actually worried about noise, safety issues, and property values or just trying to extort a station sooner than demand justifies."

Nor is a station planned for Brevard County, which is north of Indian River County. However, Brevard set aside its beef and "has established itself first in line for a station when demand dictates," Howard wrote.

The Federal Railroad Administration released a Draft Environmental Impact Statement for All Aboard Florida in 2014 and presented the final report in August 2015. The report covered twenty-two categories—including major environmental topics—such as air quality, cultural resources, economic impacts, effects on marine navigation, noise and vibration, rare species, traffic and safety (grade crossings), and wetlands. The report issued a "finding of no significant impact."

Critics also point to delays at railroad crossings which could affect response times for emergency personnel. The effect on first responders is of special concern in the Jupiter and Tequesta areas of northern Palm Beach County. The FEC tracks are just east of Jupiter Medical Center, where about 20 percent of emergency room patients arrive by ambulance.

And while response times to emergency rooms are of critical concern, one has only to review the log of the FEC rescue train which didn't reach Matecumbe Key in time to save hundreds of World War I veterans stranded there during the Labor Day Hurricane of 1935. As mentioned in

Chapter 12, the engineer of that train was delayed leaving Miami because the Miami River bridge was up to allow holiday boaters to pass. The fifteen minutes the train was idling there might have made the difference between saving lives and getting washed off the tracks by storm surge.

Other public outcry was related to suspicions that taxpayers would end up paying for AAF, and further that there was no proof that the company has cracked the code on profitability. In another article in the *Post*, rail expert Randal O'Toole of the Cato Institute questioned the company's ability to make the service pay for itself: "I love passenger trains and it would be real easy for me to say go, go, go, but I also know the economics of passenger trains and they don't go, go, go, they cost, cost, cost."

In June 2015 O'Toole said he is not against All Aboard Florida, "if it is entirely privately funded. However, I am skeptical that they can make a profit from passenger trains in Florida."

Part of AAF's master plan is to upgrade all of the grade crossings and install new signalization and "Positive Train Control"—a GPS-based safety technology capable of preventing train-to-train collisions, overspeed derailments, and other disasters.

Construction began in 2014 on the route between Miami and West Palm Beach. That leg was financed with $405 million in private high-risk bonds which All Aboard Florida sold in June. O'Toole also questioned the interest rate on those bonds: The 12 percent the company paid on their first bond sale was "insanely high, given the current low rates on the market. I understand they want to sell more bonds at a much lower interest rate, and that some of the revenue from that will repay the high-rate bonds. But why did they agree to pay that high rate in the first place?"

Bloomberg Business said the five-year high-risk bonds had a "payment-in-kind toggle option, which allows interest to be paid in additional notes." And while these private-activity bonds are not subsidized by public money, they are issued by the government, which is how they can get a lower interest rate. In August 2015, the Florida Development Finance Corp. met in Orlando and approved All Aboard Florida's financing strategy to sell the private-activity bonds. The vote was significant, as FDFC is the entity which the state authorized to issue the bonds. The 2014 application pertained to a resolution to authorize issuing bonds to finance or refinance the cost of acquisition, construction, renovation, and equipping the intercity passenger rail system; to approve funds for debt service reserves, if any; to appropriate funds for the capitalized interest on the bonds, if any; and to pay costs associated with the bond issue. The FDFC will receive a fee of $1.8 million for its role in issuing the bonds.

FECI made it clear in 2015 that, with or without the private-activity bonds, it intended to finance All Aboard Florida. And since taxpayers are not on the hook for what it will cost, opponents are running out of ways to derail it. FECI owns the tracks and the right-of-way between Miami and Cocoa Beach, and it has acquired the right-of-way on the Beachline Expressway for the 40-mile section of new tracks from Cocoa to Orlando.

Jim Kovalsky, a veteran computer programmer, the owner of Honestware, and president of the Florida East Coast Railway Society, is an avowed proponent of All Aboard Florida. Before the company withdrew its application for a federal loan, he decried critics who doubted the company could move forward without public funds: "If they don't want any federal money to build this, they can still do it. Fortress [Investment Group] has enough money to do it, but why should they spend their own money if they can borrow it cheaper?"

The private-activity bonds are not intended for garden-variety players in the capital markets. Because the bonds are unrated, they will be presented only to institutional investors and others accredited to dive into the deep end, with a suggested minimum of $100,000.

Bank of America Merrill Lynch created the Limited Offering Memorandum, which informs prospective investors of the "Series 2015" bonds and cites "a high degree of risk" involved—based on variables such as construction delays, cost overruns, regulatory or legal problems, high debt load, and faulty ridership projections. (The latter factor and revenue estimates were provided by third-party consultants.)

AAF is projecting more than 753,000 passengers in 2017 and $32 million in revenue, according to an article written by Mike Mayo in the south Florida *Sun-Sentinel* in August 2015. He states that AAF officials believe the ridership estimates are "realistic." To Mayo, however, they sound "wildly optimistic to borderline delusional."

Writing in the *Post* in August 2015, Miller said that if the bond-sale goes well, FECI will be able to satisfy that $405 million in high-risk bonds sold a year ago. The company also has to make annual debt payments on the private-activity bonds of $105 million.

Once the government loan was removed from the equation, the critics who objected to public financing had little to pose as an obstacle. Taxpayers won't be paying a dime; the bonds will be taxable, so the state will gain those benefits.

The project may have historic ties, but it is moving at 21-century speed.

In recent years FECI invested $345 million in land purchases for three new railway stations in Miami, Fort Lauderdale, and West Palm Beach. Site preparation and depot construction are under way in various stages at all three. And if the architectural commission is any indication of the scope and quality of what AAF is all about, consider that all three stations were planned and designed by Skidmore, Owings & Merrill (designer of the new One World Trade Center tower and the Time Warner Center at Columbus Circle in Manhattan), working with Zyscovich Architects.

In Miami there has been tremendous buzz since All Aboard Florida announced its plans. An article in the *Miami Herald* in 2014 said "it might be the biggest thing to happen in downtown Miami since Henry Flagler brought his railroad south"—and the station will be in the same location where Flagler built his depot there in 1896.

The centerpiece will be AAF's Miami "Grand Central Station," a downtown complex featuring the train platform 50 feet above street level, allowing two major east–west streets to remain open beneath the station. "MiamiCentral . . . represents an ambitious and unusual all-at-once marriage of heavy infrastructure with urban revitalization that would turn a drab stretch of downtown into a bustling fulcrum of transportation and human activity," the *Herald* reported.

"We're going to dramatically change what downtown Miami looks like 24 to 36 months from now, and in an unprecedented way," said AAF president Michael Reininger in 2014.

As of September 2015, construction was well under way at MiamiCentral, where one early phase was shifting the existing freight train track for better access to build the elevated five-train track. Grade-crossing upgrades in Miami-Dade County are on deck for 2016.

By the numbers, 1,626 piles will be drilled on the eleven-acre site, each 50 feet to 100 feet deep, and all but 40 are in place. Those were being readied for completion at the Metrorail and Metromover facilities. The piles for the station represent almost 50,000 cubic yards of concrete and 2,700 tons of rebar. About 100 workers at a time show up at a site covering six city blocks in historic Overtown, where 75 train piers will form the platform for 5,000 linear feet of track. About 8,000 tons of steel will go into the V-shaped piers, each one of which is similar in size to the columns at Washington Dulles International Airport—that timeless design by Eero Saarinen which was built in 1962.

The AAF station in Fort Lauderdale, also downtown, is part of a complex covering about 60,000 square feet and will feature a multistory lobby and an elevated passenger lounge. In 2014, the company demolished existing buildings and cleared the site. Throughout 2015, work proceeded on underground foundation work and storm drainage within the FEC right-of-way. The site involves 84 piles from 40 to 45 feet deep on the eastern portion of that right-of-way. Crews also poured the concrete for pile caps and the base for V-shaped columns.

In West Palm Beach, the AAF station also will be downtown, where existing buildings were razed in 2014. The complex will cover 60,000 square feet for the station and platform. The project involves 100 piles between 40 and 45 feet deep, and most of them are in place. The rest will be set once crews build a bypass track in the west side of the right-of-way. All Aboard Florida also plans to build a high-rise tower adjacent to the station with 275 rental apartments, office space, retail, restaurants with outside dining and an 800-space parking garage.

The AAF station at the Orlando International Airport will be located at the planned Intermodal Transportation Facility, which would link passengers with rental cars, an automated people-mover, SunRail (a local commuter system), and other ground transportation. In 2014, the legislature approved a department of transportation grant of $214 million to the airport for that purpose, which is similar to the intermodal center in Miami.

Despite progress, promising cooperation, and the fact that AAF is not requesting state or federal funds, some naysayers point to the fact that the deal for building new tracks along the Beachline Expressway is only possible because of a federal partnership with the airport.

As Jonathan Nelson wrote in *Economics21* in August 2015, All Aboard Florida will pay the airport $4.5 million a year for its lease, "so Florida East Coast is not getting a free ride." Should it become profitable, AAF could be a national model, Nelson said, "allowing more Americans to go on vacation by train in a way that does not waste tax dollars."

ROAD TEST

The Florida East Coast Railway began to bargain years ago for the missing right-of-way portion west of Cocoa Beach. The state owns a critical section of the Martin Andersen Beachline Expressway (formerly called Bee Line Expressway), a 41-mile toll road between Cocoa Beach, Orlando International Airport, and numerous central Florida tourist attractions. Three agencies own and maintain the Beachline: the Orlando–Orange County Expressway Authority (20-plus miles from near US 441 and State Road 528); the Florida Turnpike Enterprise (the westernmost 8 miles); and the Florida Department of Transportation (9 miles east of State Road 520 to the Bennett Causeway at US 1).

All Aboard Florida needed permission to use the Beachline right-of-way to connect the FEC tracks to Orlando International Airport. AAF gave land to the state and the Expressway Authority so the company could start negotiating a long-term lease. In 2013 the Expressway Authority agreed to spend $12 million to buy a 200-foot-wide strip of property along the expressway. And the Florida DOT agreed to a fifty-year lease on its section, with annual rent of $275,000 adjusted for inflation.

Those actions expedited All Aboard Florida's project. And the Beachline Expressway's participation provided an already-improved roadbed for rail track construction—a far cry from the days when railroad developers had to slog through swamp and raw ridge country to carve out a primitive roadbed.

The route for AAF trains involves several bridges—among them, the New River in Fort Lauderdale, the St. Lucie River in Stuart, and the

Loxahatchee River in Jupiter. The latter drawbridge has raised the most concern, as it dates to 1925 and is not without visible corrosion. In spring 2015 an electrical glitch kept the bridge partially open, forcing a southbound FEC freight train to idle. The traffic tie-ups at three east–west road closings turned into ninety minutes of gridlock.

The Jupiter Inlet District proposed a commonsense solution—that AAF should replace the Loxahatchee Bridge before it sends an additional thirty-two trains a day over the route. The company's response has been that it will be installing upgrades on all three bridges, measures meant to shorten the time it takes to open and close the movable parts.

As for the trains themselves, all of the diesel-electric locomotives and stainless-steel passenger cars will come from California, where Siemens AG, a German company with strong ties to South Florida, is building the rolling stock at its solar-powered hub. All Aboard Florida also gave Siemens the contract for maintenance and service on the trains. The firm has maintained a regional presence in Boca Raton since the 1980s.

FECI estimated that the project will plant a $6 billion kiss on the state's economy over the next decade, and create about 10,000 construction jobs through 2017.

Donna Shalala, a former member of President Bill Clinton's cabinet, was president of the University of Miami from 2001 to 2015. She has strongly supported All Aboard Florida for the advantages that train travel will offer the state's university students and their families.

And some south Florida millennials are showing more than a casual interest in rail infrastructure—as reflected in the High Speed Rail America Club founded by Florida International University students. An article published in *Rise:MiamiNews* in July 2015 credits brothers Darius and Demetrius Villa and their friend Aleksandr Khalfin with co-founding the club. The primary goal of the club, which claims more than 650 members, is a Maglev bullet train for Miami similar to magnetic rails in Japan and China.

The 20-mile line would connect their Modesto A. Maidique campus in west Miami-Dade County with other FIU centers in Miami Beach—an apt goal at a school that lists "accelerating our student body" in its mission statement.

The club's larger purpose is to promote high-speed rail nationwide, and the founders have filmed a documentary, *The American Train,* and announced a campus premiere for October 30, 2015. The article states that club members are consulting with three firms to refine their national vision: All Aboard Florida, American Maglev Technology, and Texas Central Railway.

NEWFANGLED FLANGES

All Aboard Florida is either a reinvented wheel, jazzed-up and "smart," or a total boondoggle—depending on whom you ask.

One businessman—who has a thorough grasp of the company's financing structure, political issues, environmental concerns, and the effects on lifestyle—was willing to flip a coin about the project's game plan: "Twenty years from now, it will be either the most brilliant idea of the century, or the dumbest idea ever. But they should just do it."

Given the backgrounds of railroad developers who literally paved the way for what FECI is building, All Aboard Florida has large loafers to fill. But the boots guarding this "fortress" are MBAs, not grade-school dropouts who worked on steamboats for a bunk and a biscuit and grew a personal fortune. The folks pressing this campaign don't have watch fobs tucked into a vest pocket, they consult an iWatch; they don't pen directives with quill and ink, they relay decisions via touch-screen notebook.

The professionals pulling the trigger on All Aboard Florida are not so much starstruck moneyed visionaries as they are professional go-for-it, make-it-happen types who see dollar signs but are not blinded by them.

Fans of the project have lined up in recent years to sing its praises and explain why passenger rail service is necessary to the state's economy: "While we continue adding new places for visitors to stay and visit, what we really need is a way to bring them here in greater numbers. That's where All Aboard Florida comes in—perhaps the most noteworthy game-changer for our destination and the region," so said Jorge Pesquera, president and CEO of Discover Palm Beach County.

In fall 2013 *Florida Today* writer Scott Gunnerson addressed the future of passenger rail, including Amtrak's long-term plan to upgrade its Florida route. The article quoted Department of Transportation Secretary

Ananth Prasad, who said that All Aboard Florida "will be the genesis for continued expansion of passenger rail."

The headline on Eric Jaffe's piece in *The Atlantic*—citing Gunnerson's article—was quite a tease: "Is Florida About to Enter a 'Golden Age' of Rail?" Jaffe attributed the sea change "in large part to a belief that there's no other way around the state's awful highway congestion."

That dilemma continues to frustrate transportation planners who understand that the number of Florida's roads and highways is not multiplying as fast as the population and the visiting public. Jaffe offered 2012 statistics for Amtrak ridership: 84,000 passengers boarding in Jacksonville and 94,000 boarding in Miami.

Passenger rail is a profitable enterprise in the Northeast corridor, so why could it not make money in Florida? Some say perception versus reality is driving that argument—that Floridians have become conditioned to the comfort and immediacy of their air-conditioned autos and SUVs, and they are not ready for rail travel the way New Yorkers accept the subway.

Prasad told Gunnerson he believes "the real challenge is getting society to accept trains as a primary mode of transportation again, but a transformation to a European-style dependence on rail travel is too lofty a goal." Yet anyone who has toured a European country by rail readily appreciates the speed, punctuality, convenience, and comfort those trains provide.

Florida has a sizable Hispanic population, doing business here and visiting family, especially in south Florida. And much of the perceived ridership will be international visitors arriving in Miami from Cuba and Central and South America—either to see relatives or tour the city. Often those people also rent a car to take in Disney World, Universal Studios, SeaWorld, and a myriad other attractions, as well as museums, galleries, and events at the Orlando Convention Center. Given that these people come from countries where rail travel is not an anomaly, All Aboard Florida would hold plenty of appeal.

Pesquera concurred, pointing out that more than thirty million passengers arriving in southeast Florida land at airports in Miami and Fort Lauderdale, "with more than one-third being international visitors who are accustomed to the use of public transportation."

"We are excited at the prospect All Aboard Florida presents to enhance and ignite the economic ties between Florida's largest market-places and the robust, influential Hispanic business communities that thrive there. Hispanics do business and visit family throughout the state, while our in-bound Latin and South American visitors have made Florida a travel destination of choice."—Julio Fuentes, president and CEO, Florida State Hispanic Chamber of Commerce.

The service is also geared to businesspeople who commute to meetings from one end of the state to the other, as well as the capital in Tallahassee. For them, All Aboard Florida poses great advantages over a car trip. As one man in West Palm Beach described the challenge, "You play Russian roulette trying to get to a meeting in Miami on time, using I-95 or the Turnpike."

I-4 between Orlando and Tampa can be a brutal ride as well, taking a driver from relative peace of mind into an abyss of clenched jaws.

Compare that experience to rail. As riders can attest, one makes the journey simply enough, collecting one's thoughts on the train, reading a book, listening to music, or preparing a presentation for a meeting with a client. Tri-Rail is what people would call "close enough for government work," which we can safely assume is a less-fabulous outing than one provided by private-sector professionals whose jobs depend on providing excellent transportation and hospitality.

Each of the AAF trains will have Wi-Fi communication. At about 900 feet long, trains are expected to clear an intersection in less than 60 seconds. They'll travel about 80 mph from Miami to West Palm Beach, then increase to 110 mph.

As well reported in the state's major newspapers and TV stations, AAF has sparked a lot of comment, pro and con. The "con" diminished as the company clarified its non-public financing plans, leaving most of the opposition in the lifestyle court. According to Jim Kovalsky, "Obstacles are fear of change and distortions of the facts. The lifestyle concerns are manufactured."

The voices "on board" with All Aboard Florida are those of business people, scholars, media, and advocates for upgraded infrastructure:

"Florida is home to the most interesting transportation project in the country," Mark Howard wrote in *FloridaTrend*. "We'll end up with a fast train that traverses the state, and [its] creation will be integrated with urban real estate development in the same way as private transportation companies did 100 years ago, to good effect."

"All Aboard Florida is an economic engine that will help drive Florida's new economy; as was done by Henry Flagler one hundred years ago," when Orlando was just beginning.—Shari Dingle Sandifer, CEO, Orlando Regional Chamber of Commerce.

"Sometimes government needs to do things the private sector can't—run prisons, build roads and bridges, operate airports and ports . . . Sometimes, though, private industry can do what government can't. Like run an efficient, affordable, convenient passenger rail service between two of the state's major cities . . . I'm on board, how about you?"—Michael Putney, WPLG (an ABC affiliate in Miami).

"Having passenger rail service make a comeback means a future stop here is a greater possibility than it ever was before. Let's not lose sight of the possibilities a project like All Aboard Florida can bring."—Jim Rathbun, businessman and resident of Indian River County.

"It's time to get on board with All Aboard Florida. Florida's economy is 'transportation-based' and our quality of life is dependent on a reliable and varied transportation system. The return of passenger rail—an efficient mode of transportation for moving people in great numbers—is not only exciting but needed and long overdue."—Matthew Ubben, president, Floridians for Better Transportation.

"All Aboard Florida will be a great asset . . . Having seamless travel service as an option to and from Orlando will make Broward County and South Florida an even more competitive business location as the new service provides efficiencies for business people traveling around the state. Another benefit will be the private investment surrounding the FEC stations that will drive large capital investments and create numerous new jobs."—Bob Swindell, CEO of the Greater Fort Lauderdale Alliance.

Cities owe their "cultural and commercial heartbeats" to that synergy between advanced rail infrastructure and those capital investments in real estate development, Mark Howard wrote.

And with All Aboard Florida, much of the private investment surrounding its stations falls in the wheelhouse of Flagler Real Estate Services LLC, a commercial property entity within FECI. Like the parent firm, it is based in Coral Gables and has a long history in the state.

Names associated with Flagler Real Estate Services include Armando Codina, a well-known Cuban American who is prominent in Miami business and in civic circles. Codina, a real estate developer and longtime friend of former president George H. W. Bush, invited Jeb Bush to be his partner in a realty firm in 1980—a lengthy association that has made both of them hugely successful. Comparing some advantages of AAF with other high-speed rail concepts proposed around the country, Robert Poole said the project represents "an excellent case of 'value capture' by the parent company, since it expects to make a lot of money via its real-estate investments in and around the new stations." (Poole cited such projects as the key to success for the Mass Transit Railway Corporation in Hong Kong.)

"For more than 20 years, there has been rising demand for an efficient and timely passenger rail service connecting Miami-Dade, Broward and Palm Beach counties," but all the early discussions required taxpayer subsidies. "That is why it is so exciting that a private company—All Aboard Florida—is investing more than $1.5 billion in private capital."—Dennis Grady, president, Chamber of Commerce of the Palm Beaches.

Anticipating other rail demand, FECI also began major infrastructure expansion projects related to Port Miami, Port Everglades in Fort Lauderdale, and the Port of Palm Beach. The impetus, of course, is not unlike that of a century ago, when Henry Flagler and Henry Plant anticipated increased opportunities from the Panama Canal. Now that most phases of the canal expansion are close to completion, it means its capacity will double—sending more ships to Florida ports to connect with freight lines.

The widened Panama Canal will strengthen Florida's economic profile, said architect Rick Brautigan: "Miami is deepening their harbor to accommodate larger container ships which in turn will contribute additional traffic to the FEC . . . [which] has built a new yard at the Miami Seaport and rebuilt their track to the site. Port Everglades is doing likewise." He cited biofuels such as ethyl alcohol to be mixed with gasoline as the driver behind ramped-up freight traffic at the port in Fort Lauderdale.

Throughout the 1980s and 1990s, high-speed passenger rail service for Florida was a pipe dream operating at disparate speeds via incongruous layers of yea and nay. Lobbyists spent two decades pitching, state employees studied on the clock, and private companies proposed developments. Voters even amended the state constitution in 2000, with 53 percent of the voters approving a high-speed rail line to connect two of the state's largest cities. It was called the Florida Overland Express.

However, those dreams of state-of-the-art inter-city rails became a vapor.

In 1999, when Jeb Bush took office as the governor of Florida, he had grave concern at the naiveté behind the amendment, as he believed the public-financed project would saddle taxpayers with costs not yet revealed. As Bush said in 2003, "This little choo-choo could cost a lot of money."

Noah Bierman wrote an article in the *Los Angeles Times* in May 2015 which drew attention to Bush's position, although the headline was pointed toward him as a 2016 presidential candidate: "Jeb Bush's war against Florida high-speed rail shows his governing style."

Bierman quoted Bush's note to a Floridian during his tenure in Tallahassee: "People thought it was 'cool' to have a really fast train running from Miami to Tampa . . . No costs were discussed. The higher taxes that are necessary will dramatically change the dynamic."

His response at the time was to cut funding of $70 million a year and promote another referendum, which later defeated FOX. Not that Bush doesn't like trains. His objections seem to have centered on public funding for "boondoggles" that take away from critical programs. The *Times* article said Bush was not against the train in principle, but he would only support it if it could be built and operated with private financial resources.

Then, in 2011, Governor Rick Scott quashed a high-speed rail project for Florida when he returned $2 billion in federal rail funds to the US Department of Transportation.

Much of the current protest came from Martin County, which amassed a war chest of $8 million "to slow down the choo-choo." But the county may have shot itself in the foot on the topic of "quiet zones."

All Aboard Florida said the company would pay to install quiet zones, which are half-mile stretches of track with extra safety measures such as additional crossing gates and lights. In such zones the engineer may suspend the obligatory sounding of the train horn (two longs, a short, and a long). AAF also offered to go beyond federally required track upgrades.

Miami-Dade, Palm Beach, and Broward Counties readily accepted the offer. However, Martin County balked and let the deadline pass on the federal application, meaning that if the county decides it does want quiet zones, it will have to use public money for the expensive upgrades. As noted above, Brevard County accepted the offer.

Indian River and Martin Counties also filed a federal lawsuit to try to shut down the railroad, but the ruling went against them. The counties sought an injunction to block the sale of the $1.75 billion in private-activity bonds. In June 2015 a federal district judge denied their request. As reported in the *Palm Beach Post,* the judge said that the counties had not shown that the railroad project depended on the bonds.

BACK IN THE DAY

After a prominent marketing career in Manhattan, Jay Van Vechten now runs an organization dedicated to people with physical limitations and/or intellectual challenges. Its primary celebration every spring since 2007 brings legions to the waterfront in Boca Raton for a free fun-day, the "Boating & Beach Bash for People with Disabilities." Activities include boat rides on private yachts for children, adults, Purple Heart recipients, and their caregivers.

Van Vechten has fond childhood memories of riding trains from New York to Florida "back in the day with my parents." His thoughts about All Aboard Florida are pretty straightforward: "I wish they'd do it, but in making it a reality, they need to have train stations that are easy to reach, are fully accessible and convenient to all. Toot-toot."

AAF says the new Siemens trains are compliant with the Americans with Disabilities Act, as they feature level boarding and ergonomic seating.

Politicians are playing it safe, at least publicly, deferring to handwringers worried about noise, the environment, and traffic delays at railroad crossings. Bottom line is, FECI has the full legal right to proceed on its own tracks with its own right-of-way. They don't need state or federal permission to upgrade what they own between Miami and West Palm Beach. They cannot be sidelined, although some tactics slowed them down. So if All Aboard Florida is a fait accompli, why prolong the dust and the dust-up?

In other words, everything old is new again. You're either on board or not.

FEC WAS FLYIN' HIGH

From the beginning of the Space Shuttle program until its retirement in 2013, rail was the only possible mode for transporting the 12-foot-wide, 150-ton solid rocket-booster segments to the launch site at Cape Canaveral. They were loaded at a manufacturing plant in Utah, then shipped cross-country in customized train cars.

Several railroads handed off the precious cargo, including CSX. The Florida East Coast Railway carried the segments for the final leg into Jay Jay railroad yard north of Titusville. There the NASA Railroad took over, transporting the cargo for 13 miles over the Indian River to the Kennedy Space Center.

Imagine the faces of our many railroad pioneers in the 19th century, if they had been asked whether their tracks would figure prominently into a space outing.

Good for a grin, eh?

Bibliography

Abbey, Kathryn Trimmer. *Florida, Land of Change.* University of North Carolina Press, 1941.

Akin, Edward N. *Flagler: Rockefeller Partner and Florida Baron.* University Press of Florida, 1991.

Allen, Frederick Lewis. *Only Yesterday: An Informal History of the 1920s.* Perennial Library, Harper and Brothers, 1931.

Asarch, Rhonda V. "Liberty Billings: Florida's Forgotten Radical Republican." Master's thesis, Florida Atlantic University, 2012.

Bingham, Sallie. *Passion and Prejudice: A Family Memoir.* Hal Leonard Corporation, 1991.

Black, Hope L. "Mounted on a Pedestal: Bertha Honoré Palmer." Master's thesis, University of South Florida, 2007.

Black, Robert C. III. *The Railroads of the Confederacy.* University of North Carolina Press, 1952.

Bramson, Seth H. *The Greatest Railroad Story Ever Told: Henry Flagler & the Florida East Coast Railway's Key West Extension.* History Press, 2011.

Brands, H. W. *The Man Who Saved the Union: Ulysses Grant in War and Peace.* Anchor Books, 2012.

Brown, C. W. "The Florida Investments of George W. Swepson." *The North Carolina Historical Review,* 1928.

Burnett, Gene M. *Florida's Past: People and Events that Shaped the State.* Pineapple Press, 1996.

Chandler, David, and Mary Voelz Chandler. *The Binghams of Louisville: The Dark History Behind One of America's Great Fortunes.* Crown Publishers, 1989.

Cook, David. "Arredondo Had Help in Settling Alachua." *Ocala Star-Banner,* October 11, 1992.

Cowart, John W. *Jacksonville's Railroad History.* Self-published online, 2005.

Cusick, James. "Understanding Colonial Florida." Teachingflorida.org, a program of the Florida Humanities Council. http://teachingflorida.org/article/understanding-colonial-florida.

Denham, James M. Review of *Moses Levy of Florida: Jewish Utopian and Antebellum Reformer,* by C. S. Monaco. H-Net Reviews, 2006.

Dovell, J. E., and J. G. Richardson. *History of Banking in Florida: 1828–1954.* University of Florida, 1955.

Dunn, H. Hampton. "Old Hotel Typifies Sleepy Fishing Village." Photouring Florida. University of South Florida Libraries, 1960.

Epstein, Alex. "Vindicating Capitalism: The Real History of the Standard Oil Company." *The Objective Standard 3*, no. 2 (2008).

Fenlon, Paul E. "The Notorious Swepson-Littlefield Fraud: Railroad Financing in Florida (1868–1871)." *Florida Historical Quarterly Vol. 32*, no. 4 (1954).

Fishburne, Charles Jr. *The Cedar Keys in the 19th Century.* Seahawk Publications, 1983.

Florida Memory. State of Florida Division of Library & Information Services. https://www.floridamemory.com.

Flynn, John Thomas. *God's Gold: The Story of Rockefeller and His Times.* Ludwig von Mises Institute, 1932.

Gallagher, Dan. *Florida's Great Ocean Railway.* Pineapple Press, 2003.

Gallagher, Peter B. "Hah-Pong-Ke: Tampa Red." *Seminole Tribune,* February 28, 2014.

Glover, F. H. "Henry B. Plant—Genius of the West Coast." *Suniland: The Magazine of Florida 1,* no. 5. Peninsular Publishing Company, (1925).

Gordon, John Steele. "The Other Half of Standard Oil." The American Enterprise Institute, October 29, 2008. https://www.aei.org/publication/the-other-half-of-standard-oil.

Groene, Bertram H. *Ante-Bellum Tallahassee.* Florida Heritage Foundation, 1971.

Grunwald, Michael. *The Swamp: The Everglades, Florida, and the Politics of Paradise.* Simon & Schuster, 2007.

Herr, Kincaid A. *The Louisville & National Railroad, 1850–1863.* University of Kentucky Press, 2015.

International Directory of Company Histories, vol. 8. St. James Press, 1994.

Jones, Lucy D. "Tampa's Lafayette Street Bridge: Building a New South City." Graduate thesis, Scholar Commons, University of South Florida, 2006.

Kelley, William Darrah. *The Old South and the New: A Series of Letters.* Knickerbocker Press, 1888.

Lanphear, John. "Ziba King." Southwest Florida History, 2013. http://flhistorybyjohn.com/ziba-king.html.

Lefèvre, Edwin. "Flagler and Florida." *Everybody's Magazine,* 1910.

Leonard, Elizabeth. *Lincoln's Forgotten Ally: Judge Advocate General Joseph Holt of Kentucky.* University of North Carolina Press, 2011.

Martin, Sidney W. *Florida's Flagler.* University of Georgia Press, 1949.

Matthews, Janet Snyder. *Venice: Journey from Horse and Chaise: A History of Venice, Florida.* Pine Level Press, 1989.

Matrana, Marc R. *Lost Plantations of the South.* University Press of Mississippi, 2009.

"Myths and Dreams: Exploring the Cultural Legacies of Florida and the Caribbean." Millennium Project, organized by the Jay I. Kislak Foundation, 2000–2001. http://www.kislakfoundation.org/millennium-exhibit/home1.htm.

Page, Walter Hines, and Arthur W. Page. *The World's Work,* vol. 17. Doubleday, Page & Company, 1909.

Paisley, Clifton. *The Red Hills of Florida, 1528–1865.* University of Alabama Press, 1989.

Parks, Pat. *The Railroad That Died at Sea.* Stephen Greene Press, 1968.

Peterson, Nancy M. "Jim Hill: Railroad Builder and Visionary." *Wild West,* August 2002.

Pettengill, George Jr. *The Story of the Florida Railroads.* Railway and Locomotive Historical Society, Harvard Business School, 1952.

Prince, Richard E. *Seaboard Air Line Railway: Steam Boats, Locomotives and History.*
Indiana University Press, 1969.

Redford, Polly. *Billion Dollar Sandbar.* E. P. Dutton, 1970.

Reynolds, Kelly. *Henry Plant: Pioneer Empire Builder.* Florida Historical Society Press,
2003.

Roosevelt, Theodore. "Spanish-American War: The Rough Riders in Tampa." (1899).
Florida: Essays and Poems, compiled by the Florida Center for Instructional
Technology. http://etc.usf.edu/lit2go/70/florida-essays-and-poems/4649/
spanish-american-war-the-rough-riders-in-tampa.

Sammons, Sandra Wallus. *The Two Henrys: Henry Plant and Henry Flagler and Their
Railroads.* Pineapple Press, 2010.

Sherman, Christopher. "History's Brief Sidetrack." *Orlando Sentinel,* October 7, 2004.

Shroder, Tom, and John Barry. *Seeing the Light: Wilderness and Salvation, A Photographer's
Tale.* Random House, 1995.

Shug, Mark C., and William W. Wood. *Economic Episodes in American History.* Wohl
Publishing, 2011.

Smyth, G. Hutchinson. *The Life of Henry Bradley Plant: President of the Plant System of
Railroads and Steamships and also of the Southern Express Company.* G. P. Putnam's
Sons, 1898.

The Southern Reporter, vol. 28. West Publishing Company, 1901.

Standiford, Les. *Last Train to Paradise.* Broadway Paperbacks, 2002.

State Archives of Florida.

Stimson, H. A. *Depot Days.* Star Publishing Company, 1972.

Stowe, Harriet Beecher. "From Mandarin to St. Augustine." (1872) *Florida: Essays and
Poems.* Florida Center for Instructional Technology, College of Education, University of South Florida.

Thuma, Cynthia. *Palm Beach in Vintage Postcards.* Arcadia, 2001.

"The Tribune Almanac for the Years 1838 to 1868." *New York Tribune,* 1868.

Turner, Gregg M. *A Journey into Florida Railroad History.* University Press of Florida,
2008.

———. *Florida Railroads in the 1920s.* Arcadia Publishing, 2008.

Walby, David L. *William Henry Chase, Uniquely American.* Outskirts Press, 2014.

Walker, W. M. "The Greatest Men of Florida." *Suniland: The Magazine of Florida,* vol. 1,
no. 4 (1925).

Waugh, John C. *The Class of 1846: From West Point to Appomattox.* Ballantine Books,
1984.

Westfall, L. Glenn. "Don Vicente Martinez Ybor, The Man and His Empire: Development of the Clear Havana Industry in Cuba and Florida in the Nineteenth Century." PhD dissertation, University of Florida, 1977.

Wiseman, Maury. "David Levy Yulee: Conflict and Continuity in Social Memory." Jewish American Society for Historic Preservation. Article reprinted for the University
of Florida, Gainesville, 2006.

Wright, E. Lynne. *More Than Petticoats: Remarkable Florida Women.* Rowman & Little-field, 2010.

Wyllie, Robert J. "George William Swepson." *Dictionary of North Carolina Biography.* University of North Carolina Press, 1994.

Zerfas, Lewis L. Article. "The Last Train from Fernandina." Reprinted online for the Florida Railroad Museum, 2006. Printed (date unknown) in the *Florida Frontier Gazette.* Reprinted online at www.ussforthenry.com/USSFHpdf/LastTrainFrom Fernandina.pdf.

Index

Adams Express Co., 109, 110
Adams, John Quincy, 8, 16, 164, 165
Adams-Onis Treaty, 8
African Americans, x, 2, 14, 15, 48, 67, 83, 84
Ahaya, 14
Akin, Edwin, 151
Alabama & Florida Railroad, 46, 55, 94, 101, 102, 106
Alabama & Western Florida Railroad, 100
Alabama Great Southern, 180
Alabama, Florida & Georgia Railroad, 25, 26, 106
Alachua Indians, 14
Alafia, Manatee & Gulf Coast Railway, 184, 185
Alcazar Hotel, 151, 238
All Aboard Florida, xi, 278–93, 294–95
Allen, Frederick Lewis, 234, 236, 238, 249
Amelia Island, Florida, 7, 8, 21, 69
American Agricultural Chemicals Co., 184
American National Bank, 270
Amistad, 164–65
Amtrak, 275–76, 277, 278, 288
"Anaconda Plan," 51
Anderson, Andrew, 147, 149, 156, 157
Andrews, Samuel, 137, 138
Apalachee Indians, 11
Apalachicola Northern Railroad, 23, 265, 266, 271
Apalachicola River, 5, 6, 7, 22
Arcadia Rail Road Co., 181, 182
Arcadia, Florida, 104, 106, 181–82, 235, 239, 259
Archer, James T., 38, 44
Arkwright, Preston S., 189

Armorous, Martin F., 189
Arredondo, Fernando de la Maza, 9, 10, 33
Astor, Jack, 149
Astor, John Jacob, IV, 114, 115
Astor, William Backhouse, Jr., 79–81, 114
Astor, William, 149, 172
Atkinson, H. M., 189
Atlanta & St. Andres Bay Railway, 100, 101, 192
Atlanta, Birmingham & Atlantic Railroad, 189
Atlanta, Georgia, 100, 169, 246
Atlantic & Gulf Railroad, 59, 79, 110
Atlantic and Gulf Canal and Okeechobee Land Co., 96
Atlantic Coast Dispatch, 238
Atlantic Coast Line Railroad, 123, 129, 182, 183, 185, 191, 193, 237, 238, 239, 244, 245, 246, 247–48, 250, 258, 263, 264, 265, 267, 271, 272, 275
Atlantic, Gulf & West Indian Transit Co., 82, 113, 168
Atsena Otie, 28
"Aviation City," 235, 262

Bahia Honda Bridge, 209, 222, 255
Bailey, J. C., 224
Baldwin, Abel Seymour, 38, 44, 45, 73
Baldwin, Doc, 54, 66
Ball, Edward Gresham, 266, 267, 268, 269, 270, 275
Baltimore Steam Packet Co., 241
Bank of Pensacola, 26
Bank of the United States, 25, 26
Bartow, Florida, 120

Bartram, William, 81
Battle of Cedar Key, 64
Battle of Gainesville, 63
Battle of Horse Landing, 63
Battle of Natural Bridge, 65, 70
Battle of Olustee, 62
Battle of Peachtree, 70
Bay Line Railroad, 101
"beach walkers," 159
Beachline Expressway, 286
Beardsley, William, 233, 248
Beaulieu villa, 172
Bennett, Jim, 90
Bingham, Barry, 230
Bingham, Eleanor Miller, 230
Bingham, Mary Lily Flagler, 231–32
Bingham, Robert, 229, 230, 231,
    232, 233
Bingham, Sallie, 230, 231, 233
biofuels, 293
Birmingham, Alabama, 169
Birmingham, Columbus & St. Andrews
    Bay Railroad Co., 101
"Black Seminoles," 14
Blackstone, Ellen Elizabeth, 109, 110
Blount, Alexander Clement, 177
Blount, William Alexander, Sr., 177
Bloxham, William, 95
Boca Grande, Florida, 184
Boca Raton, Florida, 236
bonds: city, 125; construction, xi, 241;
    corporate, 76; fraudulent, 74; high-
    risk, 284; investor, 74; mortgage, 46,
    77, 224, 243; private-activity, 280, 282,
    283, 284; railroads, 44, 75, 77, 78, 99;
    state, 76, 78, 79, 88
Bone Valley, Florida, 117–18, 125, 183
Boston Herald, 102, 103
Bradley, Peter B., 184–85, 242
Bragg, Braxton, 57
Brautigan, Rick, 269, 292
Breakers, The, 155–56, 230, 238

bridges: Aboard Florida and, 286–87;
    Key West, 198–99, 202, 205, 209–210,
    217–23, 239, 251, 255
British, in Florida, 12, 14
Brooksville Ridge, 4
Brown, C. K., 78
Brown, Franklin, 115, 118, 119
Brown, Harvey, 56, 57
Brown, Thomas, 44
Browne, Jefferson Beale, xi, 196, 197,
    199, 202
Bryant, Farris, 269, 270
Bryce, Crichton, 86
Bryce, George William, 85–86
Bryce, John, 86
Buchanan, James, 56, 67
Busch, Adolphus, ix, 187
Bush, Jeb, 292, 293
Butcher, Clyde, 98

Cabell, Edward Carrington, 46
Cade, J. G., 114
Call, George W., 47
Call, Richard Keith, 8, 9, 24, 27, 46, 51
Callahan, Daniel, 38, 105
Candler, Asa Griggs, 101
Cantacuzène, Michael, 172, 256
Car 91 train, 154–55, 195
*Carpet-Bag Rule in Florida, the Insider
    Workings of the Reconstruction of Civil
    Government in Florida after the Close of
    the Civil War*, 92–93
Carrabelle, Tallahassee & Gulf Railroad
    Co., 179
Casa Marina, 238
Casa Monica hotel, 151
cattle: 11, 12, 62, 90, 91, 124, 176, 182,
    278; ranching, 11–13, 90; smuggling,
    51. 61, 62, 124
"Cedar Isles," 28
Cedar Key, Florida, 28, 36, 37, 41, 47,
    48, 51, 64, 83, 85, 91, 113, 114, 119,
    249, 251

cement, designer, 211–13
Central Cypress Co., 189, 190
Central of Georgia Railway, 100, 180, 193, 265
Centralia, Florida, 190
Chaires, Benjamin, 21
Chandler, David, 232–33
Chapman, F. A., 135, 136
Charlotte Harbor & Northern Railroad, 185, 237, 239, 240, 241, 242, 244
Chase, Andrew, 92
Chase, William Henry, 25–27, 56
Chautauqua, education enterprise, 99–100
Chesapeake & Ohio railway, 272
Chesterfield and Kershaw Railroad, 170
Chestnut, Esther Serena, 41–42
Chicago & Eastern Illinois Railroad, 182, 183
Chipley, William Dudley, viii, 69–70, 94, 99, 100
Chipola Canal Co., 19
Choctaw Indians, 11
citrus products, 86, 149, 176, 249, 257, 262
Civil War: Battle of Olustee, 62; Florida and, 50–72; railroads after, 88; salt and, 136. *See also* Confederacy; US Army
Clark, Maurice B., 137
Clarke, M. J., 66
Cloisters, The, 236
coast-to-coast rail link, 35–38, 41
Coe, Clarence Stanley, 222
coffeedam, 212, 220–21
Coleman, Robert Habersham, 121
Collier, Barron Gift, Sr., 257–58
Columbia, South Carolina, 169
commuter passengers, 276–77, 278
Confederacy, 39–40, 65; Ambush at St. Marys River and, 60; Battle of Cedar Key and, 64; Battle of Gainesville and, 63; Battle of Horse Landing and, 63; Battle of Natural Bridge, 65; Florida transportation and, 51; Fort Pickens

and, 57; Fort San Marcos and, 70, 71; train service and, 58; veteran treatment following war, 69
Confederate Congress, 54; David Levy's citizenship and, 34
Congress, 54; company land grants and, 44, 45; rail development and, 10, 19, 27–28, 275; slavery and, 35; Standard Oil Trust and, 150–51
Conversation with Bertha Palmer, A, 176
Cooper, Samuel, 65
Cordova Hotel, 238
Cornwall-Lebanon Railroad, 121
cotton crops, 21, 262
Cottonwood plantation, 36, 59, 68
Craig Key, Florida, 251
Crash of '29, 249
Creek Indians, 13
Crichton, Mary Louise, 85
CSX Transportation, 40, 271, 272, 273, 274, 275, 276, 295
Cuba Railroad Co., 200
Cuba, 11; car ferries to, 239; cattle to, 51, 61, 62, 91, 124; immigrants from, 121; railroads, 200; ships to, 222, 226; tobacco crops, 126, 185, 200
Cullen, James, 71
Cutting, Fulton, 168–69
Cutting, W. Bayard, 168–69

Dalhart, Vernon, 181
Davis, Champion McDowell, 264, 268
Davis, D. P., 236–37
Davis, Jefferson, 53, 59, 67
de Avilés, Pedro Menéndez, 7, 8
Deep Lake Railroad, 258
Deep Lake, Florida, 256–57, 258
DeFuniak Springs, Florida, 99
deFuniak, Frederick R., 95, 99, 100
Delano, Lyman, 247–48
deLeón, Ponce, 7, 11
Demens, Peter, 97, 191
Denny, Edward, 59–60

Department of Transportation, 286
Depot Key, Florida, 28
DeSoto, Hernando, 11
Devereux, James H., 143
Dibble, Franklin, 75, 77
Dickers, Edward, 39, 40, 47, 82, 113, 178
Dickerson, Edward, 39, 47, 113
Dickison, John J., 63
diesel power trains, 247, 264, 265, 287
disabled people, train service and, 294–95
Disston City, Florida, 97
Disston, Hamilton, 95–96, 97, 98, 170
Dixie Limited train, 182, 183
"Dixie Route," 182
Doggett, Aristides, 178
Drew, George F., 78
Dunn, John, 240
duPont, Alfred I., 265–67, 270
duPont, Jessie Dew Ball, 265, 267
Dusenbury, W. P., 205
Duval, H. S., 199
DuVal, William Pope, 8, 16

East and West Coast Railway, 239, 240
East Coast Railway, 238
East Florida Railroad, 111
Eaton, John Henry, 8
economy: Florida, ix, 12, 60, 249, 291,
    292; Key West, 263; Tampa, 125
Edison, Thomas, 131, 193
education, segregation and, 152
Edwards, Arthur Britton, 172, 175
electricity, on trains, 123
Emancipation Proclamation, 67
End, George Kenneth, 274, 275
Epstein, Alex, 138, 141–42
Escalante Fontaneda, Hernando de, 8
Everglades, Florida, 96, 98, 200, 208

farms, Florida, 98, 101
Fenlon, Paul A., 75, 78
Fernandina & Jacksonville Railroad,
    40, 168

Fernandina, Florida, 7, 8, 41, 47, 63, 249
Ferrira, Francis, 48
Finegan & Co., 71
Finegan, Joseph, 38, 39, 40, 53, 57, 59, 62,
    63, 66
Firestone, Harvey Samuel, 193
First Coast Railroad, 40
"First Railroad War," 180
First Seminole War, 19
Fisher, Carl G., 236
Flagler and York Salt Co., 136–37
Flagler Development Co., 270–71
Flagler Viaduct, 216, 218, 220, 225
Flagler, Ann Caroline "Carrie," 134,
    145, 229
Flagler, Harry Harkness, 138, 145, 152,
    228, 229
Flagler, Henry M., viii, x, 98, 132, 133,
    144, 145, 202; bankruptcy of, 137;
    Civil War and, 136; companies of,
    138–44, 145, 149; death of, 228, 229,
    230; early background, 134–36, 165;
    estate of, 177, 228–33; family, 133–34,
    136, 144–45, 149–50, 151, 152,
    156–57, 228, 229, 233; Flagler System
    and, 231, 249; Henry Plant and, 112,
    123, 127, 147, 159; hotels of, 149,
    151, 153, 154, 155, 162–63, 192, 238;
    James Ingraham and, 147, 198; John
    Davison Rockefeller and, 126, 137–44,
    147, 165, 226, 229; Jacksonville and,
    250; Joseph Meredith and, 202, 215;
    Joseph Parrott and, 147, 148, 203, 207,
    208, 209, 213, 214, 216, 217; Julia
    Tuttle and, 160, 162, 163; Key West
    Extension and, 166, 195–227, 228;
    life review of, 165–66; Miami train
    route and, 159, 162–64; newspapers of,
    225; oil and, 137–38, 141, 143; Palm
    Beach and, 153; as philanthropist,
    151–52, 163; railroads and, 98, 147,
    156, 162; "Rambler" rail car, 154–55,
    195, 225, 277; real estate and, 147; salt

production and, 136–37; segregation
and, 152; St. Augustine and, 146, 147;
Standard Oil Co. and, 138–46, 223;
Tampa to Miami route and, 159; Trust
of, 233; William Krome and, 199–200,
203, 211, 215. 217, 218; wives of, 136,
144–45, 149–50, 156–57, 158, 165,
228, 229, 233
Flagler, Ida Alice Shourds, 145, 149–50,
156–57
Flagler, Isaac, 133, 134
Flagler, Jennie Louise Benedict, 136, 145,
151, 229
Flagler, Margery, 229
Flagler, Mary Harkness, 136, 137,
144–45, 228
Flagler, Mary Lily Kenan, 157-58, 228–33
"Flagler's Folly," 202
Flegler, Zacharra, 132–33
Fleming, George, 9
Florida: economy, 12, 52; farms, 98,
101; lumber, 28, 85, 98, 100, 149,
181, 182, 190, 192, 235, 265, 278;
martial law and, 73; mining in,
179, 184; population, 88, 193, 263;
Reconstruction and, ix, 73–93;
sawmills in, 181; secession of, 40, 50;
segregation laws, 83; statehood, ix, xi,
23, 45; topography of, 2–5; tourism,
80; Union readmission of, 67; US
acquisition of, 19; water, 4, 208, 257;
weather, 4, 22, 23, 209, 210, 211,
212, 216, 217, 222, 227, 249, 250-56,
249, 281
Florida East Coast Canal and
Transportation Co., 49
Florida Atlantic & Gulf Central Railroad,
46, 54, 62, 73, 74, 75, 76
Florida Central & Gulf Railroad, 240
Florida Central & Peninsular Railroad,
125, 168–69, 189, 224
Florida Central & Western Railroad, 168
Florida Central Railroad, 75, 76, 77, 168

Florida City, Florida, 205
Florida Development Finance Corp., 282
Florida East Coast Hotel Co., 238
Florida East Coast Industries, 270, 271,
279, 280, 283, 284, 287, 288, 295
Florida East Coast Railway, 98, 156, 162,
177, 180–81, 195, 199, 205–6, 213,
214, 215, 221, 224, 231, 233, 237, 239,
240, 243, 244, 245, 246, 247, 248,
251, 254, 264, 265, 268, 269, 270, 279,
286, 295
Florida Gulf & Central, 240
Florida Land and Colonization Co., 95
Florida Land and Immigration Co., 71
Florida Mortgage and Investment Co.
Limited, 170
Florida National Bank, 266, 270
Florida Overland Express, 293
Florida Platform, 3
Florida Purchase Treaty, 8
Florida Railroad, 28, 36–40, 41, 42, 46, 47,
52, 53, 58, 63–64, 66, 71, 72, 81, 82, 84,
91, 105, 106, 113, 178, 249
Florida Railway & Navigation Co., 168
Florida Reefs, 199
Florida Southern Railway, 104, 105, 115,
118–19, 181, 182, 244, 247, 258, 274
Florida Special train, 123, 124, 194, 244,
246, 247, 264
Florida Transit & Peninsular Railroad,
113, 168
Florida Transit Railroad, 113, 116, 119
Florida West Shore Railway, 241, 244
Florida, Alabama & Georgia Railroad, 23,
58, 65, 66, 106, 178
Florida, Western & Northern
Railroad, 242
Floridian Products Corp., 274
Floyd, Richard, 48
Ford, Henry, 193
Fort Barrancas, 55–56, 57
Fort Brooke, 117
Fort Clinch, 69

Fort Dallas, Florida, 162
Fort Jefferson, 57
Fort Lauderdale, Florida, 159, 162, 259, 276; All Aboard Florida and, 284, 285
Fort McRee, 57
Fort Meade, Florida, 184
Fort Myers Southern Railroad, 258
Fort Pickens, 54, 55–56, 57
Fort Pierce, 153
Fort San Marcos, 70
Fort Taylor, 57
Fortress Investment Group, 279, 280
freight shipments, ix, 4, 125, 149, 182, 199, 237–38, 244, 255, 264, 275, 278, 279, 293
French, in Florida, 7, 11

Gainesville, Florida, 30, 63, 104, 118
Gainesville, Ocala & Charlotte Harbor Railroad, 104
Gallagher, Dan, 198, 255
Gamble, George, 190
"gandy dancers," 83–84
Gasparilla Island, 184–85
gas-powered trains, 257
Gaster, Gordon D., 260
George A. Smathers Libraries, 60
Georgia Car & Locomotive Co., 71
Georgia Pine Railway Co., 179
Georgia Railway & Power Co., 189
Georgia Southern & Florida Railroad, 180, 237, 250
Georgia, Carolina & Northern Railway, 170
Georgia, Florida & Alabama Railroad, 179, 241
Georgia: boundary dispute with, 50; rail; train service and, 19, 23, 39, 46, 59, 65, 74, 101, 104, 110, 111, 112, 121, 179, 189, 224, 246, 271
German-American Lumber Co., 235
Glover, F. H., 129, 130
golf courses, 156, 236

Gordon, John B., 224
Gordon, John Steele, 139, 141, 144
Grant, Julia Dent, 172, 256
Grant, Ulysses S., 67, 69, 82, 103
grapefruit produce, 194
Grassy Island, Florida, 191
Great Britain, in Florida, 1, 7, 8
Great Depression, 243, 247, 250, 254, 263, 266
Great South: A Record of Journeys, The, (King), 69, 89
Great Southern Railroad, 224
Gulf Coast Development Co., 100
Gulf Coast Highway Assoc., 266

H. M. Flagler Trust, 233
Haile, Serena, 105–6
Haile, Thomas Evans, 41–42
Haines, Henry Stevens, 110–11, 112, 116, 118, 130
Hanson, John, 48
Harbour Island, Florida, 191
Harkness, David, 133, 134, 135
Harkness, Elizabeth, 133, 134
Harkness, Lamon G., 135, 136
Harkness, Stephen, 137, 138
Harrison, Fairfax, 180
Hart, Hubbard L., 86–87
Hart, Isaiah D., 105
Haskell, C. C., 102, 103
Haskell, Edwin B., 102, 103
Havana Special train, 244, 245, 246, 264
Haycraft, J. J., 252
Hemingway, Ernest, 238, 251–52, 253
Henck, Edward Warren, 102, 103, 115, 116
Hendry, A. F., 62
Henry Morrison Flagler Museum, 158, 277
Hensley, Don, 102, 103, 184, 185
Herr, Kincaid, 101, 102
High Finances in the Sixties (Hicks), 76
High Speed Rail America Club, 287–88

Hispanic population, 289, 290
Holt, Joseph, 67
Homeplace, 85
Homestead, Florida, 199, 204, 205,
    206, 209
Honore, Adrian, 173, 182
Honoré, Ida Marie, 172
horses, 12–13
Hotel Belleview, 126
Hotel Belleview-Biltmore, 246
Hotel Ponce de Leon, 150, 238
Hotel Punta Gorda, 119
Houstoun, Edward C., 46, 73, 75, 76
Hull, Joseph, 184
hurricanes, 22, 209, 216, 250; Key West,
    210, 211, 212, 216, 217, 222, 227; of
    1843, 23; of 1851, 23; of 1906, 210–11,
    212; of 1910, 217, 222, 250; of 1919,
    217; of 1926, 249; of 1928, 249; of
    1935, 227, 250–56, 281

ice, trains and delivery of, 249
immigrant laborers, vii, 18, 83, 86, 121,
    167, 179, 185, 208
Indians, x, 7, 9, 11, 13, 14, 28, 117
Indiantown, Florida, 242, 243, 275
Ingraham, James, 116, 125, 127, 147, 149,
    159, 162, 198, 200
insects, in Key West, 203
Internal Improvement Board, 44, 45
Internal Improvement Fund, xi, 38, 72, 73,
    88, 95, 96, 111, 113, 169, 178, 199
Interstate Commerce Commission, 234,
    240, 242, 273
iron rails, 58–59, 65, 66
Isle de Mai, 7–8

J. B. Bleeker boat, 48
Jackson, Andrew, 8, 16, 43, 51, 70
Jacksonville & St. John's River
    Railroad, 121
Jacksonville Naval Air Station, 262
Jacksonville Terminal Co., 250

Jacksonville, Florida, 45, 54, 118, 169, 244,
    250, 279, 289
Jacksonville, Gainesville & Gulf
    Railway, 241
Jacksonville, Pensacola & Mobile
    Railroad, 75, 76, 79, 168
Jacksonville, St. Augustine & Halifax
    River Railroad, 147, 156
Jacksonville, St. Augustine & Indian River
    Railway, 147, 149, 198, 199, 228
Jacksonville, Tampa & Key West Railway,
    118, 119
James Burt steamboat, 87
Janney, Eli, 92
Jennings, Oliver B., 138
Jewfish Creek, Florida, 205, 206, 216
Johnson, Andrew, 67
Jones, A. J., 78
Jones, Lawrence, 175
Jones, Pembroke, 158, 231
Jones, Samuel, 65
Juniper & Lake Worth railroad, 156

Keith, Minor, 101
Kelley, William Darrah, 87–88, 89
Kenan, Owen, 229, 230
Kenan, William Rand, Jr., 229, 233,
    248, 268
kerosene, 139, 143
Key Largo, Florida, 98, 204, 205, 221;
    fresh water and, 208; laborers, 206,
    207, 208, 211, 216; liquor restriction
    on, 207–8; state approval for, 213; train
    service to, 195–227
Key West Extension, 98, 195–227; bridges
    of, 198–99, 202, 205, 209–210, 217–23,
    239, 251, 255; designer cement for,
    211–13; equipment for, 203, 209;
    hurricanes and, 210, 211, 212, 216, 217,
    222, 227, 250–56; tidal wave, 252–53
Key West, Florida, 224, 239, 246, 263. See
    also, Key West Extension.
Key, Nan, 85–86

King, Edward, 69, 89
King, Ziba, 90–91
Kleinberg, Eliot, 243
Knight's Key, 204, 206, 207, 209, 214, 215, 216, 219, 221, 222, 223, 224
Krome, William J., 199–200, 203, 211, 215, 217, 218, 223

L. G. Harkness & Co., 134
LaBelle, Florida, 241
Lake City, Florida, 46
Lake DeFuniak Land Co., 99
Lake DeFuniak, Florida, 99
Lake Ewimico and St. Joseph Canal and Railroad Co., 22–23
Lake Jackson Mounds, 11
Lake Monroe and Orlando Railroad, 102
Lake Shore & Michigan Railroad, 141, 142
Lake Surprise, Florida, 205, 206
Lake Wales Ridge, 4
Lake Wimico and St. Joseph Canal and Railroad Co., 106
land grants, 9; companies and, 45; Congressional, 44, 45; federal, viii, 21, 39, 73, 88; Internal Improvement Fund and, 44, 111; state, 198
Langford, Walter Galloway, 257
Last Train to Paradise (Standiford), 136, 201, 208, 254
Laurie, Murray, 84, 91
LeBaron, Francis, 184
Lefévre, Edwin, 146, 165, 166, 195, 223, 227
Leon Rail-Way Co., 19, 21, 106
Lesley, John T., 122
Levy, David. *See* Yulee, David Levy.
Levy, Moses Elias, 10, 31, 32–33, 34, 35, 80
Lincoln, Abraham, 57, 60, 67, 86
Littlefield, Milton S., 74–76, 78–79
Live Oak, Florida, 58, 110, 111

Live Oak, Tampa & Charlotte Harbor Railroad, 115
Lodwick, Albert, 262
Long Key Fishing Camp, 238
Long Key Viaduct, 209–210, 213, 214, 215, 238, 255
Long Key, Florida, 213, 238, 251
Lord, Joseph H., 172, 175
Loughman, Margaret Josephine, 128, 129
Louisville & Nashville Railroad, 94–95, 99, 100, 101, 102, 177, 183, 185, 237, 242, 245, 271
Lower Matecumbe, Florida, 213
lumber, Florida, 28, 85, 98, 100, 149, 181, 182, 190, 192, 235, 265, 278
Lutz, Charles, 191
Lutz, Florida, 191

Mackinnon, William, 95
Mad River & Lake Erie Railroad, 136
mail service, 86, 105, 106, 109, 159, 191, 239, 244
Maldonado, Don Diego, 11
Mallory, Stephen, 53, 56, 224, 225
Manrara, Eduardo, 121–22
Manrara, Edward, 192
Marathon, Florida, 218
Margarita plantation, 36, 59
Marshy Tacky, 13
Martin Andersen Beachline Expressway, 286
Martin, Sidney Walter, 134–35
Marvin, William, 51, 67
Mascotte, vessel, 125, 126, 185
Mason, Raymond, 269, 270
Matecumbe, Florida, 206, 251
Mathews, Jean Flagler, 277
McKay, James, 62, 124
McKinley, William, x, 164
Mende people, 164–65
Meredith, Joseph Carroll, 202, 203, 205, 207–8, 212, 214, 215

Metromover, 285

Metrorail, 285

Miami, Florida, 199, 285, 295; All Aboard Florida and, 279, 282, 284; Key West route to, 166, 195–227; population, 149, 162; rail service to, 159, 161–64; route to, from Tampa to, 127

Micanopy, 14

Miccosukee Indians, 13

Middendorf, J. William Sr., 169

Middle Keys, Florida, 216

military, in Florida, 39, 58, 186, 225, 234, 235, 260, 261

Miller, Henrietta, 230, 231

Miller, William, 65, 66

mining, Florida, 179, 184

Mixon, Murrell, 85–86

Mixon, Patty, 85–86

Mizell, Morgan Bonaparte, 90, 91

Mizner, Addison, 236

Mobile & Pensacola Railroad, 57

Model Land Co., 153, 231

Monaco, Chris, 33, 60, 81

Monroe, James, 8, 16

Montgomery and West Point (Georgia) Railroad, 26

Morgan, J. P., 180, 224, 247

Moser Channel bridge, 219, 221

Mueller, Edward A., 45

Mugge, Robert, ix, 187

museums, railroad, 41, 158, 229, 255, 273, 277

Nashville, Chattanooga & St. Louis railroad, 71

National Railroad Passenger Corp., 275

Native Americans, 10, 16. *See also* Indians.

Nattiel, Dollie, 68

naval stores, 21, 28, 182, 278

Nevins, Allan, 93, 142

New Smyrna, Florida, 15

New Spain, 7, 117

Newport, Florida, 70

Newton, John, 64–65

No. 12 train, 71, 222

North Florida Highlands, 4

Notorious Swepson-Littlefield Fraud: Railroad Financing in Florida, 1868–1871, The, (Fenlon), 75

Oaks, The, 175, 176

Ocala Uplift, 4

Ocala, Florida, 168

oil development, 137

oil-burning trains, 248

"Old 447" engine, 253, 254

Old South and the New: A Series of Letters, The, (Kelley), 87, 88

Olivette, vessel, 125, 126, 185

Onis, Don Luis de, 8

Only Yesterday: All Informal History of the 1920s (Allen), 234, 249

Orange Belt Investment Co., 97

Orange Belt Railway, 97, 121, 191

Orange Belt Route, 241

Orange Grove and Ocklawaha River Steamers, 87

Orlando International Airport, All Aboard Florida and, 285, 286

Orlando, All Aboard Florida and, 279, 280

Orlando, Florida, 102, 103, 115, 130, 193, 246, 262, 276, 278, 279, 280, 283, 289, 290, 291

Ormond Beach Hotel, 149

Ormond-on-the-Halifax Hotel, 238

Osprey, Florida, 173, 174, 175

Ottawa, gunboat, 58

Overseas Railroad, 166, 197, 200, 209, 210, 214, 224, 225, 227, 238, 248, 254, 255

Pacer Channel bridge, 219, 221

Palatka, Florida, 86, 87, 104, 105, 115, 118, 121, 130, 149, 180, 193, 276

Paleo-Indians, 11

Palm Beach Hotel, 155
Palm Beach Island, 156
Palm Beach Limited train, 194
Palm Beach Railway and Power Co., 192
Palm Beach, Florida, 153, 192
Palmer National Bank and Trust
    Co., 256
Palmer, Potter II, 173, 256
Palmer, Bertha Honoré, viii, 171, 172–73,
    174, 243, 256; agriculture and, 176;
    Davies Warfield and, 173; family of,
    172, 173, 175; the Oaks and, 175, 176;
    Osprey, Florida, and, 173, 174–75, 176;
    Sarasota, Florida, and, 171, 173, 174,
    175–76, Sarasota Venice Co. and, 175;
    Spanish Point and, 173, 175; Venice,
    Florida, and, 173
Palmer, Honoré, 173, 256
Palmer, Potter, 172
Palmetto Limited train, 182, 183, 244,
    247, 264
Panama Canal, 198, 201, 292
Panama City, Florida, 101
Panhandle, 2, 5, 11, 14, 23, 51, 70, 88,
    94, 98
Panic of 1837, 26, 39, 47
Parrott, Joseph, 147, 148, 162, 225; Key
    West project and, 198, 202, 203, 207,
    208, 209, 213, 214, 216
Parson, T. W., 241–42
passenger train service, xi, 5, 151, 180–81,
    182, 191, 193, 238, 244–45, 246, 247,
    248, 251, 269, 275, 276–77, 278–93,
    294–95
"Patriot War," 19
Peace River, Florida, 184
Pembina, gunboat, 58
Peninsula Arch, 4
Peninsular & Occidental Steamship Co.,
    226, 231
Peninsular Railroad, 82
Pensacola & Atlantic Railroad, 98, 99,
    102, 106, 177

Pensacola & Georgia Railroad, 46, 65, 73,
    74, 75, 76, 78, 79, 84–85, 106, 178
Pensacola & Louisville Railroad, 94, 177
Pensacola & Selma Railroad, 98, 102
Pensacola Naval Air Station, 262
Pensacola Navy Yard, 51, 54
Pensacola Railroad, 102, 106
Pensacola, Florida, 23, 25, 27, 55, 63, 94
Perkins, George, 224
Perry, Edward, 167
Perry, Madison Starke, 47, 50, 51, 54
phosphate deposits, 4–5, 117–18, 125,
    183–84, 240
Pickens, Andrew, 54
Pickens, F. W., 57
Pigeon Key, Florida, 219, 221
Pilgrimage Plantation, 33
pirates, 28
Plant City Union Depot, 191
Plant City, Florida, 111, 191
Plant Investment Co. (PICO), 112, 116,
    118, 125, 128
Plant System, 112, 114, 116, 118, 119,
    120, 121, 125, 128, 129, 163, 172, 182,
    183, 189, 244
Plant, Henry Bradley, viii, x, 109, 120;
    David Yulee and, 113, 114, 115, 116,
    118; death of, 128, 129, 182; estate
    of, 128–29, 183; family of, 107, 109,
    110; Henry Flagler and, 112, 123, 147,
    159; Henry Sanford and, 112, 116,
    123; hotels of, 120, 125, 126, 129, 197,
    246; James Ingraham and, 116; Julia
    Tuttle and, 127; railroads owned by,
    97, 110–12, 115–24, 129, 182; Plant
    Investment Co. and, 112; "People's
    Line" and, 112, 118; railroads owned
    by, 110–12, 115–24, 129; Spanish-
    American War and, 185–87; Tampa
    route and, 116, 117; 118, 119, 122, 172;
    tobacco and, 185
Plant, Morton Freeman, 109, 128
Polk, James, 51

Pond Creek and Blackwater River Canal Co., 106, 181
Pons, Emilio, 192
population: Florida, 88, 193, 250, 263; Hispanic, 289, 290
Port Inglis Terminal Co., 240–41
Port Inglis, Florida, 240
Port Leon, Florida, 274
Port St. Joe Dock & Terminal Co., 266
Port St. Joe, Florida, 23
Port Tampa, Florida, 124, 125, 189
Powell, Legh R., 243
Pullman Palace Car Co., 123
Pullman, George, 92, 123
Pulsifer, Royal M., 103
Punta Gorda, Florida, 120

quiet zones, train service, 293, 294
Quincy, Florida, 179

Rail Administration, 233, 234, 237
Rail Management Corp., 271
Railroad Administration, 281
railroads: Civil War and, 51, 58, 88; construction, vii; embargo against, 238; oil delivery and, 138, 141; rebates, 140; segregation and, 83; World War I and, 233–36
rails: gauge, 23, 130; iron, 22, 23, 65, 80; reused, 277; wood, 5, 22, 23, 80
Raleigh & Gaston Railroad, 169
"Rambler," 154–55, 195, 225, 277
Rand, Frederic, 102
Rattlesnake Cannery and Emporium, 274, 275
real estate, Florida, 236–37, 247, 248, 249, 259
Reconstruction, Florida and, ix, 73–93
Reed, Edward, viii, 96, 113, 119, 167–68, 239
Reed, Harrison, 75, 178
refrigerated railcars, 91, 238
Reid, Robert Raymond, 8, 33

Reininger, Michael, 280, 284
religious groups: Catholics, 15 191; Greek Orthodox, 16; Jewish, 15; Protestants, 15, 132
Remington, Frederic, 90, 181–82
Remmers, John R., 60
Republican Party, 74, 87
Reynolds, Kelly, 107, 110
Ribault, Jean, 7
Rice, W. T., 272
Richmond, Petersburg and Carolina Railroad, 170
Roach, John M., 257;
Roanoke & Tar River Railroad, 170
Roberts, Edgar A., 190
Roberts, Isaac, 178
Roberts, Marshall, 39, 47,178
Rockefeller, John Davison, 127, 137; 137; Henry Flagler and, 136, 137–44, 147, 165, 227, 229; oil and, 137, 138; New York and, 144; Standard Oil Co. and, 138–44
Rockefeller, William A., 138
Roosevelt, Theodore, 150, 185, 187, 188–89
Root, Elihu, 201, 209
"Rough Riders," 185–86, 187
Royal Palm Hotel, 162–63, 238
Royal Poinciana Hotel, 153, 154, 155, 238
Runnymede, Florida, 96
Russell, Bernard, 253
rustlers, 13, 90

"saddle-bag railroad," 48–49
salt production, Florida, 52, 136
Sammons, Sandra Wallus, x, 116, 131, 153–54
Sanderson, John, 45, 54, 62, 73, 75, 76
Sanford & Indian River Railroad, 119
Sanford & St. Petersburg Railway, 121
Sanford, Florida, 104, 118
Sanford, Henry Shelton, 86, 95, 102, 112, 116, 123

Santa Rosa Island, 54, 56

Sarasota Bay, 172

Sarasota, Florida, 170, 171, 173, 174, 175–76

Savannah & Charleston Railroad, 111

Savannah, Florida & Western Railroad, 110, 111, 118, 119, 121, 124, 125, 128, 247

Savannah, Georgia, 169

sawmills, 101, 181, 189, 190

Scott, Rick, 293

Scott, Winfield, 57

Seaboard & Roanoke Railroad, 169

Seaboard Air Line Railroad Co., 40, 169, 170, 171, 172, 173, 176, 182, 183, 185, 191, 237, 238, 239–41, 242–243, 250, 256, 258, 271, 272, 275

Seaboard All-Florida Railway, 242

Seaboard Coast Line Railroad, 272, 274

Seaboard System Railroad Co., 272

Seddon Island, Florida, 191

segregation, 83, 152

Seminole Gulf railroad, 274

Seminole Indians, 9, 13, 14, 28

Seminole Inn, 242, 275

Seminole Limited train, 193, 194

Seminole Wars, ix, 19, 28, 38, 48, 69, 159

Seneca, gunboat, 58

Seven-Mile Bridge, 209, 218, 219, 255

Seward, William, 56, 57

Seymour, Truman, 60, 62

Sharon, Florida, 105

Sherman, W. C., 235

Shorr, Catherine O'Sullivan, 176

Shutts, Frank B., 225

Siemens trains, 294

Silver Meteor train, 247, 276

Silver Spring, steamboat, 87

Silver Springs, Ocala & Gulf Railroad, 106, 119

Silver Star train, 247, 276

slaves, vii, x, 14–15, 21, 31, 33, 35, 38, 67, 68, 83, 84, 164, 208

Slemmer, Adam Jacoby, 55–56, 57

Smith, John W., 272

Snake Creek, Florida, 213

South Bound Railroad, 169, 185

South Florida Railroad Co., 102, 103, 104, 115, 116, 118, 119, 120, 123, 125, 130, 272

Southern Express Co., 110, 128, 129

Southern Land and Immigration Agency of New York, 71

Southern Railway System, 180, 181, 247, 250

space program, rail service and, 295

Spain, in Florida, x, 1, 7, 8, 9, 10, 13, 14–15, 33

Spanish Point, Florida, 173, 175

Spanish-American War, 185–89

Spencer, Samuel, 180

St. Augustine & Palatka Railway, 149

St. Augustine, Florida, 19, 80, 81, 114, 146, 147, 149, 153, 239

St. Cloud & Sugar Belt Railway, 119

St. Johns & Halifax Railroad, 149

St. Johns & Lake Eustis Railroad, 90, 114

St. Johns Railway, 48, 58, 79, 80, 106, 114, 149

St. Johns River, Florida, 5, 45, 114, 248

St. Joseph Paper Co., 267, 268, 271

St. Joseph Telephone & Telegraph Co., 266

St. Joseph, Florida, 22, 23

St. Marks, Florida, 70; Ambush at, 60

St. Marys River, 5, 7, 28

St. Petersburg, Florida, 97

Standard & Hernando Railroad, 240

Standard Oil Co. of New Jersey, 144, 145, 146

Standard Oil Co. of Ohio, 138–44, 229, 230

Standard Oil Trust, 144

Standiford, Les, 127, 136, 139. 153, 162, 199, 201, 205, 207, 212, 214, 215, 217, 218, 219-20, 221, 223, 248, 252, 254

Starr, Myra, 259
steam locomotives, ix, 22, 80
steamship lines, 80, 112
Steele, A. B., 100, 101
Steele, Augustus, 28, 91
Stemper, Francis X., 191
Steward, J. Q., 66
Stimson, H. A., 194
Stock Island, Florida, 222
stock: investor, 74; railroads, 25, 44, 45, 47, 77, 99
Stone Wharf, 69
Sugar Belt Railway, 96
sugarcane, 88, 246, 278
Sullivan, Daniel F., 177
Summerlin, Jacob, 61, 62
Summerlin, Jake, 124
Sumner, W. A., 176
SunRail, 285
Suwannee River, 5
"Swamp Fox," 63
Swann, Samuel, 71, 72
Swepson, George W., 74, 75, 76, 77, 78, 79, 168
Swift, Gustavus Franklin, 92

"Tallahassa," 16
Tallahassee Railroad, 9, 21, 22, 46, 64, 66, 77, 106, 178, 274
Tallahassee, Florida, 8, 19, 46, 65
Tampa, Florida, 244; All Aboard Florida and, 279; cigar business and, 18, 121–22, 126; Civil War and, 117; coast-to-coast rail and, 36; docks in, 124, 125; Henry Plant and, 116, 117, 118, 119, 122, 126; hotels in, 125, 126; to Miami route, 127, 159; military troops in, 186, 187, 188, 189; phosphate deposits in, 117–18, 125; rail development in/to, 115, 116, 118, 119, 124, 125, 127, 130, 168, 172, 189–90, 191; Spanish-American

War and, 185, 186, 187, 188; Reconstruction and, 117
Tampa & Gulf Coast Railroad, 191, 241
Tampa & Jacksonville Railroad, 81
Tampa Bay Hotel, 126, 186, 197
Tampa Northern Railroad, 189, 190, 191, 241
Tampa Southern Railway, 244, 246
Tampa Union Station, 191
Tarbell, Ida M., 142
Tarpon Springs, Florida, 96, 241
Tavares and Gulf Railroad, 241
Tavernier, Florida, 213
taxes: corporate, 45; railroad, 79
Territorial Council, 19, 22, 25, 27
tidal wave, 252–53
Timucua Indians, 7, 10–11
tobacco, 16, 18, 88, 185; Cuban, 126, 200
Tocobaga Indians, 117
Tocoi Landing, Florida, 48, 58, 80, 81, 114
tourists, 80, 120, 170, 244, 255, 279
tram-style railways, 257
Treaty of Paris of 1763, 7
Tri-Rail, 276–77, 278, 290
Tropical Florida Railroad, 40, 82–83, 168
Tropical Peninsular Railroad, 106
Trumbo American Dredging Co., 213
Trumbo Naval Air Station, 235, 263
Turnbull, Arthur, 15–16, 69
Turner, Gregg M., 44, 45, 74, 100, 120, 125, 129, 149, 167, 178, 183, 234, 239, 245, 246, 260, 269, 270
turpentine, 85
Tuttle, Julia DeForest Sturtevant, viii, 126–27, 159, 160, 161, 162, 163, 164

U.S. Army Air Corps, 262
Underground Railroad, 68–69
unions, railroad, 268–69
United States & West Indies Railroad and Steamship, 241
Upper Keys, Florida, 216

Upper Matecumbe Key, 213
US Army, 262; Ambush at St. Marys River and, 60, 62; Battle of Cedar Key and, 64; Battle of Natural Bridge and, 70; Battle of Olustee and, 62; cattle and, 63; embargo by, 51; Fort Jefferson and, 57; Fort Pickens, 55–56, 57; Fort Taylor and, 57; Newport and, 70; Tallahassee invasion and, 64; train control of, 58; USS *Columbine* and, 63
US Department of Transportation, 280
US Navy, Key West Extension and, 213–14
US Volunteer Cavalry Regiment, 185
USS *Columbine*, 63
USS *Magnolia*, 124
USS *Maine*, 185
USS *Ottawa*, 59

Van Horne, William Cornelius, 200
Van Vechten, Charles Van, 253–54
Venice, Florida, 173, 241, 243, 244, 256
Veredura, 21–22
Vose, Francis, 178
Vose, Livingston & Co., 178

Wagner, William H., 178
Walby, David L., 26, 27, 56
Walker, W. M., 204, 211, 213, 216, 217, 227, 239
Walters, Henry, 123, 129, 158, 183, 227, 231, 234, 237, 247
Walters, William T., 112, 123, 183
"War Eagle," 63
Ward, George, 198, 227
Warfield, S. Davies, 170, 173–74, 183, 191, 234, 240, 242, 243, 256, 275
Warnell Lumber and Veneer Co., 241
Watson, Edgar J., 258–59
Way Key, Florida, 28, 85, 112
Waycross & Florida Railroad, 110
"Waycross Short Line," 111

weather, Florida, 4, 210–211. *See also* hurricanes; tidal wave.
West Palm Beach, Florida, 153–54, 242, 295; All Aboard Florida and, 279, 280, 282, 284, 282, 285
West, George M., 100, 101
Westcott, James Diament, Jr., 35, 43, 48
Westcott, John D., 48
Westerman, John, 48, 60
Westinghouse, George, 92
White, Joseph, 19
Whitehall mansion, 158, 277
Wickliffe, Nannie C., 35, 40
Wilkinson, Jerry, 197–98, 205, 209
William E. Jackson & Associates, 74, 76
William, Joy, 206
Williams, John Langbourne, 169
Williams, John Skelton Sr., 169, 170
Williams-Middendorf Bank, 169
Wilson, Woodrow, 170, 233
Wise, Louise, 230, 231, 233
Wittfield, William, 87–88
Wood, Leonard, 185
World War I, 233–35
World War II, 260-63

Ybor City Land & Improvement Co., 121
Ybor City, Florida, 122
Ybor, Candide, 192
Ybor, Vicente, 16, 17, 18, 121
yellow fever, x, 21, 23, 45, 105, 121, 122, 163
Yellow River Railroad, 101, 102
Young, Joseph W., 238
Yulee, David Levy, viii, 31–32; children of, 35, 68; coast-to-coast rail link, 35–38; in Congress, 34, 35, 43, 53; citizenship question of, 34; Civil War and, 52, 53–54, 57, 58, 59, 60, 66; Confederacy and, 39–40; death of, 40; education, 33; as a fire-eater, 31, 60; Florida statehood and, 35; homes of, 36, 59; land grants

and, 44; legacy of, 41; monument to, 41; name change, 35; railroads of, 35, 36–40, 47, 53, 58, 72, 82, 178; slaves and, 38, 48, 52, 60; "Transit Road" and, 113, 114; treason charge, 41, 67; wife, 35, 40

About the Author

Stephanie Murphy-Lupo is an author, freelance writer, and native Floridian. As a career journalist, she wrote about her experiences exploring numerous American destinations—as well as travels to Cuba, Portugal, Australia, Finland, Sweden, Canada, and Italy.

She gained extensive insight about the way other people view their own journeys—through interviews with tycoons and celebrities, scholars and scientists, musicians and artists, entertainers and athletes, analysts and policy-makers.

Among the most interesting to quiz or listen to—the late General Alexander Haig, Donald Trump, Zbigniew Brzezinski, Sophia Loren, Tony Bennett, Frankie Valli, Regis Philbin, Michael Milken, Gary Player, Dr. Murray Gell-Mann, Paul Volcker, George Plimpton, and Arthur Laffer.

Stephanie is the author of *Day Trips from New Jersey* (Globe Pequot, 2012). From 1995 to 1998, writing as Stephanie Murphy, she coauthored the first three editions of *The Insiders' Guide to Boca Raton & the Palm Beaches.*

She was a writer and columnist for the *Palm Beach Daily News* from 2000 to 2008. Her feature articles and photographs have appeared in *Palm Beach Illustrated, Palm Beach Post, Miami Herald, Sun-Sentinel, Florida Weekly, Culture, Quality Cities, Boca Raton News, Palm Beach County TravelHost,* and other publications.

Stephanie is a graduate of the University of Florida College of Journalism. She studied at the University of Colorado on a Gannett Foundation grant, and completed newspaper management training at the Knight-Ridder Institute in Miami.

A native of Jacksonville, Stephanie also lived in Fort Myers, Coral Gables, Pensacola Beach, and Gainesville. After college, she lived and worked in Orlando, Fort Lauderdale, and Boca Raton.

She is the author of two biographies in progress, including *Off the Record with Charles Calello*. In 2014 she began writing a novel and screenplay.

Stephanie and her husband, Gerard A. Lupo, divide their time between West Palm Beach, Florida, and Montville, New Jersey.